ROVING COMMISSIONS
No. 19

ROVING COMMISSIONS

NUMBER 19

Edited by
MALDWIN DRUMMOND

Angus & Robertson · Publishers

Angus & Robertson · Publishers

London · Sydney · Melbourne · Singapore · Manila

Published by Angus & Robertson (UK) Ltd, London, in 1979

ISBN 0 207 95875 0

Printed in Great Britain by W & J Mackay Ltd, Chatham

CONTENTS

LIST OF ILLUSTRATIONS

(*between pages 96–97*)

EDITORIAL ACKNOWLEDGEMENTS

The Editor is grateful to members who contributed such a wealth of material for the *Journal* and *Roving Commissions*. It was sad that all logs and articles could not be included, for the standard was particularly high.

This volume marks the beginning of a new partnership between the publishers Angus & Robertson and R.C.C. Press. It is hoped that this will mean a wider readership for *Roving Commissions* and a greater service, therefore, by members and the Club to the cruising world.

The Editor would like to pay tribute to his predecessor, Boyd Campbell, who achieved such a high standard as Editor; to Trevor Wilkinson, who looked after circulation; to Miss A. Scott-Elliott whose charts so well adorn and illustrate the cruises; and to Beken of Cowes for permission to use the photograph of *Jolie Brise*. He would also like to thank Ian Dear of Angus & Robertson for his advice and strenuous efforts to make the partnership and the book a success.

Finally, he wishes to thank Commander Ralph Swann and Captain Rupert Hughes for reading the proofs with such care.

MALDWIN DRUMMOND
Hon. Editor

FROM LOG TO JOURNAL
Keeping a log or journal

by Hammond Innes

At the time of writing this I had just returned from attending the opening of the Cook birthplace museum at Marton in Cleveland. To mark the occasion the Navy very properly sent one of their four ocean-going survey ships, HMS *Hecate*, and the day following the opening of the museum by the First Sea Lord, I was able to spend two very instructive hours on board under the tutelage of the First Officer and the Instructor. With its Automatic Data Logging equipment complete with computer and automatic print-out of time and position, its Sat-Nav fixing, its sea temperature recording and seabed coring sampling equipment, ocean survey ships have changed very considerably since the days of Cook, or even of Fitzroy of the *Beagle*.

Before his appointment to command *Hecate* Commander C. Gobey had been surveying in New Zealand waters, some of which had not been re-charted since Cook's original survey in 1769. *Hecate* herself had just spent nine months re-surveying the Dover Straits where an incredible sixty-eight additional wrecks had been located by means of ADL which enables a shadow profile to be traced. Bearing in mind that VLCCs, carefully lightened in Lyme Bay, often go through the Straits with less than six feet clearance, and that a 5° heel adds at least ten feet to the draft, the importance of accurate survey work becomes very obvious.

I mention this because yachtsmen are already involved in Pilotage guides and my belief is that they will become more and more involved in this essential work as the expensive mechanism of the fully-equipped survey ship is increasingly concentrated on vital harbours, anchorages and passages, and on the ocean seabeds. The out-of-the-way inshore waters and islands will be ignored and in years to come our own newly-born Pilotage Foundation, and any similar organisations in other countries, may be called on to fill the gap on a voluntary or perhaps slightly subsidised basis. The log of the yachtsman thus engaged will then become a more detailed and elaborate work.

On passage, of course, though the paraphernalia of survey vessels has changed over the years, the entering up of the log and the writing up of any journal of a voyage has hardly altered at all. For the yachtsman, more often than not on a voyage of relatively short duration when all on board are eager to make the most of their holiday and to pack in as much as possible, the temptation not to write down impressions as they occur is very great. I know I always found it so – perhaps for the very reason that the last thing a writer wants to do is to write when he is taking time off for sailing.

We all keep our logs as meticulously as conditions and circumstances permit, but when it comes to setting down or recording on tape the feelings and observations of the moment there is a great reluctance. Often one is too tired, too salt-weary or too sun-dazed, or one is simply more interested in a drink and the moment passes. All very well for those sponsored trans-oceaners and round-the-worlders, they're under contract to get the cameras going in a gale, flop wearily in the shelter of the doghouse and talk into the mike. They're professionals for the duration.

But bearing in mind that the recollections of a voyage are more often than not only as good as the records kept, I am of the opinion that the 'Remarks' or 'Comment' side of the log book is fully as important as the recording of navigational information. This is certainly the case when it comes to writing up the log retrospectively as a journal, whether simply for one's own sake or for publication in this Journal, in a book or as an article for a sailing magazine.

Since writing is my life I may be considered to have the edge on others whose normal occupation is totally different, but that is not the reason the Hon. Editor suggested I give my own observations on this perennial problem. My latest book, *The Last Voyage*, is a 'lost' diary of Cook's voyage in search of the North West Passage, a voyage which ended in his death after he had been through the Bering Straits to the edge of the pack where no ship had been before – in fact, almost as far north as he had been south in his two previous voyages.

The research for this book involved considerable study of Cook's journals over a period of several years and in the course of this I became very conscious that he was faced with precisely the same problems we all face when producing a journal as opposed to a straight log.

The interesting thing about Cook's journals, which cover his three voyages of discovery, is the way in which they developed. The first journal is little more than an elaborated log – an account of the ship's progress across the oceans interspersed with statements covering the various activities ashore. The second, which he wrote up during the year he was ashore in England, is more of a voyage book, the ship's progress sketched in more briefly, his mind reaching out to the islands and people he had encountered. The resulting journal was much more descriptive, much more colourful. He was learning.

The journal of the third and last voyage is different again. He was writing it up as he sailed with the 'Publick' very much in mind. Position, distance run, all the professional details that are the concern of the seaman-navigator are almost totally ignored. It concentrates in great slabs on the social behaviour, religious customs, the racial characteristics and cultures of the people of the Pacific and the Alaskan coast. It is a travel book, the forerunner of that great branch of English literature that includes Livingstone, Burton, Speke.

Cook was largely self-educated, learning from those more fortunate than himself. You may say, of course, that he had plenty of time in which to do his writing – three years on each of his three great voyages. But his ships were little longer than an East Coast sailing barge, crowded with men, livestock and stores, and in the first two voyages his 'great cabbin' was full to bursting with the scientific and artistic supernumaries the Admiralty foisted upon him. Indeed, his living conditions were little better than those of a seagoing yacht and man-management and survey problems in such confined quarters must have made the difficulties of concentration even greater.

Nevertheless, he managed to write – thousands upon thousands of words. He set the pattern of how to produce a journal from a log and, of course, if only a single page is written each day quite a body of work emerges, even from a much shorter voyage. This, as Cook discovered, then has to be laboriously worked over to make the final result readable and to give to the work form and polish.

As a general rule, descriptive detail written at the moment of experience is the most vivid, with the right adjective, the right phrase flashing to mind. Once the moment of experience is gone, gone too is the vital spark. It may be only roughly set down, but if there is no graphic record, then recall at a later date is seldom so sharp, seldom total.

The burden of writing can be relieved by the use of a tape recorder now that the hand-held variety is so conveniently small. But a tape recorder is a dangerous instrument encouraging loquacity – it is a speech machine and its use does not abrogate careful thought before recording. Also the temptation to record shipboard humour, so funny at the time, so tiresome later, is very great.

I do use a hand tape recorder on my travels, but I am very conscious that, even with careful use, the results leave much to be desired. There is really nothing as good as the written word, if only because the chore of writing wonderfully concentrates the mind. After all, the object of any voyage journal is to excite the imagination of as large an audience as possible. And since they will not have been on the voyage themselves it is the problems, observations, descriptions and general information, rather than the minutiae of the voyage, that needs to be conveyed.

Like Cook, and most others, I find it very difficult to get the balance just right, and usually it means a lot of work – writing always does!

WARE RABBIT
Stranded in the Ile de Batz Channel

by John and Mary Donaldson

Much thought and planning went into our summer cruise from Lymington to La Rochelle and back. In previous years we had cruised as far east as Sweden, but for some reason had never been south of Quiberon Bay. An account of our cruise would certainly win us no prizes, but it might demonstrate the peculiar advantages (and perhaps skills) of motor-sailing. It might even nail the myth that there is some esoteric virtue in refraining from using the engine of a motor-sailer, although none in using half the sails of a pure sailing vessel.

Friday 29 July found Mary on board at Lymington taking aboard duty-free stores. With a complement of two skippers and no crew and regulations requiring liquor to be bought in minimum units of six bottles, it had been difficult to make a selection. Eventually we settled for gin and Cinzano, hoping to add small quantities for a more varied selection in the Channel Islands.

Next day we caught the morning tide out through the Needles. There was very little wind but our metal 'sails' (Perkins 75 h.p.) brought us to Braye Harbour, Alderney, nine hours later. The new mooring buoys in the south-east of the harbour were largely occupied. We picked up the most southerly which enabled us to run out a kedge and keep *Rogger* facing the swell coming in through the harbour entrance.

Sunday took us to Treguier with a brief stop at St. Peter Port to cram in the last pint of U.K. priced diesel before reaching French waters. The night was spent on an anchor just north of Pointe Jaune in the river – very quiet, completely sheltered and good holding ground in twenty feet of water just off the main channel. The plan called for Monday's leg to take us to L'Abervrach and the tide was favourable for a dawn start. However by the time we got to within five miles of Ile de Batz the tide had turned, it was blowing N.W. F.5 and there was a very lumpy sea. The whole point of a plan is to have something which can be jettisoned. We decided to jettison ours.

The first thought was to pick up one of the visitors' buoys between Duslen Tower and Ar Chaden in the channel between Roskoff and Ile de Batz and then to carry on to L'Abervrach a couple of hours before the tide turned westwards. This would have given us the greatest tidal advantage, whilst still allowing a daylight entrance into L'Abervrach.

The plan was duly executed but the seas to the west of Ile de Batz were of a height and shortness which was most uncomfortable and the revised plan was duly jettisoned. A forty-five foot French ketch which had left shortly after us made the same decision. So back to Roskoff and a very wet night lying alongside various other yachts against the wall in Port Bloscon, the ferry harbour. This anchorage has the merit that there is much less swell than afflicts the visitors' buoys in the channel between Roskoff and Ile de Batz.

Dawn on 1 August produced a flat calm. The B.B.C. 0630 forecast gave us N.W. F.6. The baragraph had fallen during the night but had levelled out. There was talk of a slow-moving low over the Western channel. All things considered it seemed likely that we were in the centre of that low and could get to L'Abervrach before anything beastly arrived. So off we went. Five miles off Ile de Batz we met fog. Whilst it is true that we have radar, we are by nature trepid sailors and with time in hand there seemed no point in risking having to enter L'Abervrach with inadequate visibility and perhaps rapidly rising winds from the N.W. So back to Roskoff once again with the possibility, depending upon the weather, of making a further sortie later in the day.

This was our third transit of the Roskoff – Ile de Batz channel in twenty-four hours and we had been through several times in recent years. There was no wind, the sea was flat; it was neap tides and there was an hour and a half to low water. We went through under power at five knots with a one-knot tide against us. The marks seemed clear. Going east you left the black and white tower (Per Roch) which is a middle ground mark well to starboard and then passed between the red and white Duslen Tower with its conspicuous south top mark and the mauve tower on the end of the Roskoff low-water vedette jetty. A prudent seaman would no doubt have been continuously consulting his chart and pilot. But we had a ketch ahead of us which clearly drew more than we did. Where she could go, so could we. She left the Duslen Tower about forty yards to port and we steered nearer to the centre of the channel – perhaps sixty yards off the Tower.

The builders of *Rogger* make considerable claims for the ability of her engine to produce an emergency stop. We did rather better. Passing Duslen Tower we found out how to stop *Rogger* within about six feet when she was travelling at a speed of four knots over the ground. It was a traumatic experience both literally and metaphorically. It was also very noisy because everything moveable continued at four knots for as long as possible. The trick is surprisingly simple. All that is necessary is to place an unmarked rock in front of the bow. For practical purposes we had no warning. The surface of the water was undisturbed. True it is that seaweed appeared to starboard (more towards the centre of the channel) but we touched one rock and piled into another, all within three seconds of its appearance.

It was a falling tide and our first thought was to get back into deep water. Fortunately *Rogger* can be swung in her own length and we came on to a reciprocal course in less than half a minute. The next thought was that we would have to dry her out to see if we had chipped the keel. One glance below showed that this would not be necessary – the cabin was two inches deep in water over its whole length. Bearing in mind the very short time since we had hit, this indicated a large hole. Clearly we were going to have to beach and quickly. But how and where was not so clear because Roskoff harbour was a mass of drying rocks and we could see sand nowhere.

In this dilemma we headed quickly for two vedettes about 150 yards away alongside the Roskoff low-water jetty. Mary shouted that we had '*un grand trou*' in the boat but this produced little reaction until we came alongside and the vedettes skipper saw the level of water in the cabin. Things then moved fast. He jumped on board and told us to make for Porte Kernoch, the harbour of Ile de Batz about one and a quarter miles to the west. He took the wheel whilst Mary took charge of the engine controls and John tried to pass the genoa over the bows to cover whatever hole there might be. The latter operation was wholly unsuccessful. It appears that you either have to have a large crew to hold the sail against the force of the water or you have to stop the boat. Single-handed it is just not on and there was no time to stop for the forward part of the boat was sinking fast.

Within a quarter of a mile it was clear that we could not stay afloat long enough to reach Portz Kernoch. With the aid of a local fisherman in a small motor boat who went ahead, we threaded our way through the rocks on to a small sandy beach immediately to the west of Pen ar Chleguer. By this time *Rogger* was badly down by the bow and debris was floating everywhere forward of the engine compartment.

Three problems now confronted us, namely, to find out the nature, extent and, above all, the location of the hole, to plug it and to pump out before the tide turned. We had about an hour. The location of the damage was bedevilled by the fact that the fisherman had said that there was a large hole forward on the starboard side. This could not be confirmed from inside the boat and was hidden from the outside by the fact that *Rogger* had settled to starboard. Pumping out was impossible with our own resources both because of the obvious size of the hole and because our large bilge pump was fixed in the engine space, whereas all the water was the other side of a watertight bulkhead. Plugging the hole, if we could find it, would be the least of the problems but would not be easy.

Help arrived quickly. In fact part of it was already on the beach in the form of a French Army Unit steaming the rocks clean of *Amoco Cadiz* oil. To this was added three small boats heavily laden with seaweed and the local boat builder – a young man called Jean Pierre. Jean Pierre took charge of operations.

Pending the arrival of an army motorised pump, efforts were made to turn *Rogger* over on to her port side and expose the hole in its supposed position. A rope was run out to the rocks from the masthead and taken to the anchor winch. The seaweed boats attached towlines. Forty French conscripts were ordered to strip to their underwear and lift on the starboard side. The effort and the spectacle were magnificent, but in vain, for, as we tried to explain, *Rogger* weighs ten tons.

The arrival of the army pump brought new hope, but alas it was temperamental and could make no impression upon the water level. Sadly we came to realise the tide would defeat us. There followed a scramble to strip *Rogger* of such equipment as was still above water and put it on to the seaweed boats. It was a remarkable operation. Knives and spanners appeared from nowhere and even heavy items such as the radar scanner were dismantled. It was probably the most valuable cargo that the seaweed boats had ever carried. But no item large or small went astray. All were taken independently to the boat builders shop.

But there was a limit to what could be done and soon we had to go ashore in the dinghy. At Jean Pierre's suggestion the last thing we did was to batten down the hatches and lock the cabin doors. This was not to frustrate underwater thieves, but to prevent the contents of the boat floating away. In retrospect it seems an obvious step to take but in our despair we should probably not have thought of it. In the result only two plastic egg cups were lost although much was destroyed.

This was the saddest part of the whole story. As the tide rose to the spreaders we felt we had lost a member of the family. The ensign had been removed but the Club burgee flew defiantly above the waves. The French Army dried us, fed us, took us to the Marie to report our unorthodox arrival and put us up for the night. Jean Pierre planned to make an attempt to raise *Rogger* on the early morning tide, but meanwhile there was nothing to do except to inform our underwriters, Navigators and General.

One of the many precautions which we had failed to take was to arm ourselves with Navigators' telephone number. However, we succeeded in getting a message to them. They were astonished to hear that the accident had only just occurred. Apparently owners often abandon their yachts and tell underwriters days or weeks later. They responded magnificently. Within five hours of striking the rock, Peter Williams of Alan Buchanan and Partners in Jersey was advising us on the telephone, and the next day he arrived in person.

The tides were making and low water that night left *Rogger* in only a foot of water. This and the headlights of French Army lorries brought especially to the beach enabled Jean Pierre to locate and plug the hole which was in fact at the keel knuckle. The plug was far from watertight and he and two French Army sergeants spent an uncomfortable and anxious night waiting for daylight and a tow into Portz Kernoch. At one stage there had been alarm because Jean Pierre thought that there was a rock sticking through the hull. In fact this 'rock' had come with us from England. When we had bought *Rogger*, Alec Ingle, a member of the Club, had pointed out that it was not sensible to have a void space at the keel knuckle when this was the most likely part of the boat to strike a rock. We had therefore filled it with concrete. Had we not taken this precaution, *Rogger* would have sunk at once.

The rest of the story can be told shortly. *Rogger* was moved alongside the quay at Portz Kernoch taking the ground between tides. For five days we 'sued, laboured and travelled for, in and about the Defence, Safeguard and Recovery of *Rogger*' (to use the traditional words of a marine policy). *Rogger* had to be pumped out and everything moveable taken ashore and either washed and cleaned or condemned. We were not without assistance. We thought that a man who did all the pumping was an employee of Jean Pierre. Not so. It eventually emerged that he was a fellow guest at the hotel where we were staying. He said that it made a change from the usual beach holiday.

But what was quite invaluable was to have the assistance of an experienced and bilingual surveyor. Peter Williams knew what could be saved and what could not. He supervised the temporary repairs to the hull – fibre glass, cement and more fibre glass, the whole being shored to the underside of the deck. He paid off the local salvors and arranged and paid for a local trawler to tow *Rogger* to Guernsey for permanent repairs.

Before we left Ile de Batz, we had to resolve a difference of opinion between the trawler skipper and the proprietor of the hotel whose occupation, when not on leave, was that of master of a very large container ship. The trawler skipper wanted to tow us on his trawl wire. The hotel proprietor wanted *Rogger* towed on a rope. In the event we joined ten fathoms of nylon warp to the trawl chain and wire. The chain and wire provided the weight and the rope the elasticity which were needed. In addition this arrangement enabled the trawler to use its winch to 'play' *Rogger*, shortening and lengthening the tow rope as necessary.

The tow to Guernsey was accomplished on 7 August. It was uncomfortable because the trawler skipper, not having **our** faith in Peter Williams's expertise, refused to tow *Rogger* if she had a steadying sail. His fear was that the temporary repair would break and the keel drop off. That this was wholly absurd was beside the point. It was also fast – an overall speed of over seven knots. The strain on the tow rope was enormous. Secured to the mast tabernacle and led forward with four turns round the barrel of the anchor winch, it shattered the winch gears within two hours. However the mast tabernacle was made of sterner stuff and the tow was not interrupted.

Our cruise ended at Guernsey where *Rogger* began a three-month refit. The impact damage to the hull was nothing. It was the salt water and oil damage which mattered. *Rogger* has had to be stripped to her G.R.P. shell and steam-cleaned throughout. Every inch of electrical wiring has had to be renewed, so have the cooker, refrigerator, water heater, central heating installation, autopilot, gear box and batteries. Only the engine has survived, in the sense that it is an economic proposition to strip and rebuild it. The cost is horrifying and on present estimates will exceed half a century of premiums. Truly it pays to be insured and for a realistic figure.

But why, you may ask if you read the title of this contribution, why 'Ware Rabbit'? Members of the Club may think that the accident was caused by negligent navigation. We do not dissent. But no French fisherman who came aboard *Rogger* had any doubt that the cause was quite different. Our Valiant water heater had a picture of a hare on the front, that being the trade mark of the makers. To all French fishermen it was a rabbit, as a rabbit on board spelt the worst of ill fortune. We soon discovered that this was no joke. The trawler skipper who had agreed to tow us to Guernsey had second thoughts when he saw the 'rabbit'. It was not a question of money. It was simply an unacceptable risk. We had to get permission from Navigators to jettison the water heater if this was necessary in order to secure the tow. In the event it came with us simply because the trawler skipper's mind turned to other things. In fact it will have to be replaced but the latest model still displays a hare as the makers' emblem. We shall have to ask underwriters whether they consider the retention of this hare an unacceptable risk. Other members of the Club may wish to re-decorate their water heaters before the next season begins – it might avoid some accidents.

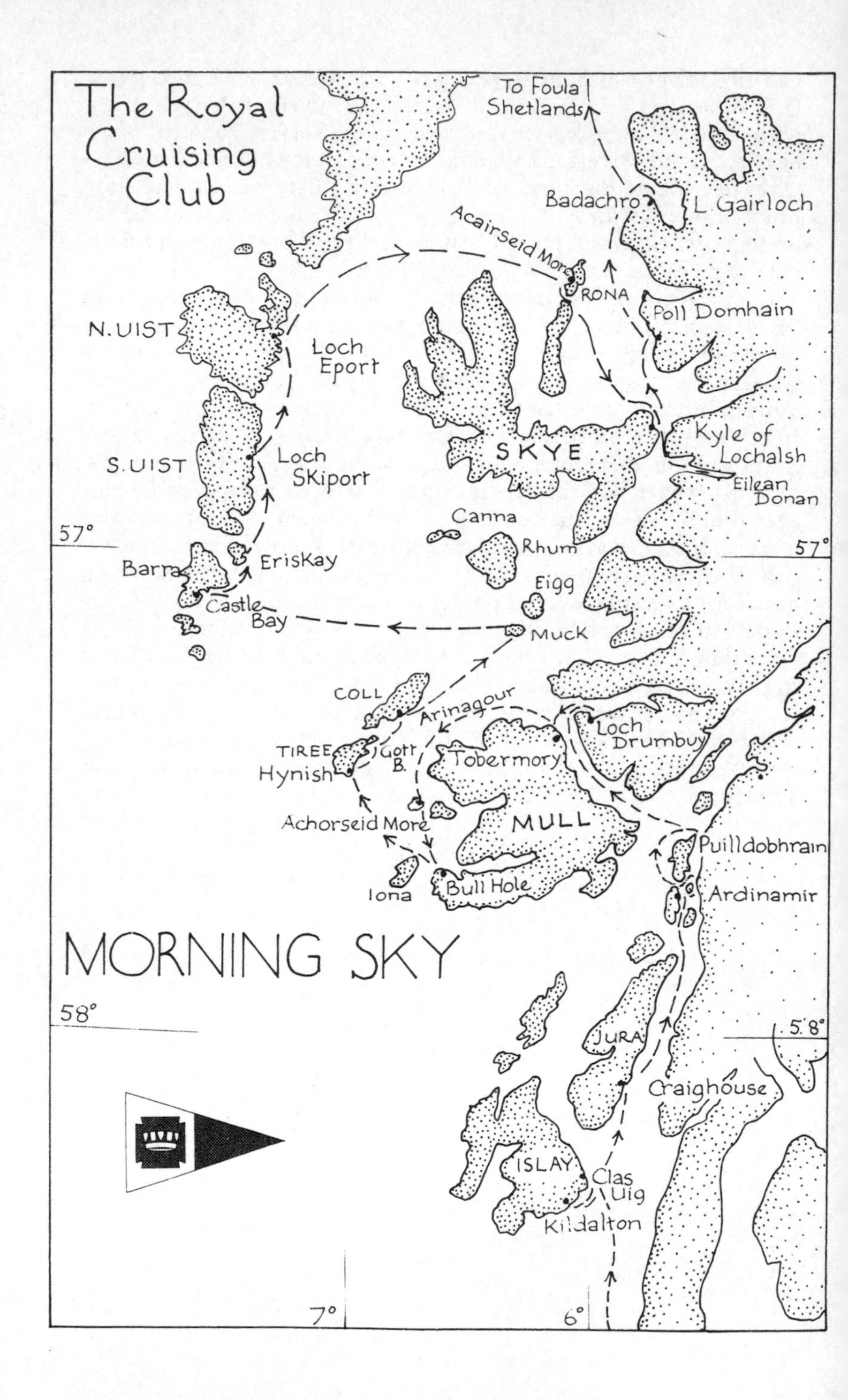
The Royal Cruising Club
MORNING SKY
To Foula
Shetlands
Badachro
L. Gairloch
Acairseid More
RONA
Poll Domhain
N. UIST
Loch
Eport
S. UIST
Loch
SKiport
SKYE
Kyle of
Lochalsh
Eilean
Donan
Canna
Rhum
Eigg
57°
57°
Barra
ErisKay
Castle
Bay
Muck
COLL
Arinagour
Loch
Drumbuy
TIREE
Gott
B.
Tobermory
Hynish
Achorseid More
MULL
Puilldobhrain
Iona
Bull Hole
Ardinamir
58°
5.8°
JURA
Craighouse
ISLAY
Clas
Uig
Kildalton
7°
6°

ROUND THE TOP
Circumnavigating Britain in Morning Sky

by Oliver Roome

Morning Sky is a vintage Nicholson 32, built in 1964 – stiff, handy, long-keeled. It was five years since our last visit to the west coast of Scotland and, in order to break new ground, we had our eyes this year on the Orkneys and Shetlands. We planned four legs – a passage up from Yarmouth, Isle of Wight, another back, and two leisurely legs in the middle, making an eight-week circumnavigation. My daughter Melanie came as mate for the whole cruise and Alex, a friend, came for all but the first leg. Others, including school friends of Melanie's, came for other legs, making a normal complement of four. And herein lay a tactical error – never sail in August, particularly within reach of a telephone, with an entire crew of 'A' level candidates.

First Leg. July 11 to 20. Yarmouth, IoW, to Portpatrick.

The wind was rising easterly, the morning sky was blue—Newbolt.

Only partly true at the outset – the blue sky came a little later – occasionally. Robin (R.C.C. member) and Sarah, a friend, joined on 11 July and we set sail from Yarmouth at 1450 near the top of the tide with a light north-easter. We had a quiet run down to the Bill in intermittent rain, passing it close at 2200, and an even quieter night crossing Lyme Bay. A foggy morning brought us to Dartmouth at 1100. After a quick run ashore, buying porridge oats (for use after cold night passages), which we must have left almost instantly as a present to a local publican, we sailed again at 1430. In fact we motored on a glassy sea, in thickening fog, until, deeming discretion the better part of valour, we put into Salcombe, picking up a mooring there at 1810.

Next morning 13 July, we slipped out at 0900, when we could see to move, and partly motored, partly sailed in fog and calm for the Lizard. At 1430 we heard the Eddystone abeam but it was not until 1930 that a little north-wester came up, the fog lifted and we made sail, anchoring at 2140 in the little cove of Parn Vose, one and a half miles north-east of the Lizard, as the tide came foul. A useful anchorage in an offshore wind, two cables north of the Lizard/Cadgwith lifeboat station. At 0300 we weighed, the men taking the watch, and picked up the first of the west-going tide at the Lizard. The wind, rather variable but generally northerly F.3, gave us a good free leg to

Land's End, which we rounded at 0730 after passing inside the Runnel Stone. The girls turned out in time to see this first major turning point. Here we became jammed on the wind, which had veered to N.N.E., and were unable to lay better than the south Irish coast, west of Waterford, but we picked up the first of the north-going tide at Land's End. By 1230 we had a lovely day of sun and freshening wind, until at 1930 we took down two rolls in the main and at 2200 two more, and changed down to the no. 1 jib. We had sailed all day on an empty sea, except for one yacht seen in the evening on the other tack, but by 2300 we had a fishing fleet for company and a satellite above. By midnight we had come seventy-one miles from Land's End and 150 from Salcombe.

The wind moderated in the night and by 0400 on the 15th we were again under full main and genoa. A fine chilly morning brought another beautiful sunny day. At 1140 we sighted the Hook L.H. on the port bow, and by 1400 we were inside the Coningbeg Lt V. dodging the rock that it guards. We had a good little beat round Carnsore Pt., passing it at 1700 inside the Tuskar. Another quiet night followed but the Welsh mountains behind Bardsey I. were in sight to the east at dawn, and Anglesey ahead by 0800. We entered Holyhead at 1700 and were quickly given a club mooring. Ashore for showers, telephoning, etc. We had come 285 miles from Salcombe in eighty hours, motoring for twenty. Our sail across these deserted seas, in contrast to our home waters in the south, allowed us to enjoy civilised meals; with our sharp tillermate at the helm and one of us sweeping the horizon every few minutes we were able to eat below in comfort.

The next day we had a quiet sail and motor-sail in this continuing light variable north-east to north-west wind to Douglas, Isle of Man. Sailing at 0710, by 1000 we looked like a Chinese laundry as the sun came through. The Isle of Man was in sight by 1500 and we entered Douglas harbour at 1945 and secured on one of those awkward star-pattern buoy and anchor systems. Luckily there were few others competing for the pleasure.

At this stage we had a day or two in hand, so on 18 July after a look at Douglas – too trippery – we sailed down to Castletown, fighting a vicious tide round Langness. The anchorage there looked very large, exposed and uninviting in the now freshening north-west wind, and we turned and retraced our steps as far as Derby Haven, where we picked up a mooring at 2030 in much better shelter. On our evenings at anchor Melanie produced excellent meals, playing with a new collapsible oven we had acquired for use with our primus, and the evenings were rounded off with hilarious games of pontoon and 'Oh Hell', a light-hearted sort of idiot's whist. Robin, with a lively wit and a well-developed male chauvinism fuelled many arguments and much rivalry, though Sarah was not incapable of returning his fire.

We decided to make Portpatrick on 19 July as the wind showed signs of going into the north. We slipped at 0820, breakfasting under way, and beat down the coast in a W.N.W. F.4–5. At 1130 we had an exciting transit of Calf Sound – between the Calf of Man and the main island – with the wind just free, a roaring tide under us and a stretch of broken water beyond the narrows. Once through, with fifty miles to go and a reaching wind, we made good time. By 1700 we were fifteen miles from Portpatrick with the wind heading us to N. by W. and the tide turning foul. We had a final beat up inshore for forty minutes and entered Portpatrick at 2045 after a very fresh, cold and wet patch at the end. The entrance is hard to identify, being just a hole in the rocks and the tidal range is large, but the harbour is snug and friendly. It is owned by a company, there are no harbour dues and yachts use it at their own risk.

Robin and Sarah left on 20 July, but not before they had stood a splendid lunch at the large Portpatrick Hotel, rounding off a light-hearted first leg with a hilarious game of bar football. Later we watered by the tedious method of carrying cans from a standpipe.

Second Leg. July 21 to 7 August. Portpatrick to Kyle of Lochalsh.

Alex and Iona (school friend of Melanie's) joined in the morning and we sailed at 1120. We motored without wind until 1445, bound north for Sanda I. off the Mull of Kintyre, or Campbeltown. The breeze came from the south-west and we set the spinnaker for two hours. There was a gale warning at 1355 and we found we were out of engine oil, so we made for Campbeltown where we arrived at 1920 and secured alongside other yachts in the harbour. Iona had not been too well, and never got her sea legs. There was a fair on in town with bumper cars – a sure crew-catcher – at which we made a forcible acquaintance with a young fisherman, who later showed us over a super modern inshore trawler. The next day it blew a gale and we amused ourselves ashore, including a visit to the excellent local maritime museum. Ralph and Ursula Fisher (R.C.C.) were in with engine trouble in *Yeong* and we exchanged visits.

Gale warnings were still in force on Sunday 23 July, but the worst seemed to be over and we sailed at 1030, with four rolls in the main and the no. 1 jib, bound round the Mull of Kintyre (not without some misgiving in view of its reputation) for Islay. It turned out to be a frustrating day. Our course was south, then west, then north. The wind did exactly the same, going from S.S.W. to N.N.W., giving us a dead beat almost all day, and even graciously dying for two and a half hours. We dodged the races off the Mull, rounding it at 1700. Eventually a small breeze wafted us up to Islay, where we entered the beautiful little pool of Clas Uig, half a mile north of Ardmore Pt., the south-east point of Islay, and anchored in two fathoms at 2045. I had been fortunate enough to fall in with Michael Gilkes (R.C.C.) in June and to have learnt of this and other delightful anchorages and passages from this expert on the area. Needless to say we had the place to ourselves, except for two sportsmen fishing from the shore as we sailed in. The frustrations of our day's sail evaporated under the charm of this spot.

The log for 24 July records 'moved onto ship's time'. For twenty years now we have put our clocks on one hour when cruising, which has many advantages, too numerous to relate here (and, to be honest, one disadvantage). Gale warnings again today, but after a scramble ashore we sailed at 1500 in a W.S.W. F.5–6 and made the short passage (seven miles) to the south-west to the little anchorage at Kildalton (Lat. 55°39′24″N., Long. 6°4′18″W.). This is a picturesque spot and snug in offshore winds at least. Chart 3116 – *Island of Islay* is just adequate to con one's way in, in good conditions. Here, following a telephone call, we were royally entertained by David and Alison, 'two of the local landed gentry' *vide* the *Journal* for 1976, *p.* 101. Aboard again eventually, after a conducted tour of much of the island.

There were still gale warnings next morning but we decided to make for Ardinamir on Luing, forty miles to the north. We had a fast sail – even a 'hairy' one in the later stages – with a following and freshening wind, anchoring for lunch behind Goat I. in the Small Isles (Jura). The afternoon was notable for the first of a number of 'sardine watches' as they became called – the skipper on watch, the rest of the crew flaked out, packed like sardines, in the saloon. We handed the genoa in a particularly strong gust off Ardinamir at 1900, followed by the main, which had already been reefed, and took this tricky entrance rather fast under bare poles with the engine going astern. By now it was blowing a gale and the anchorage was pretty full, but inside the entrance we luffed smartly and let go two anchors to windward of the fleet. Mercifully they held, but elsewhere there was a certain amount of dragging, fending off and unravelling of knitting. Teeming rain later. Alex was by now quickly becoming a useful hand and Melanie was well bitten by the cooking bug – lucky us.

July 26, dawning fine and clear, started with a call on Irene MacLachlan – a must for any visitor to Ardinamir – and a walk over the hill to Culliport, an interesting old slate-quarrying village, active until only a few years ago. Bill and Audrey Speirs (R.C.C.) came into Ardinamir this morning in *Aeolian* with some of their family, having sensibly spent the night in the small bay at the north end of Shuna I., nearby. A pleasant two days of shared anchorages followed, during which Bill lent us charts and gave valuable advice on the Shetlands. We weighed at 1550 and had a very quiet sail through Cuan Sound to Puilladobhrain. A few years ago there would be three or four boats in this charming anchorage – there were now over thirty here. We took an evening stroll over the hill to the notable old Clachan bridge, and its popular nearby hostelry, the Tigh an Truish.

Annoyingly the night and morning forecasts were for gales again, and all the signs were in the sky. We wanted to go to Iona, but decided we must tackle it east-about round Mull. We were away at 0830 and had a fast sail across the Firth of Lorne and up the Sound of Mull in a south F.5 and freshening wind. We beat into Loch Drumbuy (in Loch Sunart) at 1345 in a very gusty wind and anchored on the south shore near *Aeolian*. Very heavy rain on passage and all afternoon, but we eventually braved it for a walk ashore on the Morven (Argyll) coast. The burns were in torrents and we sighted the occasional seal.

July 28 dawned better and we sailed the seven miles to Tobermory for supplies, fuel, water, baths and a launderette – the only one of these we managed to find during the cruise. H.M.S. *Cleopatra* came in and Alex and I visited her for a forecast, as their transmitter had blotted out our 1455 one. We sailed at 1800 to catch the fair tide round the north of the island, *en route* to Iona. We had a light W.S.W. breeze, which died before dark, and after motoring for an hour we inched our way into the little anchorage of Acairseid More on the north-west tip of Gometra I. just before dark. A good little anchorage, not in the C.C.C. handbook, which we had thought of using on an earlier visit up here. Chart No. 2652 – *Loch Tuath and the Isles* shows all the dangers and is adequate to pilot one's way in.

An easy sail next morning took us the eleven miles to Iona, where we visited the restored abbey, a cradle of Christianity in the British Isles. We moved across the sound to Bull Hole for the night, having used Tinker's Hole before. We have always hit off fine weather here and one wonders which anchorage would be best in a blow. Remarks in the C.C.C. sailing directions about the existence of rings for warps to the rocks tend to sound a rather ominous note.

Sunday 30 July was something of an action-packed day. A light breeze took us the twenty miles to Hynish on the southern tip of Tiree where, on Michael Gilkes's advice again, we anchored off the stone pier and harbour (the latter now silted up) which were built as a preliminary to the building of the Skerryvore lighthouse some 140 years ago. The pier is still as good as new and even the small jib, presumably used for loading the stone blocks for the lighthouse, is still there though rusted up. And here I made another tactical error – Alex strode off to find his godfather, who farms locally, while we arranged to meet him later at Scarinish, Gott Bay six miles north, with a hopeful view to supper ashore. I have always found it fatal to let one's crew wander off with the intention of joining up again later. Today the wind freshened and Gott Bay was uncomfortable so we landed Melanie, with some difficulty, to find a telephone and urge Alex back aboard. This accomplished we weighed at 1940 and sailed the twelve miles to the snug anchorage of Arinagour on Coll, where we beat in and anchored at 2230. Sunset. One of the advantages of our ship's time.

After a run ashore next morning a fresh but moderating northerly breeze took us the sixteen miles to Muck, one of the Small Isles, where we anchored in Port Mor with only one neighbouring yacht. Although the C.C.C. sailing directions say 'not recommended for strangers' careful attention to the directions gives a safe and not too difficult approach. We had an interesting walk ashore visiting the old, now destroyed village and its derelict graveyard, with some poignantly maintained graves. There are now only three or four families living on the island, with some developing accommodation for summer visitors. Although not far from the mainland the island has a nice remote feel about it.

August 1 saw us set for a crossing to the Hebrides, and with a good forecast we sailed at 0945. The wind briefly died and then became increasingly fresh from N. by W. We had a wet and bumpy ride but in bright sunshine, virtually close-hauled, ending with seven rolls in the main and the no. 2 jib. We anchored in Castle Bay, Barra at 1845 and went ashore for baths and refreshment. A day to blow away the cobwebs.

Sadly, that was our last sight of the sun, or of any good visibility for our three-day sail up the islands. We visited Big Harbour, Eriskay; Wizard Pool, Loch Skiport and Bay Bioran, Loch Eport, all delightful Hebridean anchorages. And then on 5 August we made an early start and sailed round the north of Skye with alternating calms and light airs to the beautiful little anchorage of Acairseid More on Rona. Alex is something of a climber and he dragged us up all the local hills wherever we landed. In fact at Loch Eport we misread the chart and climbed a steep, rocky, heatherclad slope thinking it to be a 1,130-foot monster only to find later, to our chagrin, that it was a baby brother. So here on Rona we scaled the highest crag (398 feet) where we found the inevitable trig point.

Next day, Sunday 6 August, the usual northerly (What a year of northerlies!) blew us south at last – we even had the spinnaker up for two hours – to Kyle of Lochalsh and then on to Eilean Donan in Loch Duich, where we visited the photogenic Macrae Castle, in which we claim some clannish family interest. August 7 was changeover day at Kyle of Lochalsh, six miles back. Iona caught a train and Dido (another school friend of Melanie's) joined.

Third Leg. August 7 to 25. Kyle of Lochalsh to St Abbs.

We sailed at 1800 and beat a short way up Inner Sound to the attractive and sheltered anchorage of Poll Domhain where we anchored at 2130. Drizzle and low cloud. The next day we beat on to Badachro harbour, Loch Gairloch. Here we not only had friends ashore but also found Murray Bell (R.C.C.) in *St Kilda* and visited him.

We set off again on 9 August with the north-east wind still in our teeth. At 2150 we tacked off Pt. of Stoer and decided reluctantly to sail on for the Shetlands and forgo seeing more west coast anchorages. At dark the wind veered and freed us and we made better time. Cape Wrath was abeam two miles at 0330 – we would have liked to have seen it in daylight. With the dawn of 10 August, Stack Skerry came up on the port bow, followed by Sule Skerry, but the wind eased. Hoy, in the Orkneys, came in sight to starboard at noon and later Noup Hd. was visible eighteen miles distant. By 1730 the wind had gone and we motored on a glassy sea till 0500 on 11 August when we picked up a faint northerly. Foula, the westerly outlying island of the Shetlands, came in sight ahead at 0530 and we entered the short narrow Ham Voe, which affords the only landing place, at 0930 and secured to its small pier with an anchor out astern. Porpoises welcomed us, playing round the bow as we approached the island. We had a quick walk ashore and met a seasonal resident, who told us the island musters some forty inhabitants. There were many birds, including large numbers of great skuas, for whom this is one of the very few breeding grounds in the British Isles. The island, which rises steeply on the west side to sheer cliffs, is described in various books as possibly the most isolated inhabited island of the British Isles, often cut off for weeks at a time in winter. It did not really seem so today.

We were away again at 1120 and picking up a nice north-easter sailed to the village of Walls, behind Vaila I., whose entrance lies among striking cliffs and caves, fifteen miles from Foula. We beat up the winding channel and anchored off the village in the pool at the head. An attractive green spot, rather reminiscent of Denmark. It had one excellent shop that supplied virtually all our needs and introduced us to a local landlady, for baths. Indeed we found everyone in the islands here most hospitable and friendly.

We only had five nights to spare for the Shetlands so next day we drifted and ghosted to Papa Stour where there are reputedly some of the best caves in the country. None of us were 'cavers', but having selected one at random we anchored and rowed into it in the dinghy, until the crew feared for their lives. So on their insistence we returned aboard, armed ourselves with torches and tried again, getting a bit further in but with the same result. Bumping our heads on the rock roof as the swell surged in did not help our peace of mind, and the tunnel being too narrow in parts for rowing we soon decided enough was enough, and returned thankfully into the blessed light of day. Still no wind, so we motored on sixteen miles to Hamna Voe (North Mavine) and anchored in the large but sheltered pool there at 2200.

The highest hill in the Shetlands was round a neighbouring headland and up a long narrow Voe, so needless to say we had to go there and climb it. Ronas Hill, via Ronas Voe – 1,472 feet. We sailed at 0715 on 13 August and anchored at the foot of the hill at 0945. The climb was not difficult, but cruising is not good for the leg muscles so we did feel it a bit. The summit is extraordinary; it is a large plateau littered with pink boulders, and cairns built by earlier intrepid climbers. On a fine day the view from the top would be fabulous, but there was little visibility today. By 1245 we were off again, bound round Muckle Flugga, the northernmost tip of the British Isles, thirty miles on. The wind came up from south of east and we had a fast sail north in increasing rain and mist. The crew, after the morning's exertion, took a sardine watch. We rounded Muckle Flugga, looking suitably rugged in the murk, at 1800 with all hands on deck and then beat on down to Balta Sound, ten miles on, anchoring in Balta harbour near Sandison's wharf at 2100. The harbour is large but it should always be possible to find a lee for anchoring. In Balta we found one of the very few visible signs of the oil boom – the 'local' was full of contractors, airmen and the like, and the airport was in use as an alternative to busy Sumburgh in the south. Otherwise we saw little sign of 'King Oil' and most of his activity is, one understands, concentrated at Sullom Voe, which we took pains to avoid. In the next two days we had a windy sail to Mid Yell on the island of Yell, and a quiet sail on to Lerwick, where we lay in the good small-boat harbour. Lerwick is a busy, bustling town – perhaps oil has had its effect on the pace of life here.

We wanted to get on to Fair Isle next day, 16 August, but after setting out at 0820 we stopped first at the island of Mousa, ten miles south of Lerwick. Here there is the best-preserved broch, or Pictish fort, of the 500 or so of these dry stone structures of which traces remain in Scotland and the northern isles. We anchored in a small bay nearby and found this fort or refuge – it is not really known which – in an amazing state of preservation after some 2,000 years. We weighed and sailed again at 1300 and passed Sumburgh Hd. at 1450, just making out Fair Isle twenty-five miles ahead before it was lost in a cloud bank. Cloud and rain came in from the west, blotting out the land and the wind veered to north-west. The crew, on sardine watch, showed a leg at 1800 as things started getting out of hand, and we took six rolls in the main and changed to the no. 2 jib in a surprisingly rough sea. We ran into North Haven, Fair Isle at 1920 and looked like running out of water before being able to let go the anchor in the small and narrow space available between the mailboat *Good Shepherd*, the pier and a large rock to the north. Unfortunately a small rowing boat was moored in the one recommended spot for anchoring. We eventually moored with two anchors to minimise our swing. Later we were ashore for a quick run on this delightful island, and visited the famous bird observatory and talked to some of the inmates (human).

Next morning we walked the island visiting the post office, the local shop (closed on Thursdays, but it opened for us) and two of the last few remaining houses where weaving or knitting are still done. We even managed to buy a length of tweed woven on a 200-year-old loom, and order a Fair Isle cardigan – for delivery in six months' time. This was our first good drying day since Rona, and everything was on deck and in the rigging for airing. Aboard again we left at 1440, bound, if possible, for Sanday, Orkneys. There was very little wind and we motor-sailed, but we ran out of daylight and anchored in Linklet Bay – large and exposed to the east – at the north-east tip of Ronaldsay. It was, perhaps, not very suitable for the approaching depression that we could see coming. Two friendly fishermen came and chatted to us on their way home. Melanie's 'A' level results should have been out today, but they weren't. Gloom.

We made an early and fast passage next morning, the 18th, to Papa Sound, Stronsay, arriving at 1000. We anchored off Whitehall village, a sheltered spot for a blow from the south, which was forecast. In fact a sunny day developed, with strong to gale winds. We went ashore and headed for a telephone. Melanie's results were in – elation, but Alex's were not – gloom. Dido strong-mindedly decided to open hers when she got home. We teak-oiled and varnished after lunch and had a good walk ashore after tea – through low, rolling agricultural land with friendly people.

We spent 19 August at anchor with strong winds and gale warnings – our first day in since Campbeltown four weeks ago. Annoyingly, while we were ashore at one time a gust capsized the Avon dinghy and dunked the outboard. Alex's results came through at last – all well, and life can return gradually to normal. Sunday 20 August dawned better and developed into a warm, sunny day. Weighing at 1040 we had a pleasant sail in a wind four points either side of south down to East Weddel Sound, by one of the Churchill barriers at Scapa Flow. We wanted very much to get into the Flow, but with the weather turning unsettled we had to start south in earnest the next day. In any case, with the highest spring tide of the year this was not perhaps the best day for sailing in the Pentland Firth. We anchored at 1610 among fishermen's moorings. Two rusting block-ships made an eerie setting. We had a long walk after tea to St Mary's, over three of the Churchill barriers – Dutch-type dykes joining small islands, and blocking off the Flow. The Flow itself looked a splendid area for sailing.

We found great differences between the west coast of Scotland, the Shetlands and the Orkneys. In the first, fine scenery with many small isolated anchorages, often without habitation. In the Shetlands much bigger anchorages, always houses and usually moorings, but again high cliffs and hills. By contrast, Ronaldsay in north Orkney resembles Holland, with a low skyline, the highest things in sight being the houses, but higher ground and cliffs appear as one goes south. Tides round the Shetlands are not too strong except in the sounds, which time prevented us from exploring. The Orkneys, though, had strong tides round the outside and fierce races or roosts, which cannot always be avoided.

We set off on 21 August past Duncansby Hd. and across the Moray Firth full of hope with a fresh south-west veering west forecast, bound for Peterhead or Aberdeen, or further. In fact for two days we had light head winds and calms by day and better, fairer winds at night. It started to rain in the evening and the only relieving feature was a splendid school of porpoises that gambolled round us, and others out to the horizon leaping clear of the water. The sky cleared at midnight and Peterhead was abeam by 0700 (22 August). We beat slowly down the coast all day until our fairer night breeze came at dusk, and we started reeling off the miles again. When Melanie and Alex handed over the watch at 0300, Montrose was on the quarter and the Bell Rock not far ahead. A final short beat at dawn brought us to the Isle of May, in the mouth of the Firth of Forth, where we anchored in little East Tarbet Bay surrounded by noisy gulls and shags and inquisitive seals. This attractive island, one mile long and a nature reserve, has an anchorage on each side. With today's fresh westerly our bay was quiet and sheltered. The island boasts three lighthouses, two of which are now disused. The oldest, a square castellated building, is reputedly one of the last survivors of the coal-fired beacon era. The modern lighthouse complex includes a foghorn at each end of the island, operated by piped compressed air from a central power station. The nature reserve warden and the lighthouse keepers are the only residents.

Next day, 24 August, we had a fast sail to the little harbour of St. Abbs, twenty-two miles on, in a fresh north-westerly. There is a one-fathom pool in the south corner of the harbour, but coming in near low water we spent some time aground just inside the entrance. We had used this harbour before, but it is reputedly uncomfortable in a blow and Eyemouth, two and a half miles south, might prove quieter. August 25 was changeover day and Dido left after breakfast to catch a train south. She had been an inexhaustible and cheerful companion, determined to do (and doing) everything on board and ashore, and if there was nothing to do, just talking. The ascent of Ronas Hill was the only event that wore her down to silence – briefly.

Fourth Leg. August 25 to September 3. St. Abbs to Yarmouth, IoW.

Hugh, a doctor and regular sailing companion, arrived and we set off at 1000 with a light north-easterly for company. We set the spinnaker for the fourth and last time in eight weeks, until the wind left us at 1630, shortly after sailing through Staple Sound in the Farne Islands. We motored till 0140 (26 August) when a north-north-westerly breeze appeared, which freshened and stayed with us – good progress at last, and by morning a considerable sea was running. We set twin headsails for six hours, and passed Flamborough Hd. at noon and Dowsing Lt V. at 2130. Exhilarating sailing. By 0230 (Sunday 27 August) Dudgeon Lt V. was abeam, and Haisbro' Lt V. at 0530. Hugh had been scheduled to get off at Lowestoft but we passed it at noon and pressed on to Harwich, where we anchored, after a sharp beat in, by Shotley piers at 1900. This was our best sail of the cruise and we did 100 miles during the last sixteen hours. (291 miles in fifty-seven hours, nine hours engine).

Hugh had to leave us next morning and we had a leisurely and light-air passage across the Estuary to the Medway, where we had booked a scrub up-river. In fact, we only managed to make an anchorage just past Sheerness by dark. We spent two days at Upnor, on the Medway, shopping, scrubbing and polishing (topsides), repairing the outboard and seeing old friends, this being a former home port of ours. A quiet and fair-wind passage on 31 August took us to Ramsgate by dark, where we found facilities much improved since our last visit five years ago. The inner harbour has a large number of yacht berths for visitors and there are pontoons in the outer harbour too.

An 0630 start next morning and a reasonable north-wester took us to Newhaven by 2030 where my mate leapt lightly for the marina pontoon, but alas, too lightly for the oilskin trousers she was wearing. Alex appeared, no doubt erroneously, to be merely watching the spectacle, albeit with interest, and my encouragement to him to fish her out caused frosty relations until we found time to review the event in a calmer atmosphere over a glass of gin. Alex of course had some impeccable reason, which now escapes me, for just standing there at that moment.

When Grandmama fell off the boat
And couldn't swim and wouldn't float,
Matilda just looked on and smiled.
I really could have smacked the child.

The Coral marina at Newhaven is also a great improvement for yachts from the days, not many years ago, when one was actually refused permission to enter. A much lighter north to north-east wind took us only as far as Chichester the next day by way of the Looe channel. We motored away from there in a flat calm at 1030 on Sunday 3 September. It seemed a pity to end the cruise in this way, but the gods looked down on us and sent us a gentle header off Hampstead Ledge. We beat down to Yarmouth for the last forty minutes and arrived home at the exact time that we had sailed fifty-four days before.

In just under eight weeks we had made good 2,120 miles (2,250 through the water), motored for 128 hours and visited fifty places and anchorages. Light northerly winds and cold overcast weather seemed to have predominated, but we had had a splendid and entirely enjoyable cruise. Why else do we go?

Pilotage publications

In addition to Admiralty charts, tide tables etc. the following Clyde Cruising Club publications are recommended:

West Coast of Scotland – *Sailing Directions and Anchorages*
Shetland – *Sailing Directions and Anchorages*
Orkney – *Sailing Directions and Anchorages*
North and North-east Coasts of Scotland – *Sailing Directions and Anchorages*

Table of Distances

Date			Distance	Time h. m.	Engine Time h. m.	Remarks
July	11/12	Yarmouth – Salcombe	99	23 50	9 45	via Dartmouth
	13/16	Salcombe – Holyhead	285	80 00	21 00	via Parn Vose Cove
	17	Holyhead – Douglas, IoM	51	12 35	0 00	
	18	Douglas – Derby Haven	13	4 20	3 35	via Castletown Bay
	19	Derby Haven – Portpatrick	57	12 25	0 00	
	21	Portpatrick – Campbeltown	41	8 00	3 00	
	23	Campbeltown – Clas Uig, Islay	46	10 15	2 30	
	24	Clas Uig – Kildalton, Islay	5	1 35	0 00	
	25	Kildalton – Ardinamir	40	8 30	0 00	via Small Isles (Jura)
	26	Ardinamir – Puilladobhrain	9	3 40	0 45	
	27	Puilladobhrain – Loch Drumbuy	30	5 15	0 00	
	28	Loch Drumbuy – Acairseid More, Gometra	23	6 40	1 00	via Tobermory
	29	Acairseid More – Bull Hole, Iona Sd	12	4 05	0 00	via Port nam Mairtir, Iona
	30	Iona – Arinagour, Coll	39	9 35	0 15	via Hynish and Gott Bay
	31	Arinagour – Port Mor, Muck	17	3 35	0 00	
Aug.	1	Muck – Castle Bay, Barra	44	8 15	0 00	
	2	Castle Bay – Eriskay	13	3 30	3 30	
	3	Eriskay – Loch Skiport	18	6 05	2 00	
	4	Loch Skiport – Loch Eport	17	4 20	3 00	
	5	Loch Eport – Acairseid More, Rona	46	12 20	7 00	
	6	Rona – Totaig	24	5 45	0 00	via Kyle of Lochalsh and Eilean Donan
	7	Totaig – Poll Domhain	15	4 40	0 30	via Kyle of Lochalsh
	8	Poll Domhain – Badachro	23	6 40	0 00	

	9/11	Badachro – Foula I.	193	48 00	14 40	
	11	Foula – Walls	17	3 40	0 00	
	12	Walls – Hamna Voe (N. Mavine)	29	8 20	6 15	via Papa Stour
	13	Hamna Voe – Balta Harbour	50	9 30	1 45	via Ronas Voe
	14	Balta – Mid Yell	14	2 40	0 00	
	15	Mid Yell – Lerwick	31	8 00	5 15	
	16	Lerwick – Fair Isle	40	8 50	2 00	via Mousa
	17	Fair Isle – Ronaldsay	27	7 30	7 00	
	18	Ronaldsay – Stronsay	17	3 45	0 00	
	20	Stronsay – E. Weddel Sd	25	5 20	0 00	
	21/23	E. Weddel Sd – Isle of May	174	45 00	10 15	
	24	Isle of May – St Abbs	23	3 05	0 00	
	25/27	St Abbs – Harwich	291	56 40	9 15	
	28	Harwich – Lower Medway	43	12 15	5 30	
	29	Lower Medway – Upnor	8	2 15	0 00	
	31	Upnor – Ramsgate	41	8 25	0 00	
Sept.	1	Ramsgate – Newhaven	72	13 30	0 00	
	2	Newhaven – Chichester Hr	35	8 15	4 15	
	3	Chichester Hr – Yarmouth	23	4 05	4 00	
		Totals:	2120	505	128	

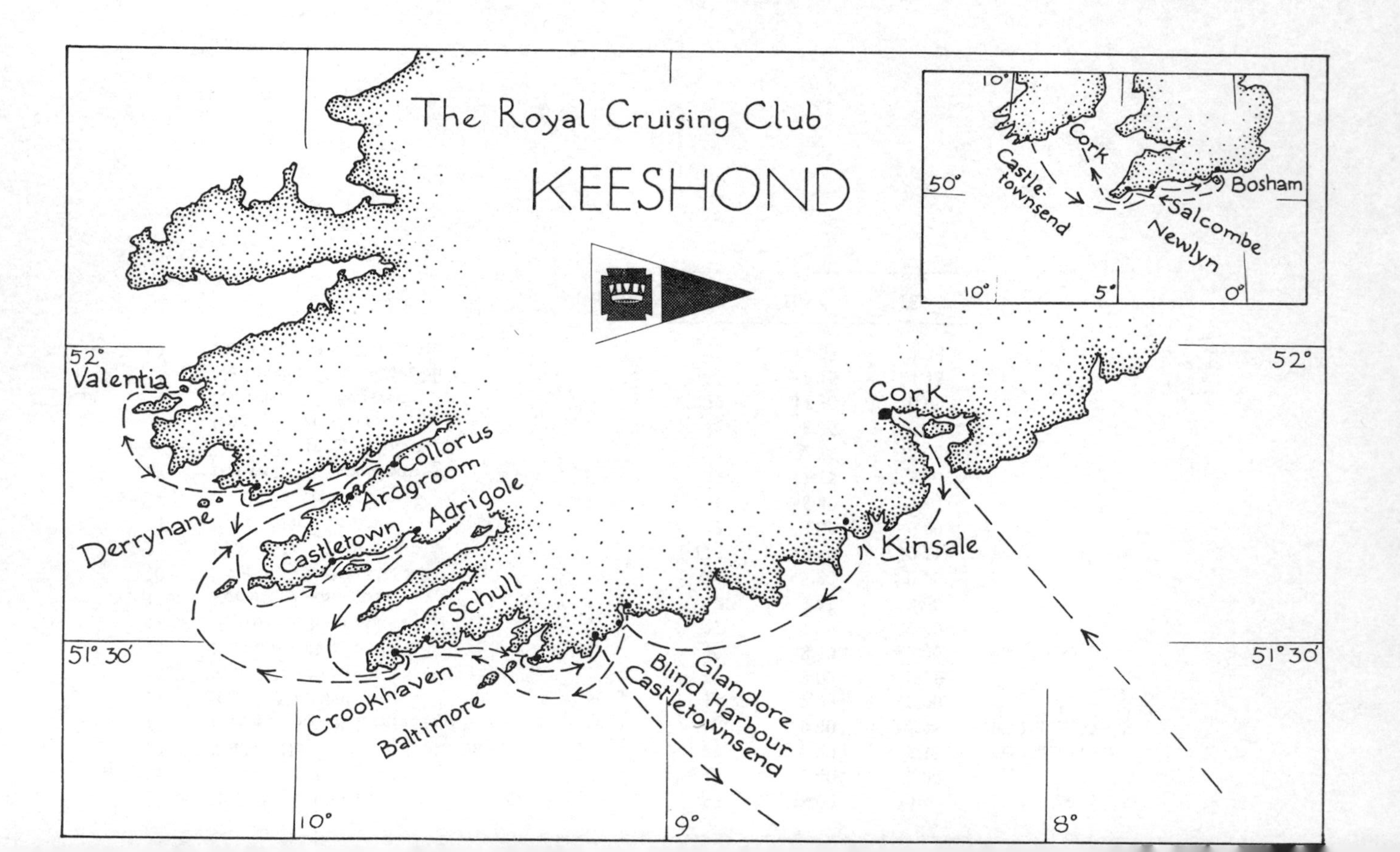
The Royal Cruising Club
KEESHOND
Valentia
Derrynane
Collorus
Ardgroom
Adrigole
Castletown
Schull
Crookhaven
Baltimore
Glandore
Blind Harbour
Castletownsend
Kinsale
Cork
52°
51° 30'
10°
9°
8°
Cork
Castle-
townsend
Bosham
Salcombe
Newlyn
50°
10°
5°
0°

FAMILY CRUISE TO THE EMERALD ISLE

by Peter Price

Keeshond joined the family in 1977. She is a 35-foot Super Sovereign designed by Holman and Pye, a sturdy ketch with an electric self-steering gear, which is such a help when cruising with a small family. After our first round of modifications we felt it was time for a gentle cruise to the Emerald Isle.

For the first few days of the holiday I was fortunate in obtaining a strong and jovial crew to help me out to Ireland, consisting of Avian Case ('Uncle' as he is known in the services), Barry Olford and Mike Butterworth. The rest of the holiday including the return journey to Chichester was with my standard crew: Gill, my wife, Colin, aged twelve and young Alan, aged six.

Our adventures started on Friday 29 July, when the crew joined at Chichester and we slipped down the creek to take a mooring at Hayling ready for a quick start next day.

July 29. Sailed out of Chichester at the crack of dawn with a light southerly breeze which came and went at regular intervals. The log reads: 'engine on, engine off, sails up, sails down, please dear Commodore, we really are trying!'.

This was a disastrous start as I had been determined to use the engine as little as possible, this being one of the main reasons that we had sold our reliable nine-ton Hillyard. The elements had other ideas for the first few days but gave us plenty of wind once we got to Ireland. By midday we were under power again some seven miles S. of Anvil Point when the engine stopped with a sickening thud and all the rigging vibrated with the shock. The sea being a glassy calm we soon hauled out the end of a long rope which was securely wound round the prop. 'Uncle' promptly volunteered to go for a swim and, bearing in mind that he is seventeen stone and that we had no power available, I was somewhat apprehensive. However, we streamed warps, took down the sails and prepared for the splash. With his usual skill he soon had the rope clear and to my amazement we hoisted him aboard with no trouble at all. Amid sighs of relief we re-started the engine but to our horror the whole boat shook violently again. With visions of bent shafts or worse, I soon located the real trouble which was a broken coupling between engine and prop shaft. The rope had wound so tightly that it had effectively extracted the shaft and hence the rubber cylinder from the coupling casting. We tried to re-insert the rubber with a vice, with levers, nuts and bolts and brute force but all to no avail. My practical crew then suggested that we should cut the rubber cylinder in half, feed it back in either side of the coupling and bolt it up again. This was quickly done and the repair lasted the whole season without any further trouble.

July 30. We had a pleasant day alternately motoring and sailing but decided to put into Newlyn to top up with fuel which we had mistakenly believed to be much more expensive in Ireland. *Irish Mist* swept past us and a cheerful owner informed us that he had just bought the boat and wasn't trying, that one of his crew had broken his arm and his navigator was ill below. We decided our more sedate progress had its advantages. Shortly before arrival we tore the no. 2 genoa on a mast cleat but Uncle got out the needles and we soon had a workman-like patch fixed. We anchored outside Newlyn to avoid the crush in the harbour and had a very peaceful night.

July 31. Up early to listen to the forecast N.4/5. We went into Newlyn for fuel and at the same time phoned St. Morgan for an up-to-date forecast. We were given a severe warning against setting off as a high was building up over the Atlantic and squeezing the low over France, giving strong northerly winds. Sure enough it was soon blowing N. F.7. We spent the day talking to fishermen and removed the offending cleats from the mast.

August 1. Up early for the forecast and spoke again to St. Morgan who still gave a depressing outlook. Uncle decided to phone the local stations at the Scillies and Hardfast Point in order to make our own judgement. There was still a confused weather pattern but after plotting our own chart we decided that the worst was probably over and that by keeping to the Lundy side as long as possible we should get some easterly in the wind. The afternoon forecast was N.6/8 in Fastnet decreasing 5, and E.5 in Lundy so we now seemed to be in broad agreement with the Met. Office. The crew were called from the showers ashore and we rapidly prepared for sea. We made our departure at 1438 motorsailing to catch the tide round Lands End.

August 2. A murky day and we got lots of D.F. practice, finding St. Morgan and later the aero beacon at Cork (343.0 KHz) as two very useful stations. The wind was on the nose and we were bashing into an uncomfortable sea, annoyed that we couldn't square away for Bantry as we had agreed to meet the family at Cork.

Eventually sailed into harbour at 2310 and carefully positioned ourselves over the shallows at the entrance to Crosshaven, by means of back bearings on the lights, where we anchored for the night. (The leading lights into Crosshaven were not operating.)

August 3. After a good night's sleep we explored Crosshaven Yacht Club which has all the facilities but is rather expensive at £4.00 per day. We made the best of it and in the afternoon re-fuelled at the small jetty near the entrance. It seemed doubtful if we would ever be served since there was only one pump and this was re-filling a tug at three gallons a minute. The skipper had informed us that he wanted 900 gallons! However, seeing our plight he very kindly handed over the hose and we topped up with our five gallons. In the evening we had a good meal at the Pier Restaurant run by a couple from Fulham who were trying almost too hard to provide a good service. At one stage Barry Olford suggested in jest that he really preferred to listen to Beethoven rather than 'Top of the Pops'. Sure enough, the next record was Beethoven's *Fifth*!

August 4. Made enquiries at Crosshaven Boat Yard as to their lay-up charges with a view to staying over for next year's rally. I was sufficiently frightened by the cost to be convinced that we must return to England at the end of our holiday. We also scoured their stores for two eye bolts with which we mended the lavatory seat. We had learned to our cost on the crossing that with a heavy male sitting on a fore and aft toilet the seat pivots are at distinct risk in the event of a sideways lurch. The eventual repair was clearly much stronger than the original.

After lunch we had a lovely sail right up the river to Kings Quay near Blackrock Castle, just opposite where the ferry docks from Swansea. It was a perfect evening and we dropped the hook near the boat club out of reach of the mainstream traffic.

August 5. Exactly on schedule the ferry berthed at 0730. We waved at the family and proceeded to moor just down stream. In a matter of minutes the crews were transferred. The returning party had a safe journey to Swansea where they picked up my car and drove home. They had been an efficient and very jovial team. At times my sides were aching with laughter and their skill made the passage out a lot more enjoyable and a lot less worrying.

Suddenly *Keeshond* came alive again with the patter of little feet rushing everywhere, exploring all the lockers for goodies which had been hidden by Gill before departure. Up with the sails and we were off down river, stopping for a while at Cobh alongside a very rickety and dangerous pier with timbers swinging to and fro in the stream. Having obtained our stores we set off again straight down the harbour, passing the entrance at 1100 where the ferry overtook us.

Then we had fun semaphoring *bon voyage* to our late crew. We always use this means of communication whenever we can as it is clean, clear and silent and I think it is a great pity it has been dropped from the Ocean Masters syllabus. Uncle obviously received the message safetly but our thoughts were elsewhere as we rushed onwards with a fair wind S.W.5. We had a hard sail and at times hit eight knots. It was a little unfair on the crew's tummies but it was nice to be on our way. We roared up the impressive entrance to Kinsale but were a little disappointed at the number of boats everywhere which had been attracted by the sailing championships for the new windsurfing craft.

We explored ashore and retired excited at the prospect of new cruising grounds ahead.

August 6. Under way at 0920. We had a lovely sail to Old Kinsale Head in W.4 rolling in some reefs we went close into the Head to avoid the race. The wind promptly fell light and enabled us to have a gentle sail to Glandore. This was an important day for us since Alan had not been too happy on the first leg. This stemmed from a very rough sail we had had at the end of the 1977 season which he had remembered all winter. Now he was all cheerful again, eager to know how many 'points' we would have to round before reaching our destination, then doing his own imaginary navigation at the chart table. We entered Glandore spurning Adam and hugging Eve (as shown in the Handbook). The marks just inside, placed there in 1820 by John Barry, a wealthy landowner, as his gesture to help the local fishermen, were a little confusing. The red pole is to starboard of the entrance and the black to port with the rocks in fact lying between the poles. We met an American inside who after crossing the Atlantic had entered Glandore without any large-scale charts or harbour instructions and had really wondered if he was seeing things, but luckily had obeyed the rules and survived. We anchored under sail in this lovely harbour at Union Hall, in 12 ft. with only three other vessels and plenty of room. There is a good quay which would be suitable for drying out, a tiny beach and in the village more pubs than houses. That evening we noticed the evil smell of diesel on board and discovered a small leak in my home-made fibreglass reserve tank. Luckily this was located on the lid and showed how much we must have been rolling about on the previous day. We cleared the bilges with soapy water and laid another layer of fibreglass across the top to stop it happening again.

August 7. After a peaceful night, we went ashore for a good walk on the south side of the harbour. There is a patchwork of small fields with stone-wall boundaries and mushrooms everywhere, which we picked in quantity for lunch. At 1500 we set forth again under sail having first found the anchor well dug into muddy sand. A perfect sail around Adam and inside High and Low Islands we soon crept into Blind Harbour where we anchored in eleven feet. Colin set all types of complicated fishing lines and the family went ashore for a walk whilst I serviced the engine. Later Alan started to read his first big storybook, copying Colin who was engrossed in a *Biggles* adventure. We enjoyed seeing the anchor down on the bottom in clear water and the peace of being all on our own. This harbour would be hopeless in a southerly wind but is fine in off-shore breezes. There are also some interesting caves which I intend to explore on my next visit.

August 8. Anchor up, and under sail at 0950. We had a lively sail tacking off Kedge Island and again to Cascanane Sound. We saw the Commodore, obviously bound for South Harbour on Cape Clear Island and all waved like mad and believe we had made contact. The scenery was now magnificent, rather like Scotland but a little less grand and much greener. We engaged in some interesting rock hopping as we swept through the Sound and had a lovely sail in sheltered waters on to Crookhaven. Passing some three miles inside the Fastnet Light I regretted we had not done a circumnavigation but my faithful 400 mm telescopic lens recorded yet another lighthouse for my collection. It never ceases to amaze me the results that can be obtained with such a powerful lens at 125th of a second even on a wobbly platform. Crookhaven has an impressive entrance under the conspicuous lighthouse and is a perfect landfall harbour. We crept in under sail to anchor off the village. There was one other yacht flying the Red Ensign and we regret not having made contact as this was the only time we were in the same harbour as another English boat. As usual, the other seven craft in the harbour were all Frenchmen. We had a walk ashore to look for Marconi House where the great man had set up his aerial to try unsuccessfully for his first trans-Atlantic call, and took some pictures before the rain came then decided that the beach at the head of the harbour warranted some exploration and a day in port.

August 9. We awoke to a grey morning and listened to the cheerful voice of the Irish forecaster. He has an easy manner and an accurate forecast which covered such things as drying conditions for haymaking (and in passing, damp clothes as well!). After this we listened to Valentia in order to get the full synopsis and were glad we had decided to stay. We packed our lunches and rowed to Rock Island to explore the shellfish pens and packing sheds. These had been deserted recently, the French owners having finally given up the uneven struggle as the lobsters had been overfished. Such a pity when the rest of the village was obviously prospering. It was noticeable all along the Coast that there was an improvement in the living standards which we understood resulted mainly from E.E.C. Grants which were clearly having a beneficial effect on the area.

Leaving Gill and the boys ashore I tacked our dinghy (we do not have an outboard) to the beach at the western end of the harbour. The crew climbed the ridge along the north shore, Alan finding the going rather hard as the ground was covered with a prickly mixture of gorse and heather. They found hot sheltered areas out of the wind and passed three lakes all covered with water lilies. We met at the beach for lunch and the boys then walked to the famous Barleycove Beach. Their report was favourable so Colin sailed the dinghy a mile back to *Keeshond* to fetch swimming togs and flippers. Eventually after further manufacture of sandcastles and a quick dip in the icy sea, we all piled into the dinghy and ran back at speed to *Keeshond*. After tea, Colin made friends with a pleasant family in the village and this was later to prove of great value. Alan was exhausted and gloriously peaceful, reading, writing and colouring. A lovely day, the crew had settled down and were enjoying their holiday in delightful surroundings.

August 10. Up anchor, under sail again at the sensible hour of 0915. A very muddy chain and Alan kindly winched lots of it down the hawse pipe whilst Colin was fetching a bucket to clear up the mess. I wonder if I will ever convince Alan that we will have a disaster one day if he will insist on winding up our chain. (All neighbouring yachts beware!) He loves to help and takes a great interest in all of the practical side of sailing, learning faster from his big brother than from his parents. With the big genoa up and Colin working at clearing transits (without being asked), we rushed towards Mizen Head. It was such a thrill to realise that Colin had taken in the navigation wrinkles and was enjoying applying them.

We had intended going to Bantry Bay but the following breeze S.S.E. 4/5 was too good to waste and we decided to keep going. At 1415 we reached Dursey Sound, seeing gannets swooping everywhere. We saw two other boats pass the entrance and bearing in mind comments in previous logs that the cable car had been under repair, we wrongly assumed it must be closed again. After a brief discussion as Alan was looking rather pale and the sea was distinctly lumpy, we decided to go round Dursey Island and inside the Bull, Cow and Calf Islands. As we rounded the point Alan recovered, even though it was getting rougher which showed that his problem was one of apprehension rather than *mal de mer*. Suddenly we all realised we were thoroughly enjoying a magnificent sail up the Kenemare River. Colin decided to cook a hefty lunch, soup, baked beans etc., while we rushed along at seven knots. The sun even peeped out for the first time since we started and I managed to take some telephoto pictures of the Bull Rock and its lighthouse. We roared along to Ardgroom. Outside we dropped the sails and very gingerly motored in looking for the marks. We had been well prepared for the tricky entrance after reading the log by John Power (1968) and were relieved to find that the back mark was just showing through the trees, somewhat to the left of the point indicated by John Power. Photographs were duly taken for the record.

We crept into the anchorage in the N.W. corner and had the embarrassment of dragging the anchor twice in front of two French boats. More of that anon. The forecast was S.5 increasing 8 but the glass had not moved so we thought we would stay the night and if necessary move to the windward shore in the morning. By dusk it was clouding over.

August 11. By 0100 it was blowing a full gale so I dropped over the fisherman (with warp attached) as a precaution but the Danforth was holding. We mounted anchor watch and at first light all three vessels motored to the other side of the harbour. The Frenchmen both dropped over two anchors, the first a Danforth then 8 fms. of chain shackled on to the bar of a CQR. They held without fuss. Once again my thirty-five pound Danforth dragged twice. In disgust, I pulled out my faithful sixty pound CQR, chucked it over and ceased to worry any more about dragging.

There were several interesting lessons that night:

1. Danforth type of anchors should be treated with caution on this coast and always pulled home. I don't understand why they sometimes do not bite but noticed that Mr. Knockhold had the same experience in this area in 1977.
2. The French all appear to have read the latest recommendation in the Glennan Island sailing school publications and the flat pull on a Danforth created by the weight of the inboard CQR gives the former a chance to bite home, particularly if laying out an anchor in a strong wind where it is difficult to control the backwards motion.
3. In practice I find the sixty pound CQR easier to handle than a smaller Danforth and for that reason we used the former for the rest of the cruise without any further difficulty. By 1600 the wind had died but the visibility was still very poor.

How we wished for the sun. More splendid cookery by Colin before we set off under mainsail alone. We crept out and round the corner into Colorus Harbour, Colin using a paddle to ensure that we did not have to start the engine. Lovely clear water and oncc again we were the only boat. Notwithstanding the I.C.C. warning about the poor holding ground our faithful CQR bit first time. The crew of a small fishing boat came out to welcome us providing the first real Irish hospitality we had experienced. Our normally jovial met. man informed us that we had just had 2 ins of rain in six hours and still sounded very miserable about the outlook. Alan retired to bed and Gill and I stayed in the cockpit enjoying the lovely scenery overshadowed by Knockanougarish mountain. A powerful launch approached and the owner invited us to visit his house ashore should we want anything. I asked if they were going fishing. There was a long pause, then the skipper said that the boat had an uncanny knack of steering to the nearest pub, and asked whether we would like to join him. Like an idiot, I refused.

August 12. We went ashore to the house and filled our water can. We also chatted with the owner who made us feel very welcome. He indicated that he was very against French boats at that time because one had recently broken his mooring and left litter all over the foreshore. We also learned that the Dutch were buying up many of the best cottages and about the story of the local Dutch tugs. These had been left at Bunaw, blocking the quay (and more important, the pub). The locals were very fed up and suddenly there were mysterious 'wee breezes' causing the mooring lines to come adrift. One tug was eventually towed to Ardgroom where another 'wee breeze' caused it to drift on to the rocks and sink. It now lies just to the north of the leading marks.

We walked over the hills amidst breathtaking scenery to find the rear mark at Ardgroom. We also noticed a lovely little cove, well worth exploring, just below the hotel. On the way back we spoke to the owner of a well-kept bungalow who kept bees, goats, ducks, hens, in fact virtually enough to be self-sufficient. He was an Englishman who had escaped the rat-race and it was clear that the whole family were very happy and surprised how they had adapted to their new life. Their children were apparently very well educated at Castletown and travelled there every day by bus.

At 1410 we sailed out of this lovely anchorage with good intentions of visiting Sneem. Outside we found the wind funnelling up the river so we set to, tacking for Derrynane, leaving Sneem for another time – a nice sail but hard work. The entrance to Derrynane is formidable with a swell swooshing between the rocks in the narrow entrance. Two minutes of engine were required to find a suitable anchorage, the harbour being relatively crowded. This really is an incredible natural harbour, a huge swell outside but so completely calm inside we listen to the chain rattling down at 2045.

August 13. We revelled in the glorious coves and beaches, little hills, heather and pools all beautifully sheltered. Colin went fishing and lost all his tackle in the weeds. The forecast was for an occluded front crossing the area and the crew agreed to a quick dash to Valentia just to please the skipper with the object of meeting the cheerful weather man at the radio station. At 1215 we left in the middle of a rain storm which made visibility so bad we very nearly turned back, but instead proceeded on short compass courses between headlands. With six rolls in the main we were soon going at seven knots into a filthy sea and even Colin looked a bit pale but he cheered up as we counted puffins off Puffin Island. I prepared an escape plan should the visibility get any worse but all the landmarks turned up one by one except that we got slightly confused by the entrance to N. Valentia Sound. The Admiralty pilot pictures would give one to believe that North Valentia was steep too. However, when approaching along the coast from the west it appears to come right down to the water in a very long low point. The masts of the radio station are the best mark if they can be seen. Doulus Head to the east is very much higher and quite sheer when viewed from the west. On entering the Sound we saw the lighthouse with some relief, and were swooshed into the harbour to anchor opposite Glanleam House. Colin and I went ashore to try and walk to the radio station but it was too late and we had to return with our objective unfulfilled. We were the only boat until a Frenchman came and anchored right on top of us, however, she was a lovely vessel and Colin rowed round and round hoping to be asked aboard. No such luck; even though he had praised their vessel in excellent schoolboy French.

Another horrible forecast which ended with an apology by a reader for the very poor outlook. The glass was falling and another low was on the way.

August 14. Awoke to the sound of our Japanese alarm at 0600 after a wet and windy night and with visibility not much better than the day before. Under way at 0655 with working jib and six rolls in the main. The crew sensibly stayed in their bunks. With visibility less than one mile we were escorted round a fishing net by two boats as we left the harbour. By 0810 we were motor sailing, Colin was up but young Alan was stuffing himself with biscuits in his bunk. The Skelligs were visible but unfortunately this was not the weather for a visit. We rounded Bolus Head and pointed for the gap between Lamb Head and the N.E. end of Two Head Island in order to get clear run for Derrynane where we dropped anchor at 1140. Alan popped up and declared that as we were in harbour he would now get dressed.

In the afternoon we walked to Catherdaniel which turned out to be considerably further than the two miles shown in the I.C.C. Handbook. When halfway there we asked the way and were told it was merely a further three quarters of an hour's walk. We arrived at the one main shop, a typically Irish store called 'Freddy's'. It had everything from milk to juke boxes, a bar and even a room for the children. We sat outside with our Guinness and fizzy lemonade to regain our strength. On our return we discovered a much easier route through the grounds of Derrynane House. After tea, Alan had his first solo row in the dinghy on a long rope. I fear he still has a lot to learn.

August 15. After a quiet night we decided to have a day in harbour, went aboard a French boat and watched them eat salmon which they had caught in a net during the night. Had a barbeque lunch round a roaring fire of drift wood on Lamb Island and in the afternoon we all sailed in the dinghy to the north-east corner where we landed to explore the lobster pens. Back on board to listen to the forecast. Absolute silence is normally demanded during forecast time and Alan had developed the ritual of returning to his bunk with a weather book by Alan Watts, and we would then hear mumblings of bright periods and snow storms over Southern Ireland with strong gales and black clouds. Poor chap, like us he was getting a gale complex. During supper he got very excited as he had invented an automatic toasting machine which required a flat fire run with flat wood. He always managed to come up trumps with something amusing after a bad weather forecast.

August 16. Forecast bad again with another deep low on its way. We decided to leave and make a decision whether to run for Sneem or carry on when at Dursay Sound. Once again we set sail in a heavy rainstorm but were sorry to leave this lovely sheltered harbour. With the wind S.W.3 we had a good sail in a sea which was getting progressively bigger as we approached Dursay. We sailed through meeting another yacht just at the narrowest point which was only eighty yards wide. By 1245 we had the genoa boomed out as we headed for Castletownbere. The sun came out, the sea went down and this was the best weather we had had so far. There was even a hint of warmth. We sailed right into the harbour using two minutes engine as we came alongside a newly-painted fishing boat at 1500. Ashore for water and to find fuel in case we decided to make our departure from Bantry. I called at the Co-op and was directed to the High Street to ask for 'Patrick O'Sullivan' who would get us the fuel. In the main street every shop was called 'O'Sullivan' but eventually I found the redoubtable Patrick running the grocers and just as I arrived the lights went out as a result of a strike. This meant the fuel pumps were all out of action and that was that. Luckily, I persuaded the local garage owner to find a handle, take off the front of his pump and work it manually so we got four gallons without difficulty. A queue quickly gathered once the idea got around. We liked this harbour which was much better than we expected, with bright shops (when the lights were on) and lots of activity.

At 1730 we set sail and had a lovely evening coasting inside Bear Island, drifting gently to the superb anchorage of Adrigole. We carefully positioned ourselves right behind the Island taking bearings to make sure that we would miss the one fm. rock. What a beautiful place to have to oneself!

August 17. Woke after a peaceful night surrounded by seals sitting on rocks just below the surface and other wildlife all around us. Full sail and off we went at 0845. We put up the large genoa but soon had it down again and were close-hauled first with the no. 2 genoa and then the working jib as the wind increased to S.W.5. Saw Dr. Sergal in *Sequel RCC* flying past as we plonked into a head sea. Eventually we got round Mizen Head and though I had intended going further I was faced with a mutiny as we tried to go past the beaches and Crookhaven, so we anchored under sail off Crookhaven at 1700. What a delight to have room to maneuvre! The fast moving scud above confirmed the synopsis with a low 500 miles west of Iceland 971 with all its horrible fronts rushing forward. Colin went ashore to meet his chums and swim and later they all came aboard.

August 18. With grey skies, strong wind and rain, we were rolling even in the sheltered harbour of Crookhaven so decided to go ashore for baths to cheer us up. To our dismay the hotel said they could not help because of the power cuts, indicating that all the hot water was required for washing clothes. Just at our lowest ebb we bumped into Colin's newly-made friends, a cheerful family of seven. They offered us baths at their flat and we were all very grateful for their hospitality. Feeling much brighter we were just getting into the dinghy when we were told of Crookhaven tummy. It appeared the water was being blamed and we had unfortunately just put two cans into our tank from the local supply. I put a dozen small purifying tablets into our fifty-gallon tank but as the instructions said one per pint the effect, if any, could only have been psychological but I am pleased to say it worked.

In the evening I phoned the U.K. to hear that they were basking in a heatwave. It seemed we had better get back as quickly as possible. I checked over the storm jib and mizzen roller reefing in preparation for our possible return.

August 19. Set off under sail at 1005. Found a dead calm outside with an uncomfortable swell after the gale and unfortunately had to use engine to get behind Long Island. To our surprise there was less swell in that position than in Crookhaven and a beautifully sheltered channel led to a good anchorage behind Coney Island where we stopped for lunch. The Island was alive with rabbits and with no foxes or other predators they must be multiplying like fun. The boys explored an old copper mine before we set off again under sail.

Rounded up in style in Schull Harbour at 1400. We rowed ashore and I decided to fill up an empty jerrycan. Eventually located Mr. O'Reilly who lives opposite the green tanks *en route* to the town and our can was filled from these with gas oil *domestique*, but for larger amounts he apparently would use the tank on the quay. Gill and the boys voted the town the best for shopping we had found on this cruise.

The sun was shining again as we set off for Baltimore passing between Middle and East Calf Islands, then east using the white entrance tower (at Baltimore) to help miss the Mullin and Torren rocks. This was the perfect day to see these rocky passages, at the top of an exceptional spring tide. We wiggled our way into the north entrance holding our breath as we were swept rapidly under the power cable. Having sailed around the harbour looking for a sheltered spot, we eventually dropped the anchor near the lifeboat slip at 1820. An exciting day.

August 20. We were determined to use every minute we had left to do some exploring and had chosen as our target the Frolic Point passage at the head of Roaring Water Bay at the N.E. corner of Hare Island. This passage was previously mentioned in the log by Mr. Knockhold (1977). Once again we were lucky to be able to see the passage at an exceptional low water springs. The north passage from Baltimore itself looked very different at low water as we sailed through to anchor at Hare Island. We dumped the boys ashore whilst Gill and I worked hard with the lead plonking away and the camera clicking as we plotted the reefs on our carefully drawn chart. At 1030 we decided we must have the courage of our convictions and we motored through shortly after low water. The depth on the north-west side of Frolic was somewhat nearer the original charted figures and as we had not had time to complete this section we turned and with full sail sped yet again through the north passage and out through the Baltimore entrance. We looked forward to explaining the Frolic passage to those who will be attending the grand gathering of 1979. At 1740 we anchored in Castletownsend. The evening was spent preparing for the passage home, filling in tide tables, plotting courses, checking D.F.

stations and all the 101 items which have to be done so carefully particularly when sailing short-handed. The forecast sounded fair and I was sorry we did not have time to go ashore to visit Annies Bar, but that pleasure will have to wait for another trip.

August 21. Gill and I woke up at 0430 and had a cup of tea to give us strength. The fishing boats were creeping out feeling their way as there were no obvious leading marks in the dark, and, following them out, we were surprised by the very weak light at the entrance. This would obviously not be good for a landfall in anything but very fair visibility. At 0600 we took our departure and by 1000 were bowling along in S.W.5. The boys got up but Alan immediately retired to his bunk to read, later followed by Colin who by now had graduated to a Hammond Innes thriller. We took in six rolls, put on the no. 2 genoa and dropped the mizzen. I played around with Consul and the Cork area D.F. beacons trying to plot the position of the oil rig or was it a gas rig? It is obviously becoming increasingly important to obtain the latest information on these monsters from the Notices to Mariners as there are a lot of unlit buoys surrounding such rigs. At 1430 I managed to get four quick sextant readings with Colin's help. We were really travelling, yawing all over the place as we busied ourselves with the usual navigational problems, and ate our corned beef hash admirably cooked by young Colin. The boys retired to bed by 2100 and we were still roaring along finding little difficulty in appreciating how cruel this sea would be in a real blow. At 2300 we managed to get a quick fix on Round Island with its cheerful red light blinking out of the gloom. Colin woke at 0200 and was keen to do his turn on the wheel, he was obviously enjoying the passage.

When approaching Lands End on a narrow angle from the N.W. the only good navigational aids that one can use in poor visibility, apart from the soundings, are Consul and a running D.F. fix on Round Island. I was able to obtain St. Morgan D.F. quite clearly but since the line from this runs along the edge of land it seemed sensible to treat the bearings with caution. In practice, it turned out that the results were good.

August 22. Longships was abeam at 0950. We had done 168 miles in twenty-eight hours. For the last twenty minutes we had motored across the very busy shipping lane as the wind had suddenly dropped and the visibility was closing in again, fog horns going everywhere. We passed the Runnel buoy and put everything up as the crew decided that they would like to continue in the now pleasant conditions with a light southerly wind. The whole vessel was festooned with bits of string as we goose-winged every conceivable sail whilst Colin experimented with the different rigs. How we longed for a spinnaker! The sun was shining brightly and with fried egg sandwiches appearing from the galley we really felt we were on the way home. Alan was out and about again informing us that his plastic boat (which is always towed much to everyone's amusement) was just going into hyperspace. Gill was sleeping down below as we all enjoyed this lazy day. By 1725 the Lizard was abeam and we had mackerel for tea, being the first fish that Colin had ever gutted by himself. I regret to say that nos. 2 and 3 got away. By 2300 we were coasting along at two knots but needed a little engine as we eventually lost steerage way near the Eddystone.

August 23. Colin came out for his watch and together we took a moonsight at 0300. We were both keeping a good lookout when we suddenly saw a yacht gliding past some fifty yards away with no lights on and apparently nobody in the cockpit. We had not seen anything although we had been looking all around continuously and the visibility wasn't too bad. This was the second time in one trip – a similar incident had taken place on the way across. In that case there were three hands on deck at the time and we had just turned on the spreader lights to help a sail change when immediately another yacht much too close for comfort turned on his lights. At least he had been keeping a watch and presumably preserving power but it is very easy to react incorrectly when a light suddenly appears so close. I hope these incidents are not a trend and that the offenders were not U.K. vessels. They both gave me a considerable fright and I was thankful our reflex actions were correct.

At 1017 we anchored off Salcombe beach. We visited friends, had supper ashore and young Alan retired to bed at 2230 – still full of beans – which proved that he had slept well during the passage.

August 24. A pleasant sunny day on the beach, the only excitement being when I boarded a nice motor sailer to let out more chain as she dragged gaily down the harbour. After visiting various boats, including *Little Eila* and *Norissa RCC*, we set off at 2100. A little apprehensive as to what would happen with the visibility, but had a pleasant trip to Poole harbour dropping anchor off Brownsea at 1825 on the following evening. We still find night passages the best way to cover ground with a young family even if we are a little tired next morning.

August 26. Sailed to Cowes to participate in a rally where we swapped tall stories with friends who had just returned from their holiday.

August 27. Back to Chichester to complete a lovely cruise. Rather windy but we had had some glorious passages, visited twenty-four different anchorages in twenty-eight days and sailed some 1,016 miles. Our one regret was that we had not met any R.C.C. boats whilst in Ireland. Perhaps they were all waiting for the gathering in 1979?

KEESHOND

Table of Distances

Date			*Distance made good*	*Time h. m.*	*Engine h. m.*
July	29	Chichester – Newlyn	195.0	36 30	24 00
Aug.	1	Newlyn – Crosshaven	157.0	32 32	28 00
	4	Crosshaven – Black Rock	8.0	2 00	0 10
	5	Black Rock to Kinsale	18.0	5 30	0 10
	6	Kinsale – Glandore	32.0	7 38	0 10
	7	Glandore – Blind Harbour	5.0	1 20	0 00
	8	Blind Harbour – Crookhaven	24.0	7 15	0 00
	10	Crookhaven – Ardgroom	45.5	9 15	0 20
	11	Ardgroom – Collorus	3.5	1 55	0 05
	12	Collorus – Derrynane	15.5	6 35	0 01
	13	Derrynane – Valentia	22.0	4 30	0 30
	14	Valentia – Derrynane	22.0	4 45	3 00
	15	Derrynane – Castletown Bere	33.5	5 10	0 00
	16	Castletown Bere – Adrigole	9.5	2 00	0 01
	17	Adrigole – Crookhaven	24.0	8 15	1 00
	19	Crookhaven – Coney Island	7.5	2 00	1 00
		Coney Island – Schull	2.0	0 30	0 00
		Schull – Baltimore	9.5	1 40	0 00
	20	Baltimore – Castletownsend	13.50	3 35	0 35
		via Frolic Point	135.0		
	21	Castletownsend – Salcombe	240.0	52 45	4 30
	24	Salcombe – Poole	88.0	21 25	5 00
	26	Poole – Cowes	30.0	8 35	2 00
	27	Cowes – Bosham	21.0	5 05	1 45
		Total trip	1027.5	231.45	71.51 (31.6%)
		With family alone	664.0	159 36	20 28 (12.8%)

BALTIC SUMMER IN *QUICKSILVER*

by Arthur Beiser

Even as a boy, long before my first visit in 1963, the Baltic fascinated me, and ten cruises there have not diminished its magnetic pull. In particular, I find sailing in the archipelagos that fringe the Baltic shores of Finland and Sweden to be crystalline joy, the profusion of routes and anchorages there an inexhaustible treasure. True, the weather can be dreadful, cold and damp with bitter winds, but it can also be warm and sunny for weeks on end. So not the least of the attractions of having a new yacht built in Finland was the prospect of taking delivery there and spending another summer in those magic waters.

A year earlier we had decided that a smaller yacht would serve our purposes better than *Minots Light*, the 58-foot ketch on which my family and I had sailed perhaps 50,000 miles since I bought her in 1960. A fine vessel in every respect, in good shape and up-to-date in her equipment, *Minots Light* was nevertheless simply too much boat for Germaine and me to be comfortable with now that our three daughters were grown up and leading their own lives. To be sure, each of them usually spends a month or so sailing with us every year, and we have many friends who are good shipmates, so we do not lack for crew, but for us the pleasures of cruising are enhanced by the feeling of independence that comes from being able to manage by ourselves on any venture we might undertake, from a day sail to an offshore passage. Although we had made a number of successful cruises alone on *Minots Light*, more often than not we felt afterward that there had been little to spare and a run of bad luck could have had unpleasant consequences.

After much consideration we settled on a Sparkman & Stephens-designed and Nautor-built New York Yacht Club 48, which is basically a Swan 47 sloop with a shallow keel plus centreboard instead of a deep fin keel and with a somewhat different interior arrangement. *Quicksilver* is 47 feet 9 inches overall, about 37 feet 6 inches on the waterline, and 13 feet 9 inches in beam. Her draught with her stainless-steel centreboard up is about 6 feet and with the board down it is nearly 10 feet. *Quicksilver's* displacement is about 16 tons of which half is represented by her external lead keel. Her sail area (mainsail plus 100% foretriangle) is 1,115 square feet, larger than standard because I prefer a big rig for shorthanded cruising – the jibs do not need much

The Royal Cruising Club
65° N
65°
60°
60°
55°
55°
10°E
15°
20°
25°
SWEDEN
NORWAY
FINLAND
Pietarsaari
Vasa
Åland
Isls
Hangö
Helsinki
Lovisa
L. Vänern
Kristine Hamn
Motala
Stockholm
L. Vättern
Göteborg
Laesö
Anholt
DENMARK
Copenhagen
Baltic Sea
U.S.S.R.
POLAND
EAST
GERMANY
QUICKSILVER

overlap and so are easier to handle, and the mainsail is large enough to be useful downwind.

After ordering *Quicksilver* and specifying 147 modifications and extras, we spent the summer of 1977 on an Adriatic cruise, and then put *Minots Light* on the market. She was sold in February; when she left the Mediterranean port where we lived two months later with her new owners, it was the first time I had ever seen her sailing whilst not on board, and I felt stricken. In May, Germaine and I drove up to Pietarsaari, which is in the northern part of the Gulf of Bothnia, to take over our new ship. Meeting us in Helsinki were Jim and Juliet Rickards, R.C.C., old friends who had made a number of cruises on *Minots Light* and now were generously helping put *Quicksilver* into commission.

The four of us, plus several of Nautor's craftsmen, took eleven days to check out all the equipment, to modify items that had not turned out as planned, and to stow and restow the mountain of gear that belongs on a yacht meant to be self-sufficient under all circumstances. The builders and the weather were most cooperative, and we were delighted to find that a nearby motel could provide both saunas and fine food. Other Nautor yachts were being readied for departure at the same quay, and we were a bit rattled when the first of them to leave returned to report that the Gulf of Bothnia was impassable due to floating ice. Usually the ice is mostly gone by this time, but the winter had been a severe one. A few days later they tried again and did not come back, so under the assumption that they had not sunk without trace we set 28 May as our departure date.

A cold north wind greeted us on the morning of the 28th, fine for a passage south. However, by the time we had gotten everything ready, been cleared by customs, and said goodbye to our neighbours at the quay and to various Nautor people who had come down to see us off, it was noon and the wind had gone around to the southwest. Once clear of the harbour we made sail for the first time in earnest, and to our relief and pleasure all went well: the sails set beautifully, the self-tailing winches (all fourteen of them) performed as advertised, and the centreboard reduced leeway to a barely perceptible amount. *Quicksilver* leaped forward as though she knew exactly what she was doing (which was not quite true of us), and our spirits rose as the temperature fell below 10°C. Soon we began to encounter ice, lovely sculptured floes that glistened in the sun. Dodging them in darkness did not appeal, and we headed west toward Sweden in order to spend the night there. Most of the time we had no trouble spotting floes far enough away to avoid them easily, but this was harder when the sun was hidden by clouds. Once we found ourselves surrounded and had to push our way through a group of small floes to get clear. The ice thinned out near the Swedish coast, and we anchored at midnight in a cove a few miles north of the island of Holmö.

The next morning provided cold rain and a southerly of F.4 as we motored with the main up through the channel inshore of Holmö. This part of the coast was new to us, and we were sorry that we were able to see so little of it, on the previous night and now. Clear of Holmö we headed south-east, which enabled us to set the jib and turn off the engine. *Quicksilver* found herself a groove less than 25° off the apparent wind along which she 'vroomed' (There is no other word!) at seven knots. *Minots Light*, though considered a close-winded boat in her day, could never point higher than 30°, and was usually happier at 35°. I am not usually fond of long windward stretches, but this was splendid going. The wind gradually increased, and at 1500 it was a solid F.5. With *Quicksilver* heeling as much as 25° at times, reefing the main was in order, which took Jim and me only a few minutes with the help of those handy winches. I was surprised at how easy modern slab reefing is to accomplish, hardly more work than dropping the mizzen of a ketch – but under full sail a sloop or cutter is much more efficient to windward and downwind than an equivalent ketch is. I am sure *Quicksilver* is not far from the line beyond which a ketch is a better proposition for short-handed cruising than a cutter (since *Quicksilver* has a removable inner stay on which a forestay-sail can be set, she can quickly become a cutter when desired), but her present rig seems just right.

We could not enter the archipelago on the Finnish side of the Gulf of Bothnia outside Vasa because the buoys had not yet been put in place, so in the late afternoon we anchored off the pilot station on the island of Norrskär. A bleak part of the world. A fisherman in an outboard boat came out to invite us into the tiny harbour, but there seemed little room there, nothing of interest ashore, and he was vague about the depth. We rolled a bit, which however did not prevent Germaine and Juliet from putting together a dinner of fish chowder, meat loaf seasoned with dill, mashed potatoes, salad, and ice cream with blueberries. Stuffed, tired, and happy, we proceeded to sleep for eleven hours.

An overcast sky and a southwest wind of F.5 the next morning provided no incentive to leave, and we spent the morning on assorted chores. Lunch and naps followed, and when we woke up it was to find sunshine and a wind that had softened and veered to the northwest. We left at 1600 under main and jib, but soon replaced the jib with a Hood invention called a Multipurpose Spinnaker. This huge sail – ours is about 1,300 square feet in area – is a cross between a spinnaker and a drifter and is made from 1.5 ounce nylon. Set flying from a spinnaker halyard and tacked to the stemhead, it is far simpler to handle than a spinnaker because it needs no pole. Running wing-and-wing downwind, to be sure, a whisker pole helps the MPS stay out where it belongs, but it is not really essential and, in any case, setting a light whisker pole is an easier job than messing around with a heavier spinnaker pole and its various strings. With the help of the MPS we were doing up to eight knots in a following wind of F.4. Such nimble going is normal on today's stripped-out racing boats with their large crews, but *Quicksilver* is not light for her size in the first place and was loaded down with extra tankage, extra batteries, heavy ground tackle, a refrigeration compressor, and so forth; nor did we ever have to work very hard on deck. Even now, with the season over, I can't get over *Quicksilver*'s exhilarating speed, which was achieved with no sacrifice of seaworthiness or cruising amenities. Not that *Quicksilver* is perfect, but I find it easy to forgive her faults in exchange for her alacrity under way.

Just before dinner-time the wind freshened to F.5 and we took in the MPS. Since we were going at almost seven knots under main alone, we didn't bother to set a headsail, and in fact went through the night that way. Our course paralleled the Finnish coast about ten miles offshore, and once we had put the Vasa archipelago behind us, we saw nothing until the following afternoon – no land, no lights, no aids to navigation, no ships, not even any birds. After dinner we set watches of two hours on, six hours off. With steering easy and nothing else to do but keep an eye out, the person on deck needed an awesome amount of clothing to keep warm once the sun set. At 0400 the wind grew lighter and we set the jib, a few hours later changing it for the reacher. This sail is essentially a high-cut genoa whose clew is a little higher than the main boom. The helmsman can see under it, the lead of its sheet does not have to be changed when it is trimmed in or out, it is easier to tack or jibe than a conventional genoa, and on a reach it can be sheeted without twisting via the end of the main boom or held out on a run with a whisker pole: a formidable list of virtues. Why cruising yachts ever carry deck-sweeping genoas beats me. Though we call this sail the reacher because that is its designation in the inventory of a racing boat, it works very well to windward.

We entered the archipelago north of Turku at the Isokari lighthouse. Germaine and I had never been in this region before, and it seemed to us more attractive than the archipelago to the south, perhaps because there were fewer signs of civilization. As *Quicksilver* glided through the winding leads in the late afternoon the only sounds were of birds. Besides gulls and starlings, we met many ducks with strings of duck-lings paddling frantically behind them. The islands are all wooded here, with the light yellow-green leaves and silver trunks of the birches standing out against the darker pines. Soon the wind vanished entirely, and we furled the sails to float still during dinner. Then we motored for an hour to a sheltered spot in the middle of a group of small islands southeast of Lypertö where we anchored for the night.

Thursday was bright and clear, and, most welcome of all, warm at 22°C. A fair wind of F.4 from the north-west completed the picture. Soon we were in familiar waters, islands of grey and green all around, but in contrast to our previous visits, which had been made later in the year, no other boats were out and only a few people ashore were to be seen. We anchored at 2000 at Hamnholm, after a day threading the leads. Although these are well-marked, they are sometimes intricate with the sequence of marks not always clear until the last moment, especially where two or three channels intersect. The harmony of land and water in this region is hypnotic and we were all glad to be back.

Two more days of fine weather and fine sailing brought us to Helsinki on Saturday. Outside the harbour several races were in progress, and scores of other yachts were out just for the fun of it. We debated whether euphoria or alcohol was responsible for some of the whimsical maneuvering we saw, which more than once gave us a fright as boats would change course suddenly to dart in front of *Quicksilver*. At 1645 we tied to the wooden quay at the Nylandska Yacht Club (N.J.K.) on its island of Blekholmen in the middle of the inner harbour. A perfect spot: close to the centre of the city with fine views all around, but always quiet. A launch takes people back and forth to a landing on shore at regular intervals. The members of N.J.K. are Swedish-speaking Finns, and nearly all of them speak English as well.

Quicksilver stayed in Helsinki for a week. Finnish friends came to visit, and we took some of them for a spin one day; the engine was checked by a Volvo representative; *Quicksilver* got her official papers from the U.S. Consulate . . . there was always something going on. One day the motor-sailer *Summerwind* came in under charter to the National Geographic Society for a cruise to Leningrad, Tallinn, and Riga. Tom Abercrombie, one of their writer-photographers, was the skipper, and the crew consisted of his wife Lynn and a young friend of theirs named Stoll. The Society had been officially assured by the Soviet Embassy in Washington that they would be welcome, and Tom and company were full of enthusiasm at the prospect of being the first Americans to sail a yacht to this part of Russia. All they needed was a piece of paper said to be waiting for them at the Soviet Embassy in Helsinki, and they expected to be off in a few days for Leningrad.

We left Helsinki on 11 June headed eastward in a westerly breeze that barely ruffled the water. We set the real spinnaker for the first time, a lightweight (0.85 ounce) tri-radial affair that somehow stayed up in an apparent wind that went as low as two knots. After a while the wind shifted to the south and strengthened, and we set the reacher in place of the spinnaker. In a stretch of open water we turned the helm over to the Sailomat self-steerer, which held the course only moderately well. The trouble seemed to be that the vane was not perfectly balanced. In the late afternoon we entered the little bay off Tallbäcka where my friend Stig Eriksson has a summer place. Stig met us in his dinghy and talked me into going all the way in to pick up his mooring, which was free since his motor cruiser *Clyde* was then tied to his jetty. In *Minots Light* we had always anchored where the depth was 3 metres but that was a quarter of a mile from shore. The mooring was supposed to be safe for a draft of 2 metres, and *Quicksilver* draws something over 1.8 metres, which did not leave much margin, but Stig is a persuasive fellow. We seemed all right there, and went ashore for a welcome sauna and drinks. Later we all returned to *Quicksilver* for dinner and a discussion of Stig's plans to sail around the world in a Nautor 43 motor-sailer which he was about to order. I found myself envious, not of his project – a circumnavigation is not one of my dreams – but of his excitement, of the way the idea possessed all his thoughts.

During the night the water level fell a few centimeters and we found ourselves gently bumping the bottom in the morning. The bottom was soft mud, so no harm seemed in prospect, and since the wind was F.0 anyway, we decided to stay there for the day and hope the situation was temporary. Plenty of odd jobs remained on my list, and we took care of many of them, including balancing the Sailomat. In the evening Stig came out for dinner again, which was followed by a walk on shore through the forest in the long June twilight. The tang of wood smoke from a nearby sauna spiced the air. We learned that Stig had hired a Danish girl who had lived in the U.S. to spend a few weeks improving his English in preparation for his voyage, since Finnish and Swedish are not the most useful languages for a world traveller. We promised to return to check her command of English.

Tuesday saw us afloat, but as we motored out we ran hard aground. Swinging Jim out at the end of the boom heeled *Quicksilver* enough for us to get off. The wind was easterly, on the nose, but as usual *Quicksilver* loved it, and with the board down, only a finger on the wheel was needed. We tried the Sailomat in one of the broader channels, and it now steered a beautifully steady course. Neither a windvane self-steerer nor a compass-controlled autopilot (ours is a Neco) is particularly useful in these complex waters, and we did not use ours very much during the summer, but it was nice to know they worked. We had never taken the 2 metres channel north of Pellinki before because of *Minots Light*'s 2.4 metres draft, and this seemed a worthwhile shortcut now. The board had to be raised, but the wind here was not too far forward and leeway was not excessive. Unfortunately one of the marks was missing, cut loose by a log tow that had preceded us, and we came to a shuddering halt for a second time. For all *Quicksilver*'s relatively shoal draft we seemed to be going aground more than ever before.

Not long after getting off we were sailing up the unmarked passage that leads to Johan Björksten's place at Fantsnäs, just west of Lovisa. Since we had negotiated this passage many times before with *Minots Light* we were really safe enough, but we were unnerved by our experiences earlier in the day and very careful about following my old pilotage instructions. A sample: 'Head N. keeping 100 m. away from the rocks awash to starboard until the big tree at the end of the long, narrow island to port is in line with the birdhouse on the little round island past it, then turn NW.' We got in with no trouble and anchored near Johan's Folkboat *Aganna*. Two days later Jim and Juliet left for England and home, having been with us for a month that had seemed only half that.

Four years had passed since our last stay at Fantsnäs, which meant a lot of visiting back and forth with our friends there to review what had been happening to all of us in the meantime. One day, while the engine was being run to charge the batteries, the alarm rang and clouds of steam emerged from the exhaust. I shut the engine down and went through the usual procedure for finding a fault in the cooling system, but I could find nothing amiss. I proceeded to curse the engine, a French-built Volvo MD21A, which I had not wanted in the first place but which Nautor refused to consider changing. Since I liked everything else about the NYYC 48, I had reluctantly accepted the engine, and now it seemed my worst fears were materialising. After a while, I realized that one element of the cooling system had not been checked, the inlet seacock. I opened the strainer and then the cock, but only a trickle of water came in. Aha! After disconnecting the hose to the cock, I poked a bit of stiff wire into it, to be rewarded with a fountain of water and half of the fish which had been stuck inside.

On Monday 19 June, we sailed back to Helsinki. We know this passage by heart, but always enjoy the varied scenery along the way. At N.J.K. we found *Summerwind* again, her crew considerably less ebullient than before. To their surprise – but not to mine, because I had tried in vain some years before to get permission for a similar venture to Russia – the Soviet Embassy claimed never to have heard of *Summerwind*, and indeed were dubious about the very existence of an embassy of theirs in Washington. Much cabling and telephoning to Washington and Moscow had no effect, and the Abercrombies had to be content with a visit by cruise ship to Leningrad and Tallinn, hardly a novelty.

The rest of the week was a blur of activity, ranging from having the laundry done to meeting the American ambassador. At a party one evening at N.J.K. in honour of the participants in the Copenhagen–Helsinki Race, Germaine and I sat next to several Finnish naval cadets. I asked them why Finland needed a navy, since clearly they couldn't expect to hold off the Russian fleet. Quite true, they replied, but Russia wasn't the potential enemy they were worried about, it was Sweden. Sweden? Yes, after all, Sweden must surely covet the Åland Islands, and one day . . . who knows?

We had planned to spend Midsummer Eve, that most important of Scandinavian occasions, at the island of Kaiholmen where N.J.K. was putting on a big party. A foul wind (in every sense) and heavy rain all day were inauspicious portents, and we agreed with the *Summerwind* people to just stay put and have our own private party, The event was not the most joyous on record; they were still unhappy about their abortive Russian expedition, and Germaine and I were not enjoying the incessant bad weather. When the rain finally stopped a few days later, Germaine and I went off for an unambitious but most delightful cruise in the archipelago between Helsinki and Borgå to the east. Having so substantial a vessel to ourselves meant comfort and convenience in life on board, but despite her towering rig (the masthead is about 67 feet above the water) we had no trouble in handling *Quicksilver* under sail, and revelled in her speed.

One day we thought we would see how Stig's English was getting along, and we sailed to Tallbäcka again. The wind expired a mile or two short of our destination, and we continued under power. After a short time the engine stopped. Again I cursed it, and Nautor too. Germaine suggested I shut up and find the trouble. After a while I saw the justice of her remarks, and discovered that the fuel tank was empty. We had been using the engine so little lately that I had lost the habit of checking the fuel level every day. I apologised to the engine (which gave no trouble the rest of the summer), switched to another tank, and went through the messy routine of bleeding the fuel system while Germaine chased cat's paws to get us to Tallbäcka.

Stig's teacher Bente turned out to be a lovely girl (we had half expected a battleaxe) who spoke fluent English. After dinner we discussed the preparations that had to be made for his circumnavigation, whose number and complexity amazed Bente. At midnight we all had a sauna, still talking about everything from the length of the lines needed for a Panama Canal transit (100 feet each) to the minimum number of anchors to take (four, we agreed). I would not be surprised if Bente decides that Stig will continue to need her help with English during his voyage.

We were back in Helsinki early in July to meet two of our daughters, Alexa and Isabel. Westerly winds of F.5 plus rain by the bucket kept us at N.J.K.'s hospitable quay for some days more, which was fine with the girls who know the city well. When we left on 11 July we also had with us their Finnish friend Titti Ramsay, who had cruised on *Minots Light* on two previous occasions. Alexa and Isabel had been respectively three and two years old when we bought *Minots Light*, and all their summers since had been spent on her. They missed *Minots Light*, but less and less as the pleasures of *Quicksilver*'s brisk performance became evident. Germaine had been apprehensive about their reaction, but in a short time they seemed as much at home on *Quicksilver* as they had been on *Minots Light*. All three girls were intrigued by the new gear, especially the self-tailing winches, and they were quite able to do all the work on deck. How nice to just sit behind the wheel and let other people handle the sheets while tacking back and forth in a narrow channel! On *Minots Light* there had been all too much heavy work that, on a family cruise, only I could carry out.

The calm and light fog of our early start from Helsinki were soon replaced by a modest south-westerly breeze. On the way to Hangö we passed many yachts returning to Helsinki under spinnaker after having competed in Hangö Race Week, including four graceful eight-metres. I was looking forward to having the wind behind the beam for a change after turning the corner at Hangö, but the wind shifted to the north-west just about then: clearly it was that kind of summer. At 2130 we were at the romantic Stor Krockö anchorage, having covered ninety-three miles. The wind was from the north at F.3–4 in the morning and we had to beat up Jungfrusund, but it was a close reach after that to the channel south of Nauro. We made the passage between Nauro and Korppo in two tacks, and then the sun came out and the wind almost died as we turned west into the channel north of Korppo. We ghosted to a small bay in the middle of the island of Vattkast which we had to ourselves. Two days of good progress and the day's sunshine made a special dinner in order: poached salmon with new potatoes washed down by a lively moselle and followed by strawberries.

Miraculously the sky was a transparent blue the next day, and we drifted westward in vagrant zephyrs by courtesy of the MPS. At noon the wind vanished altogether, and we motored the rest of the way to Enskär, an island in the Kumlinge group that belongs to Rolf and Ada von Frenckell. Most of the islands near Enskär are uninhabited and the nearest marked channel is several miles away, so Rolf and Ada have perfect peace there. Rolf's family have been master printers since 1642 and he is busy most of the year in Helsinki, but on Enskär his main occupation is fishing. When we arrived, Rolf and Ada came out to greet us; we were expected, having called them on the VHF earlier. Much talk and liquid refreshment, then all ashore for a sauna, and back to *Quicksilver* for a roast-beef dinner. The only note that fell short of perfection was the sky, which clouded over as we ate. The barograph had begun to descend, too, and Rolf and Ada had no trouble in persuading us to spend the following day there.

Saturday was a clear, sharp November day, complete with an icy northwest wind. The air temperature was 11°C, the water temperature 13°C, no conditions for a brass monkey. Rolf led us out with his speedboat; the routes to Enskär are unmarked, and while the eastern approach is clear enough, the western one is tricky. We set the forestay sail to supplement the jib, and had a joyous sail south of Mariehamn and then across the Åland Sea to enter the Stockholm archipelago between Söderarm and Tjärven. At 1900 we anchored in our usual spot at Tjockö in front of the red house at Sten and Hilka Brag. Finding a dozen boats tied to the shore opposite the Brag's house was a shock, since we had had the anchorage to ourselves on previous visits. July is the Swedish holiday month, and it seems that every Swede is out in a boat then. We were about to inflate the dinghy when Åsa Brag, Sten and Hilka's daughter, rowed out to welcome us and invite us to have a sauna. Though the Brag's sauna is one of the very best anywhere, hot as hell and right at the water's edge, we had been cooked enough at Enskär and declined with thanks. Sten and Hilka were away for a few days, and Hilka's brother Immu, who had sailed around the world in a Swan 37 a few years before, was not expected for another week. We were sad to miss them all, but it was nice to see Åsa again.

Three marked channels lead south from Tjockö. We took the outer one because it is the least populated with houses and motorboats, and ran downwind under main and MPS wing-and-wing. During a jibe the MPS decided we were not according it sufficient respect, and it wrapped four times around the headstay. The yachts we had just passed with a condescending wave now passed us, their crews generous with insincere expressions of sympathy. The smooth rod headstay made it fairly easy to unwrap the MPS, an unexpected advantage of rod. In mid-afternoon our old friend the rain returned, and shortly after hail began to pelt down. We ducked behind Nötholmen, a small island not far from Stockholm, and picked up the mooring there. To our surprise nobody was on the island, the first time we had ever found it thus; usually three generations of the Dalén family are represented there all summer.

On previous Baltic cruises our custom had been to go for a swim before breakfast whenever the water temperature exceeded 18°C, which was normally the case; indeed, in a good summer, such as that of 1973, we regularly found water as warm as 24°C. In the morning Germaine and I moaned about how much we missed these dips, and Titti responded that for a Finn the present water temperature of 14°C was entirely adequate. Challenged, she dived in – and climbed out at once. Poor girl, some of her *sisu* (Finnish hardiness) must have evaporated during a week with us. The north-west wind was light at first but later grew to F.6 and backed, so what started as a reach ended with us reefed and hard on the wind. What a day! *Quicksilver* just loved it. When we reached Nynäshamn at about 1600 none of us really wanted to stop, but mail was waiting for us there.

We left Nynäshamn on Thursday and had a busy day close-hauled in a south-east wind of F.3. Hundreds of boats were everywhere, and, at narrow places in the channel, traffic jams sometimes occurred. All the pretty anchorages we had used in the past were now crowded, and we finally left the channel south of Oxelösund to find ourselves a quiet spot among some islands. Our mast must have been visible from the channel because soon a few other boats arrived and anchored nearby. I think it is dreadful to play a radio or tape on deck when any other boats are within hearing, but it was just the evening for Vivaldi and a cigar in the cockpit after dinner, and it was *our* anchorage after all, so I went ahead.

An early start on Friday had us at Mem by 1500, where we went through the sea-lock of the Göta Canal and tied up just past it. Here we bagged the jib, covered the mainsail, stowed the sheets and snatch blocks, dug out all the fenders (we had eight, but ten would have been better), and otherwise got *Quicksilver* ready for the canal. This was to be our sixth transit of that charming waterway across Sweden, which is nearly a century-and-a-half old. There are plenty of locks – thirty-seven on the way up to Lake Vättern, then twenty-one on the way down to Lake Vänern – but all of us were old hands at coping with locks, and we had an uneventful journey. When we got to Motala, at the eastern end of Lake Vättern, Titti had to leave to take up a summer job back in Finland. Over the years we had come to think of her almost as a member of the family, and we were sorry to see her go. The headquarters of the canal are in Motala, and we learned there that the canal had just been sold for one krone to the Swedish government by the private company that had owned it. The canal itself seems to be a losing proposition (despite the dues of 700 kroner we had to pay), although income from the land bordering the canal, which also belonged to the company, is an off-setting factor. About 6,000 yachts were expected to pass through the canal in 1978, seventy per cent of them in July. A good month, July, to be elsewhere.

On Saturday 29 July we left the last lock at Sjötorp and went on to Mariestad in Lake Vänern. The visitors' berths were all too small for *Quicksilver*, so we tied to the inner end of the main quay near a sign forbidding this. A number of other yachts joined us there later, and nobody seemed to mind. Alexa and Isabel left two days later to return to the U.S. where they had much to do before returning to their universities in September.

Tuesday was so fine that Germaine and I sunbathed as *Quicksilver* sailed the twenty miles to Läckö Castle under autopilot – a real summer day at long last. We were joined there by the sloop *Indigo* with Herman and Gudrun Schaedla and their three sons on board, a *rendezvous* that had been arranged some months earlier. Herman owns Abeking & Rasmussen, the German yard where *Minots Light* was built and where we kept her for six winters before bringing her to the Mediterranean. We had much to talk about, not least of all Herman's miniature folding motorbike that looks like a toy, but isn't.

Thursday provided a south-westerly, making it a dead run to Kristinehamn at the north-east corner of Lake Vänern. Herman left early and soon had *Indigo* festooned with huge sails. We were slower off the mark, but once we had *Quicksilver*'s reacher set on the whisker pole to port with her mainsail to starboard, her larger size told and in a few hours *Indigo* was almost out of sight astern. Ordinarily I might have allowed Herman, who cares about such things whereas I don't, to arrive first, but on our last cruise in company he had soundly beaten *Minots Light* and revenge is always sweet.

At the entrance to the long, narrow inlet that leads to Kristinehamn we noticed what seemed to be some sort of huge totem pole. We later found out it was, of all things in this part of the world, a Picasso statue. We anchored near a bathing pavilion on the theory that it would be safe to bathe there, and had a welcome swim in 22 °C water. Since the water was virtually fresh, Germaine took advantage of the occasion to wash her hair in it. Later *Indigo* arrived and rafted to us. Jimmy and Hans, the elder Schaedla boys, rowed to a nearby yacht basin to look for their Soling, which Herman had sent ahead by trailer.

Friday morning, on the way into Kristinehamn, I did something so stupid that the memory of it is still painful. As the larger vessel, we were going in first, and we had borrowed Hans to give us a hand in case tying up presented any problems. I was so busy talking to Hans that I overlooked the buoy marking the start of the dredged entrance channel, and we gradually came to a stop. The bottom seemed soft and the situation merely comical at first. When we were still there an hour later, despite two anchors out and *Quicksilver* heeled over to reduce her draft, things were less funny. By now it was pouring as well, and when a small harbour tug appeared and offered to pull us off, I felt that enough was enough and asked how much. 'For nothing' was the reply, and soon we were afloat in the channel; our own failure to get free had been due to inadequate sounding of the shoal, so that the anchors were in the wrong places. The tug's skipper kindly offered to recover the anchors, two 35-pound Danforths (*Quicksilver* also has a 60-pound CQR in a stemhead roller and a 55-pound fisherman), but these were so deeply buried that raising them was harder than it had been to get us off. I gave the tug's crew our thanks and a bottle of whisky; they really deserved more, but seemed quite happy. In the harbour we tied to a derelict motor cruiser with *Indigo* next to us. Soon after the Schaedla boys brought the Soling over and tied her to *Indigo*, almost blocking the channel. It made quite a spectacle, but in the rain nobody was there to notice.

The rain continued intermittently on Saturday, which did not stop the boys from taking the Soling out for a sail. In the evening we walked to the train station to meet a friend of the Schaedlas who was coming from England and some friends of ours, Are and Karen Mann, who were coming from Germany. By coincidence they were on the same train from Göteborg. The next morning our fleet moved to a bay west of Kristinehamn. The rain was still with us, and later in the day I made a gallon of Moose Milk – a hot beverage of remarkable restorative powers (rum, brandy, and whisky are among its ingredients) whose recipe I learned one winter in Alaska – which was well received by all hands.

Monday brought a light breeze from the north-east and a clearing sky, and we decided to head south. The northern end of Lake Vänern, though in no way unpleasant, was not especially attractive either, and we had no reason to hang around there. We said goodbye to *Indigo* and left under mainsail and MPS. The sky cleared entirely in the afternoon, and we had an easy sail to the Lurö archipelago forty-two miles away where we anchored just north of Husön. The ambiance was that of the Maine coast, lacking only a passing fisherman to sell us lobsters just out of the sea. The wind was from the same direction in the morning but stronger, and we ran before it to Vänersborg. Are and I were in favour of setting the spinnaker, but the ladies were not enthusiastic, pointing out quite correctly that we were doing seven to eight knots under main and poled-out reacher while sunshine and the Goldberg Variations filled the cockpit, which should be enough for anybody.

We spent Wednesday in Vänersborg, where a laundromat and shops of all kinds are near the yacht harbour. I changed the engine oil, topped up the water tanks, and exchanged an empty propane tank for a full one. The Manns treated us to dinner at the best restaurant in town, but unfortunately the cuisine was as undistinguished there as it is elsewhere in Sweden. Even though it bore the Carlsberg label, the beer was locally brewed, and disappointing compared either with the real thing or with the fine beers of Finland.

On Thursday we went through the six locks of the Trollhätte Canal and down the Göta River to Göteborg. We tied up in the Lille Bommen basin and spent Friday exploring the city, which was only a short walk away. On Saturday we left Lille Bommen, but the weather was pretty dreadful and we got no farther than the Långedrag yacht harbour a few miles away. The man who took our lines turned out to be Sven Lundin, and we went with him to see both his old *Bris* and the new one in the garden of his mother's house nearby. Sven had made a remarkable voyage to North and South America in the first *Bris*, a wooden twenty-footer he had designed and built, and it was interesting to see the fruits of his experience manifested in her successor, also his own creation. The new *Bris* is 19′6″ × 19′6″ × 8′ × 4′6″ with a plumb stem and a long bowsprit, and is solidly constructed of welded aluminium with no fewer than twenty-one triple-glazed windows. Despite her size, *Bris* is fully equipped: a Saab diesel with a range of a thousand miles, a refrigerator, full B & G instrumentation, an automatic pilot, and so forth. No ascetic, Sven was looking forward to the arrival of two French girls who were to be in charge of the gastronomic end of his forthcoming voyage to San Francisco via Cape Horn. Are was fascinated by the whole project, to Karen's horror.

Rain and winds of F.5 and 6 from the south-west kept us at Långedrag for the next three days. On one of them we had the pleasure of meeting Sven's crew of Elizabeth and Martine, who had been recruited by means of an advertisement in a French yachting journal. Otherwise it was a dreary wait for the weather to improve. Local yachtsmen agreed the summer – which they referred to as the 'green winter' – had been the worst they could recall, which made us feel better about our many delays waiting for reasonable conditions; although we have always been pretty soft sailors, at least we were not getting any softer.

A cold front was expected to pass through the Kattegat on the afternoon of Wednesday 16 August, but the morning was reasonable for a change and we set out for the Danish island of Laesø in the hope of getting there in time. We lost the race, but the wind did nothing more than go from F.3 to F.5 when the squall line reached us, and then faded back to F.3 after twenty minutes. We tied alongside in the inner harbour of Østerby at 1700. We found the village a dull place; it even lacks a bakery, the one mentioned in the F.P.I. having closed a few years earlier.

Those who are in charge of the weather must have heard us scorning Wednesday's front, because on Thursday, on the way to Anholt, we were blasted by a squall with F.7 winds and torrents of rain that turned to hail. We hove to until the drama subsided. An hour later an arrogant cumulonimbus cloud complete with lightning strokes and waterspouts was moving purposefully toward us, and we altered course by 90° in a successful effort to avoid it. Only a few miles from Anholt a third squall materialised which we could not evade, and we again had an exciting time for a short period.

In Anholt we were lucky to find a good berth and made fast with *Quicksilver*'s bow to the inner breakwater and an anchor out astern. According to the harbourmaster, about 200 yachts were in the harbour, most of them German. It looked full to us, but he said that the record, which had been made on August 3, stood at 410. The number of yachts steadily diminished during our stay, with only twenty remaining when we left two weeks later. Because cruising sailors tend to be civilised, the mob scene was not as bad as it could have been, and, of course, the miles of sandy beach that rim Anholt can absorb any number of people. This beach, together with the relative inaccessibility of the island and its unspoiled interior, make Anholt unique in this part of the world, and we always pause there when we are in the Kattegat.

On Friday the Manns left on the daily ferry for Grenaa and then a train home. We are ambivalent about cruising with other people: with the right shipmates (such as Karen and Are) it is fun, but it is also fun to be by ourselves. We spent the rest of the day drying sails and inspecting the other yachts, a motley collection that ranged from ocean racers to bundles of planks held together with baling wire and chewing gum. Unaccountably we failed to recognize *Lene*, the varnished double-ender of Hans and Birte Bagh, but Hans had spotted us and later we had dinner with them in *Quicksilver*'s cockpit.

The next few days were glorious with blue skies and bright sunshine, and Germaine and I (like everybody else there) spent them on the beach and in the water. Hardly a bathing suit was to be seen. One morning Hans introduced Germaine to a fisherman he knew from whom she bought no less than five kilograms of the small lobsters called *jungfruhummer*; the price was so reasonable that Germaine was carried away. Though my dream of paradise includes an unlimited supply of *jungfruhummer*, I must admit I was not sorry when we ate the last of them nearly a week later.

Our original plan had been to sail to Aarhus where our friends the Brocks live, but we were reluctant to leave and instead invited them to join us in Anholt. Although they do not live so very far away, like most Danes they had never visited Anholt. Anxious to make up for lost time, Axel, Wibeke, and their daughter Kristine set out the day after their arrival to walk around the island, which took them until evening and whose rewards included meeting a herd of amiable seals with many pups. Germaine and I stayed on the beach, intent on soaking up the maximum of sunshine before the weather reverted to form. A wise idea, because the Brock's departure was followed by many days of rain and cold winds.

Anholt in the rain is pretty much a total loss, but we were prevented from leaving by a case of flu that knocked me out. With exquisite timing the Webasto heating plant chose this moment to give up, which surprised me since the same model on *Minots Light* had proved reliable for nine years. (The trouble turned out to be a too-powerful supplementary fuel pump, and a pressure-relief chamber was later installed in Copenhagen which cured the problem.) We spent a dismal week waiting for my recovery. Although I was still a little shaky, we left on Saturday 2 September, with a fair wind from the north-west. Under mainsail alone we averaged seven knots to Gilleleje, the Sailomat steering all the way. It felt great to be sailing again.

The wind shifted farther to the west on Sunday, giving us a run to Helsingør and a reach to Skovshoved, the yacht harbour just outside Copenhagen. *Quicksilver* was the fastest yacht on the Sound that afternoon, clearly as happy to see the return of the sun as we were. I was glad we were arriving at Skovshoved in such style because our friends there had all thought us crazy or worse to replace *Minots Light*. 'Next you will sell your mother,' one of them had said. Still, no welcome could have been more cordial. Willing hands helped us tie up, bag the jib, cover the main, and open the whisky. We had dinner at the Royal Danish Yacht Club with Børge and Mitzi Holte, and to cap a full day *Summerwind* came in later with many adventures to report.

A few days afterward our eldest daughter Nadia arrived with her friend George, who had been introduced to sailing the previous year with a largely idyllic passage on *Minots Light* from Venice to the south of France. The return of rain and gusty winds enabled us to show George the other side of the picture day-sailing out of Skovshoved. As her sisters had, Nadia approved of *Quicksilver*, which pleased Germaine and me. According to the Danish newspapers, this was the coldest, wettest September since 1725. I believe them.

Quicksilver's first season ended with her being hauled out for the winter at a Copenhagen yard. She had exceeded our expectations by a great deal, but the weather, despite a few good patches, had taken much of the edge from our enjoyment and had led us to truncate our plans for a more extensive cruise in Danish waters. Still, there are always rewards to be found in the Baltic, and we look forward to going back next year.

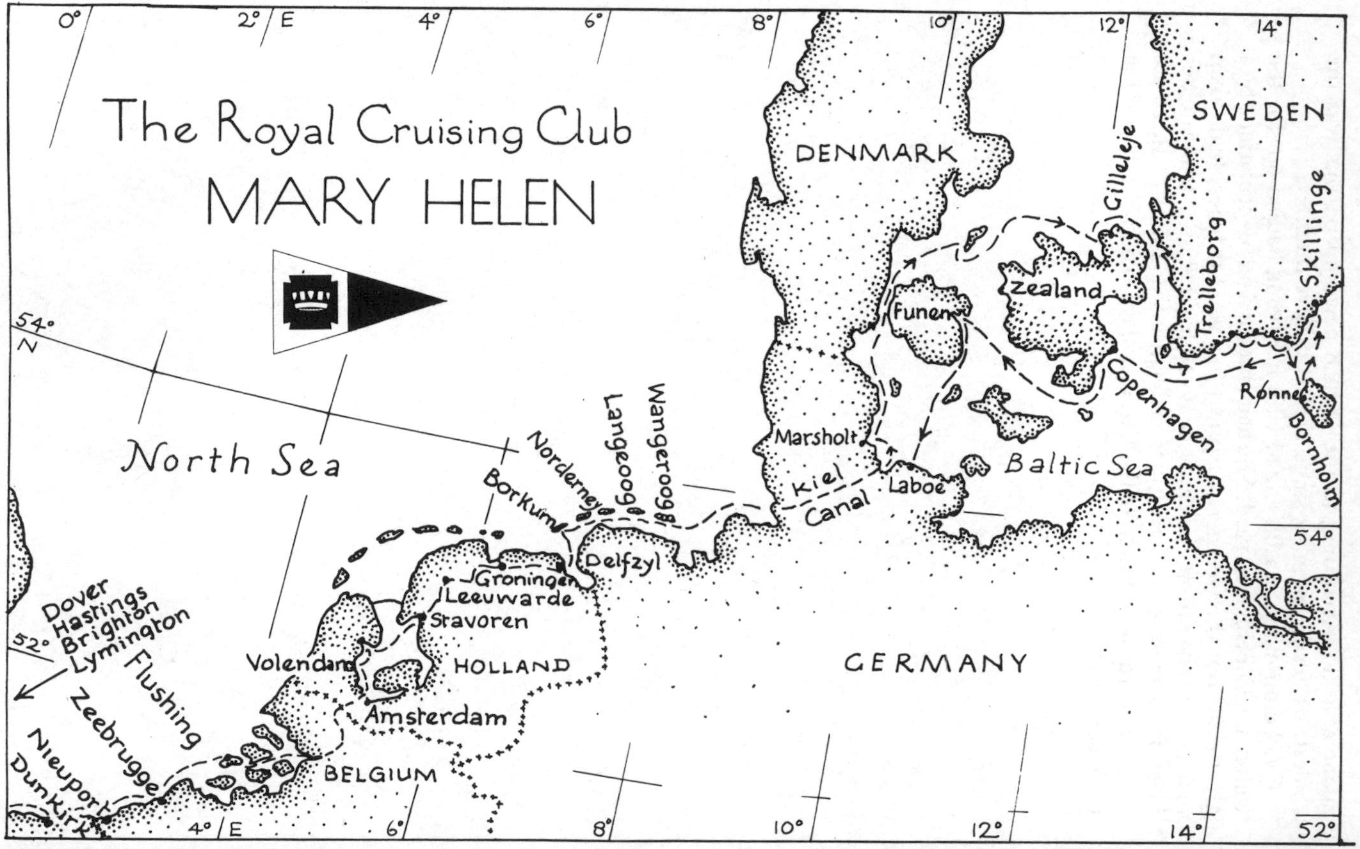

The Royal Cruising Club
MARY HELEN
North Sea
Baltic Sea
SWEDEN
DENMARK
GERMANY
HOLLAND
BELGIUM
Gilleleje
Trelleborg
Skillinge
Rønne
Bornholm
Copenhagen
Zealand
Funen
Marsholt
Kiel
Canal
Laboe
Wangeroog
Langeoog
Norderney
Borkum
Delfzyl
Groningen
Leeuwarde
Stavoren
Volendam
Amsterdam
Flushing
Zeebrugge
Nieuport
Dunkirk
Dover
Hastings
Brighton
Lymington
0°
2° E
4°
6°
8°
10°
12°
14°
54° N
52°
4° E

MARY HELEN REACHES THE BALTIC

by Helen Tew

Mary Helen was first described in the 1938 journal, and more recently in 1969, but for the benefit of newer members here are her vital statistics: 26′ O.A., 23′6″ L.W.L., 8′3″ beam, 5′ draft, 6.5 T.M. She was designed by my late husband, John Tew and built by the late Percy Mitchell at Port Mellon, Mevagissey during the winter of 1936–37. She cost £250 and was paid for out of our wedding present cheques! It costs more to buy her a new sail now! She is still the handsomest yacht afloat and gets admired wherever she goes! Her only electricity is a hand torch.

This year my son Ian (R.C.C.) had leave from Singapore, and fortunately for me wanted to have a cruise in *Mary Helen*. As British 420 Association president, I wanted to attend the 420 World Championships at Jyllinge, Denmark, so we decided to sail *Mary Helen* there. Accordingly, at midday on Sunday 11 June, Ian and I set sail from Lymington with a light fair wind in bright sunshine, and had a pleasant sail up the Solent, hoping to make Bembridge for the night. We were a bit late on the tide, so decided not to risk the entrance, particularly as the engine would not start and it would mean tacking in; so we anchored in 2.5 fathoms off the Lifeboathouse – another yacht behind us went on in and stuck!

Off at 0706 on the turn of the tide, bound for Brighton, via the Looe, with a northerly breeze, mainly force 3–4. An uneventful sail, and we tied up in the Brighton Marina at 1630, and ten minutes later had paid our £3 harbour dues! Everyone very efficient and friendly. The entrance was quite easy and obvious; they assured us that the entrance was feasible at all times, and certainly, once inside one would be safe enough, but with a strong onshore wind I should be frightened! One cannot help but admire the foresight and imagination of those who said 'Let's build a Marina at Brighton!'

After shopping at the Marina chandlery and stores, we were off next morning with the tide, and had a quiet, rather cool day's sailing close along the shore, tacking as necessary, the wind varying between N.E. and E. Eventually we anchored off Hastings pier, at dusk, the tide having turned and progress very slow. Ian records, 'Hot ham and fresh vegetables, 1971 *vino*; V.G.' We rolled gently, but slept soundly, and were away soon after 0500 with a fair tide and light north-easterly

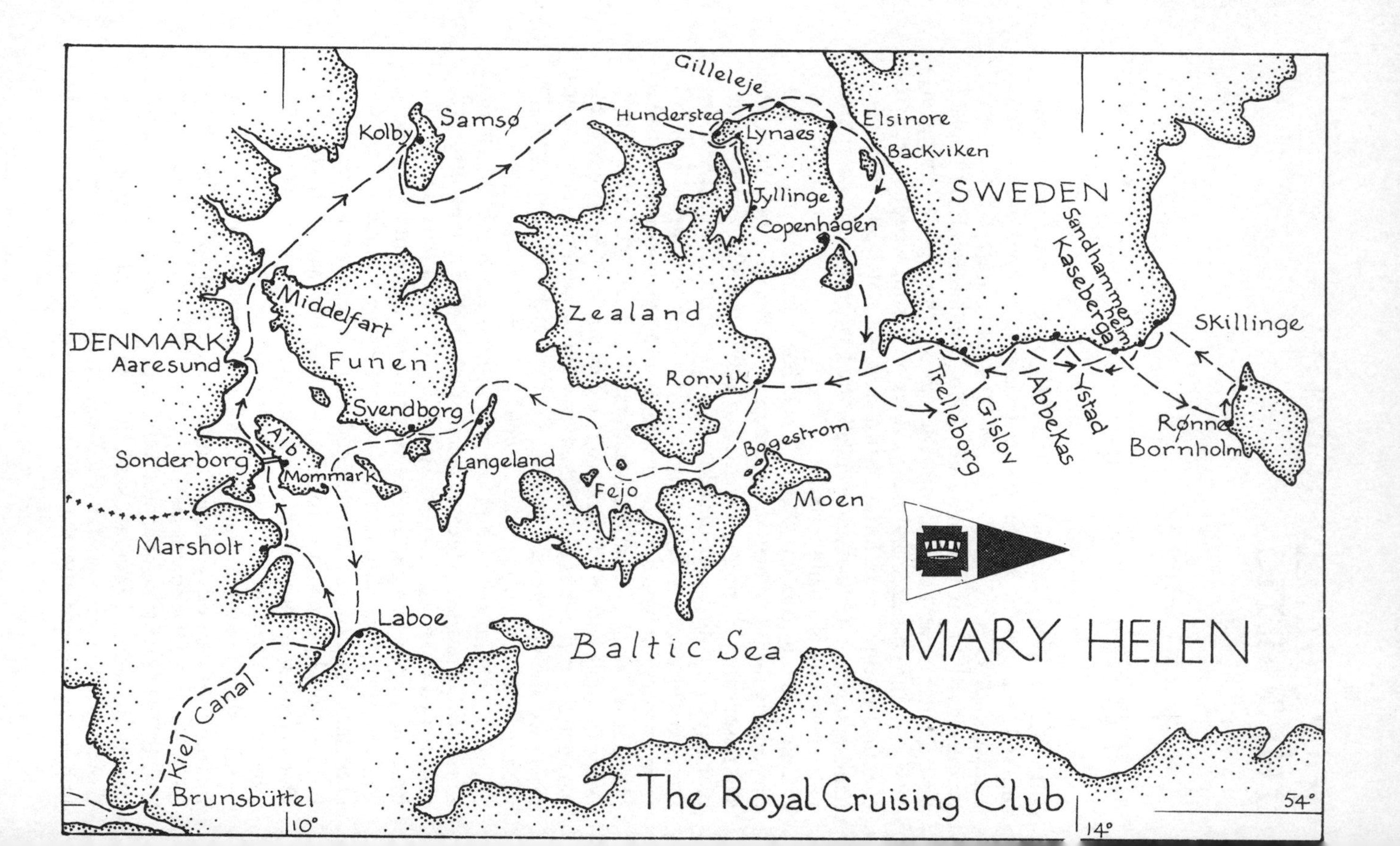
MARY HELEN
The Royal Cruising Club
SWEDEN
DENMARK
Baltic Sea
Zealand
Funen
Gilleleje
Hundersted
Lynaes
Elsinore
Backviken
Jyllinge
Copenhagen
Sandhammen
heim
Kaseberga
Skillinge
Rønne
Bornholm
Ystad
AbbeKas
Gislov
Trelleborg
Ronvik
Bogestrom
Moen
Fejo
Langeland
Svendborg
Middelfart
Kolby
Samsø
Aaresund
Sonderborg
Alb
Mommark
Marsholt
Laboe
Kiel Canal
Brunsbüttel
10°
14°
54°

breeze – cool but sunny. The wind freshened in the afternoon, and it was jolly cold beating along the coast. As we tacked to make the Dover West entrance the watch there immediately gave us the entry signals, which we appreciated, as it would not have been much fun hanging about. We anchored off the town and soon were fed and turned in.

Another 0500 start and similar weather conditions as we sailed across to Dunkirk, intrigued as ever by the Dover straits traffic. We tied up at 1430 alongside a German yacht who recognised us from Eric Hiscock's first *Cruising Under Sail*! It turned into a very wet evening! Sailing out next morning we were scared stiff by six enormous French tugs apparently charging us! They missed of course, just, but we were truly 'storm tossed' as their wakes hurled us about! Outside we found a light southerly air and about two miles visibility – bliss to have a fair wind! At 1050, off Nieuport we lowered sails and the tide gauge showing 3.6 metres, motored in and tied up to a Dutch yacht off the Yacht Club de Nieuport. There is another huge marina on the east side of the peninsular – whole place quite unrecognisable from my last visit in 1965! The next two days were spent at Nieuport with north-easterly gales, we took the train out to Nieuport Baad and watched some small boats literally surfing in; a nasty steep sea and we could not have sailed (or motored) out, and if there had been more north in the wind I think the entrance would have been impossible.

By Monday 19 June the wind had eased and the forecast was less alarming, so we slipped anchor and sailed gently along to Zeebrugge with a variable, mainly northerly wind. There were harbour works going on off Blankenburg, and Zeebrugge seemed larger than in 1965; there are shops near the yacht pontoons now, which is convenient.

We awoke to thick fog, but it soon cleared and we were off at 1125 with a light north-westerly breeze and a fair tide. Another pleasant sail with sunshine, and at 1500 we put on the engine for the locks at Flushing. We stopped at the yachthaven while Ian went ashore for charts, and then went on to Middleberg. There are now two bridges here, and one cannot lie alongside the quay as we had before, but there is a yacht haven to port where we tied up at 1910 – very convenient for the town, and a good chandler on the quay. The engine refused to start next morning, so Ian found a mechanic, who, after fiddling about with it, said there was an air lock and that the engine would have to be taken out. Ian did not think this was a good idea, so after the mechanic had been paid fifty guilders and gone, Ian tried again, and the thing went!! – talk about being bewitched! It was 1700 now, so we slipped and motored to Veere old harbour – at last somewhere I recognised from forty years ago!

Thursday 22 June, we woke to rain and gale warnings all round, so were glad we had decided to take the inland route and not made a passage up the North Sea! We had a hectic sail in a strong S. Wester down the Veerse meer and along the old Zandcreek, sometimes with five rolls in the main, sometimes no main at all – at times it was really rather foul. We anchored for lunch off Middleplatten nature reserve, sounding to find a suitable depth inside the line of withies; it's fairly steep-to and we touched but quickly blew off. It was rather pleasant to be the only boat for a change, and we enjoyed watching the numerous birds. Later in the afternoon we motored on to the Kortegne Delta Marina, having looked at the one opposite and thought it dreary. Next morning still raining with gale warnings, and we motored on to the locks, which, after hanging around for some time, we entered in company with a lot of other yachts, at 1030.

We then had a somewhat hairy and exhausting sail to Willemstad; it was a fair wind, but strong and squally, with thunder, lightning and hail, often under bare poles, sometimes small headsail only or with a very reefed main. It was wild and bleak, with a lot of yachts about, all wet and bedraggled! We had a good dinner at the Hotel Bellvue on the quay. Still no let up in the rain next day and a force 9 gale warning, and at 0930 we sailed out of Willemstad under headsail, hoisting a much reefed main when in the Hollandsch diep, which we had to lower for a very fierce squall. All this up and down sail very hard work for Ian and tough on his oilskins! We reached Dordrecht after lunch, and after some shopping were whisked away inland by some friends of Ian from Singapore. We returned next afternoon, Sunday 25 June, and were off up the Noord canal towards the Hollands Issel. There was a strong current, a force seven S.W. wind and it was really quite rough! At times we had to tack along the waves to keep the engine going! It was a bit hair-raising going under a twelve metre bridge, with an 11.5 metre mast. The bridge in Hollands Issel showed no sign of opening, so we turned into a sort of 'Barges Corner' to starboard and lay alongside one. Ian explored ashore and reported 'Cafes not suitable for you mum!' so we dined on board and listened to poor Holland losing the World football cup!

Up to catch the 0600 opening of the bridge and locks. Unfortunately at the critical moment the gears jammed and the engine stopped, but we managed to drift through; once through the locks we hoisted sail, hoping to sail to Gouda and find an engineer. About two miles up we saw a large notice to port – 'Yachthavn Zandra' so we rounded up into it, tying up to a convenient pontoon and had breakfast. It poured with rain. Ian walked for miles in the wet for stores and an engineer. The harbourmaster, who also owned the marina, was very helpful, and Ian nearly bought an outboard from him, he was so fed up with our engine! Eventually an engineer was found, who took off the carburettor to his workshop to clean up. He returned later in the afternoon, but still the machine would not go, then he noticed that the magneto cover was adrift, so he tied it up with string, and the engine started up at once! Was it afraid of Ian's threat of an outboard? It was 1800 by now, but off we went, the engine almost purring, and did not stop till we tied up at

Alphen on Rhine at 2300, after a bridge keeper had commented on no mast-headlight – we had sidelights on, of course.

It was 1030 before we got off next morning, and immediately ran aground! We were soon off, mostly motoring with a northerly breeze, and though cloudy it was not actually raining. Soon we were going through the Brassemer, which looked a fascinating lake with lots of small boats sailing around. We had to stick to the buoyed channel, but it could be fun to explore in a 420. We tied up alongside the road at Oude Wettering for lunch, an attractive little holiday place with numerous small boats and a sailing school. Then on, till at 1712 we stopped at 'Nederlands Pumpencentral' a large garage, where the friendly pump attendant gave me a couple of *eau de cologne* sachets! We drank coffee and beer at an adjoining cafe and sat admiring our ship in front of us! The Haarlem route now has a fixed bridge across it, so we had to go via Amsterdam and its 0200 railway bridge. What with waiting for the Schiphol road bridge to be mended, and negotiating all the others, it was midnight by the time we were through Amsterdam, which looked absolutely fascinating with all its bright lights and reflections in the canals. We waited in the pool before the bridge which opened at 0240. It was a bit alarming with big barges about, and all the time we were afraid it would shut before we got through; but all was well, and soon we were tied up in the Sixhaven and turned in for a well earned sleep. It rained all morning and Ian visited his friend's tug, getting back in time to cast off at 1616, still raining and a fresh S.W. wind. Got safely through the Orange Sluicen and out into the Zuider Zee (Yes, I know it's called Idsselmeer now!) which looked very dreary with about one mile visibility, just enough to pick up the buoys. We rounded up in Volendam at 2103, alongside another yacht, too late to feed ashore so supper on board and turned in. Volendam still very much geared for tourists, but we found it attractive all the same.

Sailed to Enkhuizen next day, still raining and poor visibility, the locks just before were new since my last visit (1938!). We went into the Buithaven, feeling attracted by the large new marinas, and had supper ashore. I don't think it stopped raining all day! It was still raining next morning, Friday 30 June, and a fresh S. wind, so we decided to cross to Stavoren and keep in the canals a bit longer. Accordingly, we sailed away at 0900, and into the Stavoren locks at 1130, the keeper kindly holding the lock gates open for us, and he broadcast a weather forecast in English as we lay in the locks. The sun came out and we had a pleasant afternoon alongside a beautiful old Dutch barge yacht, built in 1905. We had been hearing rumours of bridge closures, so Ian consulted with the lock-keeper who even took the trouble to ring up and check. An early tea and we sailed off along the canal, the various bridges all opening to our three hoots. It was delightful sailing along the lakes and canals, rather broad like we imagined, with rushes, reeds and ducks abounding, and Friesian cattle browsing in the fields. We finally tied up at Heeg, in time to have an excellent meal in a small local hotel.

Saturday 1 July. Ian had a lot of 'up sail, down sail' as we sailed through various bridges and the Sneekermeer, which looked fascinating. Then, approaching another bridge we tried to start the engine to be more maneuvrable with a fair wind and current, but it refused, so, under bare poles, we steered close to a small holding jetty and Ian leapt onto it with a line to hold us; alas, it parted and Mary Helen drifted onto the bridge, leaving Ian marooned on the canal. I frantically waved a line at a passing motor boat who kindly towed us clear at some speed and went back to pick Ian up, and then dropped the line so that we were in the same fix as before, but this time we had more way on so were able to luff across and get alongside a wooden jetty at the middle of the bridge. The bridge then opened and the keeper pulled us through to the other side where we tied up to collect our wits! Ian had another go at the engine which started straight away! This delay meant that we arrived at the first Leeuwarden bridge a quarter of an hour after it had shut till Monday!

It rained solidly all Sunday and was still pouring as we motored through the bridge at 0615 on Monday. Now that we were moving, Leeuwarden looked quite pleasant, with a rather attractive leaning tower. We were held up by a bridge at Birdsaad, where we tied up alongside a convenient little shop for stores, though it was too early for bread, but Ian found a garage for petrol. At Dokkum, again while waiting for the bridge, we were given a bag of 'goodies' – literature, toothpaste, local peppermints, dominoes, coloured chalks, a bag of soup crisps and two tins of what we thought was butter, but turned out to be cheese spread! After the bridge we saw an R.C.C. burgee alongside so hailed her. It was *Janet Mor*, but as we were in a hurry we could only wave 'hullo' and 'goodbye'. We understood she was on her way to Denmark and wondered whether we should meet later on.

By midday we were through the locks and into the Lauwers Zee, and as the weather was foul were not tempted out, so navigated the narrow winding reed-lined channels through this rather bleak looking now tideless sea, to the Riet Diep canal. At 1600, in giving way to a barge, we ran hard aground, almost in the middle of the canal. There was a fresh southerly wind, so we hoisted sail to try to get off, but no luck. However, the barge, seeing our predicament, turned round and came back to tow us off. It was jolly decent of her, but she had so much power that we came off suddenly and went slap into her with our bowsprit! No damage to her, but a crack in our decks by the bits! However, on we went, safely negotiating the remaining bridges till we reached Groningen, where they had shut for the night. We tied up to a convenient barge, and went ashore for supper. The Groningen bridges opened at 0930 and by 1040 we had got through all nine of them and were into the Eemskanaal, wide and tree-lined. At lunch time we were moored at the entrance to the sea locks, by a notice '*ligsplatten* not more than six hours'. One of the other waiting yachts reported that the locks were soon opening, so, though Ian had time to get some petrol, he did not have time to visit the attractive looking cafe nearby! Our port bollard carried away in the locks – almost a last 'nip' from the canals! At 1420 we were moored in the Nautilus yachthaven, according to the harbour masters' instructions, and were glad to see the red ensign immediately hoisted on our arrival! Being Tuesday, it was early closing, but we had a walk along the big dyke and enjoyed seeing sea and sand again! Had dinner at the expensive Ems Hotel and agreed with F.P.I. that it was worth it!

Although it was a pity the weather had been so foul, the canals etc. had been great fun, but perhaps *Mary Helen* is not the most suitable type of boat for them; her engine certainly wasn't! Anyway, soon there will be no more routes through for fixed masts, and they told us the barge trade is dying out.

Wednesday 5 July. The tide was not right until after lunch, so we had a busy morning shopping, washing (an excellent launderette) and refuelling and at 1400 slipped for Borkum. It was a beat at first; later the wind freshened from the west and we had a good sail, though off Borkum it fell away and we had to motor in. We were fascinated by the huge flocks of birds feeding on the uncovering sands. We found a convenient-looking berth alongside an old converted fishing boat and enjoyed a meal at the cafe overlooking the harbour. *Mary Helen*'s first visit to Germany, and we were very conscious of being in the Riddle of the Sands area!

We woke to the usual rain and slipped at 0600 with a light southerly breeze, and the engine going to keep up to schedule for the watersheds. However, we soon had it off as the wind freshened from the N.W. and we had to put four rolls in the mainsail and change down headsail. We just touched crossing the sands as now we were early, but we 'eased' across safely into the main Delfzijl channel. A somewhat hectic sail winding about in these narrow withy-lined channels, sometimes under headsail only, sometimes the mainsail with seven rolls! It was great fun and exciting, but a pity it was so wet. We made an error at the Nordeney entrance which was somewhat obscured by several large ferries, and grounded! We barely had time to say 'bother' and back the mainsail before a little bright red and green tug appeared and towed us off. The engine started and we motored in safely, tying up to a German yacht who had been in difficulties outside of the town and had had to be towed in by the main lifeboat; it appeared that the little tug was the equivalent to our inshore rescue craft. We spent the next two days in Nordeney with a N.W. gale, and though, from the comfort of a seaside cafe, the seas looked magnificent we were very glad not to be out in them.

Sunday 9 July. Though still raining the wind had moderated so we slipped at 0953 with a moderate N.W. wind. This soon freshened so we took down the mainsail as we were sailing too fast for the first watershed, behind Nordeney, where we just touched. At 1120 we rounded Nemmerseel, nasty looking breakers out to sea! Still a bit too early for the Baltrum watershed and touched again for about ten minutes; a lot of yacht and ferry traffic. Approaching the entrance to Langeoog the outside channel looked impassable and we found quite a swell, though it was quiet enough behind the island. They have dredged out some of the northern part of the harbour and there are now yacht pontoons there, and withies mark the edge of the mud on the eastern side. We found three feet at low water, very soft mud. Overlooking the yacht pontoons is a small clubhouse-cum-cafe where we had a reasonable supper of steak and ices. We noticed that the ferries and other boats, all gave the western arm a wide berth. The large stakes, except the one by the pontoon, were all well on the mud, and the inner withies were also dry at lower water. We liked Langeoog with its horse-drawn 'taxi' (no cars allowed except the police car), and little train to meet the ferries.

Next morning we woke to find sunshine streaming into the cabin! Ian went shopping by train but had to walk back, only to find he had left half the stores behind. Nothing daunted he borrowed a bicycle and cycled back to collect them! We were away after an early lunch, and had a very pleasant sail amongst the withies with a light northerly breeze and sun. We had to motor a bit to catch the tide on the Spiekeroog watershed, and found eight feet an hour after H.W. Finally we tied up in the Westlanger harbour, just inshore of the ferries in two-and-a-half fathoms, two hours after H.W. There were several other yachts in, moored on both sides of the harbour. There was nothing at the harbour except the ferry trains and the harbour masters hut on stilts, but outside there appeared to be work strengthening the dyke protecting the road. There was a new yacht harbour for small boats, but the channel, marked by withies, was dry at half tide! A wild, unspoilt corner, good for walks and lots of sea birds to watch.

Thursday 11 July found us under way at 0345, in company with another German yacht, who later turned back. There was a moderate north-westerly breeze and we kept the engine on to help in the channel as there was still quite a nasty sea on the bar. Once clear we hoisted all sail and turned it off. Though cold it was good sailing, and the sun actually broke through by midday. It was good to be back at sea and rather exciting to be sailing up the notorious Elbe! We made good time so decided not to stop at Cuxhaven but carry on to Brunsbuttel, and by 1640 were off the Kiel canal entrance, in company with lots of other yachts. We had to hang around for about an hour, but eventually we were let in, it was almost as if the yachts had taken over, there were sixteen of us and one barge in the lock. Ian, when in the harbourmaster's office, overheard the keeper say into the telephone 'No, I've too many yachts to cope with!' By 1830 we were tied up at Brunsbuttelkoog alongside a Swedish yacht, we'd had no formalities, and no request to see proficiency certificates, only money needed! The cafe recommended in F.P.I. must have changed hands, there is still the view, but only snack food, and that revolting.

Were away from Brunsbuttelkoog at 1950, in company of several other yachts. To conform to the 'black inverted cone' regulation I made one from a black plastic dustbin bag with a wire coathanger and duly hung it in the rigging when we had the sails up as well as the engine going, no one objected so it must have looked O.K.! Our sails with the fair wind helped both our speed and fuel consumption, it would have been terribly tedious with a head wind. We enjoyed the canal with its very varied scenery, and the sight of the little red-roofed villages clinging to the wooded hills of Schleswig Holstein reminded me of Rupert of Hentzau's Ruritania, there were numerous yachts but not nearly as much commercial traffic as I had expected, but the huge liner 'Royal Viking of the Sea' fairly dominated everything as she slowly overtook us, she seemed enormous! As we approached the locks, still some distance off, we saw they were open so put on full speed hoping, but not really expecting, that they'd wait for us, and they did, though the lights turned red when we were almost there, but we carried on and all was well! I was really thrilled that at last, forty-one years old, *Mary Helen* had reached the Baltic! We went round to the B.F.K.Y.C. as instructed by friends at home. Unfortunately, they were in the middle of some yacht training session so were very busy, but we had lovely hot baths and the use of the bar, where there is a fine painting of an R.C.C. gaff cutter, but the secretary did not know who she was. We were also interested to see *Andrillot*, the original *vertue*, tied up there.

We slipped round to Holtenau next morning for stores, the N.A.A.F.I. not being available for civilians, and as the club was busy we did not want to be in the way. We sailed away from Holtenau at noon, and had a good sail with a westerly wind, fresh at times, to Marsholm. The entrance was a dead beat and it was raining so we motored up the narrow channel and into the big Marsholm marina. It seemed chock-a-block but we managed to tie up alongside a motorboat in the N.E. corner. How desolate and bleak the low-lying entrance had seemed in the rain! The marina is three years old; a convenient stop for the night, close to the attractive old village with all ordinary shops, a bank (open 0800–1200), and post office, but the nearest petrol is at Kamplen up the river. Ran down the channel under jib in a fresh, cold westerly, and outside hoisted the main and then had a long, at times very wet, beat up to Sondeberg. It was good sailing, but cold. We finally tied up at Sondeberg alongside a Dutch yacht, a Cornish crabber in fibreglass! There was a chandlery on the quayside so Ian slipped ashore to buy an N flag for the bridges and a washer for the primus. He also managed to get some petrol from a nearby garage.

The wind was still fresh, N.W. next morning as we slipped at 0915 flying our smart new N flag, and, after hanging about for half an hour were safely through the bridge and hoisted a reefed main and working jib, but kept the engine going to help us through the narrows. Off Stagvig we hoisted the small jib, turned off the engine, and had a hard sail in a steep rough sea. At 1515 off Halk Hoved were glad of a bit of shelter from the land! An hour later we were through the narrows of Aarosund; by now it was gusting force 8, and the sight of a handy harbour tempted us, so we downed sail, got the engine started and nosed into the narrow entrance of Aarosund. The tiny harbour seemed full, but with an efficient harbour-master and lots of cheerful people to help with our lines we managed to find a berth alongside a friendly motorboat, and the sun came out! There is no longer a shallow S.W. corner as the harbour has been dredged to two metres. Ian took the ferry over to Aaro, where there was another marina, but he thought we had chosen the better spot, particularly with the strong N.W. wind. Away from Aarosund in the early hours (0530) with a reefed main and small jib and had a pleasant close-hauled sail up to Brandso Island in spite of some heavy rain showers, wind W.N.W.4. We then shook out the reefs and beat up the delightful wooded sound to Middlefart, imagining ancient Vikings beaching their longships on the sandy strands, surrounded by forests for fuel and shelter.

There was quite a strong adverse current running under the bridge so we had to help with the engine. Kongebro seemed full but the town marina even fuller, so we went back to Kongebro and managed to find a berth with the help of a friendly Danish yachtsman, who very kindly promised to look after *Mary Helen* whilst we went home for a week for the wedding of my eldest son Donald (R.C.C.). It took less than twenty-four hours to retrace five week's hard work!

Got back to *Mary Helen* in the early hours of Friday 28 July and were away soon after 1100, with a very light easterly air. There were no harbour dues to pay at Kongebro as we had not been there for three weeks! We thought this very generous. The visibility was hazy but adequate and it was just a case of motoring from buoy to buoy, and we decided on Kolby Kaas, seeing that what wind there was, was easterly. We did manage to get a couple of hours peaceful sailing and tied up in Kolby at 1930. An easy approach with conspicuous black and white vertical stripes on the entrance dolphins, between which one passes and then head up past the ferry terminal, which looked rather like a big yacht! and moor where one can find a berth. There was petrol at the village stores past the 'Country Hotel' and ferries to Aarhus and Kolundrul. It would seem a safe harbour in all weathers.

Woke next morning to thick fog, but this soon cleared to a fine weather haze and we were off under power at 0800. It was a day of alternate motoring and trying to sail with about three miles visibility, and by the time we tied up at Hundested we had made good fifty-eight miles in twelve hours, only having been able to sail for four of them!

Although a large commercial port it seems mainly taken over by yachts, and the ferry terminal is outside, so there is no disturbance in the harbour. It is convenient for petrol and stores. There were a few fishing boats in the harbour, but not much activity.

Saturday 30 July. A gorgeous sunny morning, mirror-calm with the reflections of the gaily coloured yachts, sails and masts making a beautiful picture. Ian was ashore early for bread and milk (the shop opened at 0700!), but it was nearly 1100 before we slipped under light weather genoa and sailed down the channel to the Roskilde fjord. At 1150 the fairway buoy was abeam, and with a force 3 easterly we had an exciting beat through the narrows into the Roskilde fjord in company with many other yachts, a bit hair-raising at times! We anchored off the shore for lunch, and hoisted my 420 flag to the crosstrees as we motored off again, with a dead head wind and a very wiggling channel to negotiate. By 1600 we were through the Fredricksund bridge when a Contessa, *Eller Hund*, came and hailed us, pointing to our 420 flag, saying 'Welcome to Jyllinge, we are expecting you, the channel is very tricky so follow me!' This was an encouraging welcome and we duly followed. Off the village, Ian thought it 'felt very shallow' though we did not actually stick, even the locals do not take short cuts, but follow the marked channels carefully. *Eller Hund* led us into the large Jyllinge marina, where we had a great welcome, the flag officers helping us moor in our reserved berth, we really felt we had arrived, and on the day I had said!

Here endeth the first part! For the next three weeks *Mary Helen* became the H.Q. for the British 420 team at the 420 World Championships, and while Ian had to go home, I lived on board sporting my 'presidential' hat!

On Sunday 20 August with my son James (R.C.C. cadet) and friend Francesca Pollock, *Mary Helen* was once more underway, glad to be moving, but sorry to say goodbye to my many Danish friends. It was bright and sunny but no wind as we motored up to the bridge. Once through, we were able to sail with a light westerly air as far as the narrows, where, light puffs coming from all directions, my heart failed and we put on the engine and motored into Lynaes marina. The young people went ashore, but they thought it dull – 'Just a boat park'. We motored out next morning and soon were sailing well with the working jib and mainsail in a force 3 to 4 south-easterly breeze and bright sunshine. It was very pleasant sailing along the north coast of Zealand making five knots at times in smooth water. It clouded over after lunch, looking like rain, and, having rounded the top, it was now a beat to Elsinore, so 'How about Gilleleje?' 'Why not?', so at 1530 we motored in and tied up in what looked like the only vacant berth. A fascinating little place, a large fishing harbour with a yacht marina in the southern basin. Ashore we found an ancient fishing village with lots of shops etc., somewhat spivved up for tourists. The 'season' had ended and we found nowhere much to feed, so we bought pork chops, fresh vegetables, and Danish pastries, so fed well aboard.

The bad weather did not materialise and we woke to sunshine again in the morning, and were off at 0830 with a moderate, squally S.W. wind. It was good sailing down the coast towards Elsinore, whose castle showed up after Hornbeck and certainly dominated the coastline. We put on the engine outside the northern harbour and motored in to this enormous new marina, quite unrecognisable from 1964 when I came in here with John Budget in *Fairlight*. We motored around till we found a 'Fri' berth on the S. side of the inner basin. The afternoon was spent 'doing the castle', it was hot and exhausting, but the maritime museum was worth it. James bought a spinner here, having found our fishing line was minus one. Ian and I had done no fishing so had not noticed!

We sailed for Ven next morning with a squally west wind, and, after taking down our genoa, to slow up, James caught a garfish on his new spinner. We tied up in Backviken at 1100 alongside the breakwater just beyond the yellow 'no parking' lines! We enjoyed this tiny harbour, where there were only a few yachts, although they say it is crowded in the summer. We bought ices, postcards and stamps at the kiosk on the quay and watched the harbour come to life as a ferry came in. A heavy rain shower damped our intent to walk up to the village, but Ven is the sort of place one would like to re-visit. After lunch we sailed off with reefed main and working jib, bound for the highlights of Copenhagen and tied up in Langeline harbour in time for tea. It cost us twenty kr. per night, the free berthing having ended four years ago. Had an enjoyable evening ashore with my niece and her family, and next day James and Francesca explored the city. As I'd been taken round by my Jyllinge 420 friends I had a quiet day on board.

After watching the *Malcolm Miller* with a girl crew get away under sail on Friday 25 August, we were off ourselves and sailed down the coast under working jib alone, there being a fresh squally N.W. wind. It was too windy to go on across to Sweden, so we turned into Dragor, tying up alongside a yacht on the North outer mole, the *Gastepladser* being to leeward and looking uncomfortable. The ferries have a separate harbour now and there was another large yacht marina to the south of it. Dragor is rather fascinating with its old Dutch connections and a museum on the quayside. We saw some garfish in a fishmongers so were relieved to know they are not poisonous, in spite of their emerald green bones! We dined, expensively but well, in the hotel overlooking the harbour from where we could see our ship.

We woke to a bright sunny morning and a light westerly breeze, so were off by 0615 under the genoa, hoisting the mainsail outside. Quite a few steamers about, so we gybed to cross the shipping lane at right angles, and James caught a couple of garfish. Soon the wind freshened so we lowered the sails and hoisted the working jib, under which she sailed along very comfortably in the biggish sea now running. By noon we were off Trelleborg, but as the conditions were so pleasant we decided to carry on, thinking that once round Smggenhamn we'd be able to sail close in shore in a smoother sea, some hope! All along this stretch of coast, lines of fishing nets extend up to two miles out, anchored with bright plastic buoys and having a small light on the outer ones. We went across one, where there appeared to be a gap in the buoys, but it wasn't really a gap as we could see the lines under us, so we did not risk that again. We had to put on the engine to get into Abbekas, as the fishing lines had made us get to leeward! An old fishing harbour, now mainly used by yachts, though being out of season now there were not many there. James and Francesca went ashore for stores, but found the shops shut, it being a Saturday. However they made friends with a local who took them inland to get some bread. Fertile farming country, and fairly flat.

Sunday 27 August was a rainy, blustery morning, but we slipped under sail at 0945, and by 1100 were abeam of Ystads Redd, still having to keep two miles off for the fishing nets. The wind freshened so we ran along under the old genoa. As we approached the cliffs by Kaseberga there appeared to be a row of chimney tops showing above the headland; on looking through the glasses they looked like some sort of stonehenge-type stones, and we were intrigued. Into Kaseberga at lunchtime and tied up alongside the breakwater. It was a tiny harbour, quite quiet and snug, though the sight of the waves breaking against the mole had me worried at first. The curious stones turned out to be an ancient Viking burial ship the 'Ales Stenar', one of the largest known we were told. We climbed up to look at them and I was absolutely fascinated to think of the wild Vikings buried there on the cliff-top, forever looking out over the stormy Baltic towards Bornholm, I even tried to paint them! Kaseberga seemed to be a place people visit for the day, but don't stay. It is evidently renowned for its smoked fish, and has a souvenir shop and kiosk which sold sweets and cigarettes etc., including most excellent toasted sandwiches. There were the usual 'loos' and showers here; even though all harbours now charge, they do provide some facilities! It was absolutely quiet in the evening, just a few yachts and the Viking spirits brooding over the harbour.

A sunny morning with light westerly airs, so we slipped at 0545, bound for Bornholm. Francesca did her morning 'press-ups' at 0730 on *Mary Helen*'s now rolling decks as the wind soon freshened, up to a good force 5. There was a big sea running, but it was superb sailing with bright sunshine and a fair wind. Visibility was good and the chimneys off Ronne showed up a long way, and it was exciting to watch this unknown (to us, anyway) island gradually rise up out of the sea. The wind being dead on shore she needed careful steering between the Ronne pierheads, on both of which breakers were spurting;

the actual entrance was free enough and it was immediately quiet once inside. We tied up in the tiny *buithaven* in the N.E. corner at 1130, feeling very pleased with ourselves, as it was soon blowing hard and a German yacht, who went out later, returned, finding it too rough!

James called on a Danish Naval vessel, the *Daphne*, for a local weather forecast, but they weren't very helpful, saying Bornholm was quite unpredictable!

We woke to a filthy wet windy morning, so decided not to sail round the Island, but to take a bus instead! Bornholm has been very much developed for tourists, but did not seem spoilt. Before modern communications it must have been wild and lonely, supporting inland farmers and coastal fishermen. There are numerous small harbours, still used for fishing, though we were told that in the summer season they get very crowded with yachts, mostly German. It was a pity we did not have more time and better weather to explore these ports, but the bus trip was fun, even playing crazy golf in the rain at Allyinge, and finishing up with a super dinner at a fish restaurant at Nesko, the one large fishing harbour.

By lunchtime next day it had stopped raining and the wind had eased, so we motored round to Hasle, mooring alongside the west harbour wall. Hasle was a busy fishing port with rather oily water and apart from one small motor boat we were the only yacht. There was a small inn on the quay side, evidently the fishermen's haunt, and the usual good supermarket up the hill. There were some fascinating old houses and we felt Hasle was a bit off the tourist route.

Away at 0520 next morning in the sunshine and a light northerly air, and had a pleasant leisurely sail enjoying the sun. By noon though, there was almost no wind so we put on the engine and by 1400 had tied up in Skillinge; threatening black clouds around which later turned to rain.

There was a tall radio (?) mast about two miles N.N.W. of Skillinge which we saw clearly twenty-five miles away, and the big silo tower a half mile E. of Kaseberga was much more distinct than the Sandhammen lighthouse which was rather hidden in the trees, though when the light was right, the red tower showed up O.K. The windmill mentioned in the pilot at Skillinge we never saw. There is a female statue on the mole at the harbour entrance, put there we were told by a local businessman and disapproved of by the community! We had dinner at the 'Kro' by the harbour, super but expensive. We were told it had been built for the benefit of the large number of rich German yachts who frequent this coast in the summer.

Friday 1 September. With a light westerly we slipped at 0615, leaving Francesca still sleeping! She soon emerged however and the wind quickly freshened so that, within the hour we'd changed headsails and reefed the main. Under the lee of Sandhammen the sea was relatively smooth, but by the time we were abeam and about two miles off, there was a very nasty sea and a still freshening wind. We took in another couple of rolls, but soon decided that a dead beat in these conditions was no fun, so turned and ran back to Skillinge. Two hours out, one hour back, three hours' hard sailing and nothing made good! James and Francesca went shopping with the primus, whose pump had ceased to work. In the supermarket a Swedish family overheard them trying to make themselves understood and came to their rescue. It seemed that her husband was a Jaguar repairer, but understood about primuses, so the stove was repaired and they all came back to *Mary Helen* for tea, then they took us back to their home a few miles inland for supper and baths, and we spent a pleasant evening discussing the world and our respective countries' problems. What excellent English these young Swedes speak!

Started off at 0930 with full main and working jib, but outside there was a lot more wind so we reefed the main, by 1040 we were again abeam of Sandhammen, on the outward tack. There was still a big sea but not as nasty as yesterday. At noon we tacked inshore, making in to about a mile E. of Kaseberga, and firmly tacked out again, as I was hoping to make Ystad. Alas the conditions were deteriorating; there was a large cold sea, and we reckoned we'd be very cold and tired by the time we got there, only making two knots to windward, so I relented and we went in to Kaseberga and had tied up by 1400. Were met by a friendly customs man, the first we'd seen in Sweden! We moored to the village quay as the rough sea was periodically breaking over the mole by our previous berth. In the evening when all the tourists had gone we, and a couple of other yachts had the place to ourselves, and again, one was aware of the Viking stones up the hill, and could imagine an ancient settlement in this little corner, untouched for centuries!

We were away by 0800 with working jib, five rolls in the main and a fresh westerly breeze. She was making very slow progress to windward so we shook out some of the rolls and we went better, in spite of quite a few splashes over us. By lunchtime we were off Ystad, where there were harbour works going on and some difference from the chart, so we put on the engine and motored around until we found the yacht harbour. One thing about these new marinas, the forest of masts soon shows where they are! It appears that two moles are being constructed outside the old ones, which presumably will eventually enclose the yacht marina, where at the moment a bit of a swell runs in. There had evidently been a local race as a lot of yachts came in, very reefed and very wet! We thought Ystad a fascinating old town, and Francesca found an open supermarket (it was Sunday), and a duck pond with masses of ducks. Whilst cowering under our cockpit tent next morning, in the rain, we were hailed by a chap who asked if we were the *Mary Helen* of Eric Hiscock's book, and when we said yes, and that I was still the same Mrs. Tew, he rushed home and reappeared with Eric's book for me to sign. Such is fame – this, the second time this cruise! We got away after an early lunch accompanied by our friend in his folk boat who took photos of us, a pity it was dull and not much wind. We made very slow progress with the light westerly wind, so put on the engine and bashed our way along to Gislov which we reached at 1900, securing alongside a German yacht on the west mole, the marina looking very full. It was pouring with rain. James and Francesca went ashore to look for some petrol, and were met by our Ystad friend and a pal of his who also had Eric's book. They took James and Francesca round to the marina, but it seems there is no petrol here, one must go to Trelleborg. They also gave us a kilo of 'Gul Mocca' – an excellent coffee!

Slipped round to Trelleborg early in the morning, the sun actually shone! Here we stocked up with petrol, stores and money (Sparbanken open at 0900) and sailed away at 1000 with a light northerly breeze, basking in the sunshine, with all our overworked oilskins hanging out to dry! We had a delightful warm leisurely day's sail over to Rodvig, and it was satisfactory to find that my estimated distances from the various lighthouses tallied very well with James's sextant calculated ones! We moored in Rodvig at 1725, where I nearly fainted with shock when the harbour-master wanted 35 kr., our most expensive yet, even more than Brighton! I certainly must have been shocked for James logged 'Mum has at last said "now that I'm young, we'll spend some money".' I don't quite know what I meant but we went and spent a lot on a delicious meal at the Rodvig kro, said to have been started by a pair of lovers thrown up on the shore after escaping from Sweden in a storm, having lost a friend overboard on the way. There was a birthday party going on and when they started singing 'Happy Birthday to you' we joined in too, at least I did!

Wednesday 6 September. Slipped at 0945 with a light W.N.W. wind, bound for the Bogestrom, which, with the help of the engine, we reached at noon. We kept to the middle of the channel, sounding as we went, getting a minimum of one-and-a-half fathoms. Francesca, though used to echo sounders, soon became a dab hand with the lead, it was delightful sailing along in the smooth water, and beautifully warm, though the sun was a bit hazy. We turned into the Sandvig channel and anchored off the tiny harbour for lunch, resisting the temptation to go in, as the chart only gave one-and-a-half metres. Off again under power as no wind. We had thought of anchoring near the bridge at Kalvehave, but it did not look interesting, so we carried on until at 1720 we anchored three-quarters of a cable E. of Petersvoerft quay off a wooded shore. James and Francesca blew up the dinghy for the first time and rowed ashore to explore. They reported finding a beautiful, out of the way 'garden of Eden' countryside, and as the sun set with lovely colours reflected in the mirror-like waters we might have been the only people in the world!

Away next morning at 0915, with very little wind, so a day of gently moving, partly with the big genoa the only sail drawing, and partly under power, till by 1700 we had nosed into Fejo havn and tied up to a German yacht, not risking going too far up the harbour as F.P.I. said it was shallow. In fact, it has been dredged, so there would have been plenty of water. James and Francesca found a good stores three-quarters of a mile after turning left at the main road, which they said was better than the nearer shop. There is a bank here too (but only open 0930 to 1230). Another 'garden of Eden' with luxuriant vegetation and masses of flowers and fruit.

It was thick fog in the morning, but by the time we'd shopped and re-fuelled it had cleared enough to let us out. Soon the sun came out and by noon we were sailing through Staaldyb, between Vesterby havn and Kargnaes with a freshening wind, and then we had an exciting beat through a narrow unmarked channel between Fejo Staalgrund, Skalo grund and Raago naebbe grund; it was a bit hair-raising seeing the yellow shallow water on either side – unmarked! Soon we had a fair wind again and at 1600 were abeam of Omo, it was a bit early to stop so we carried on to Lochals, Langeland where we tied up at 1900. There was a fresh southerly wind and pouring rain next morning, but at 1020 we motored out past the ferry, which now berths outside the harbour, so does not quite block the entrance. Outside we hoisted the working jib and main and sailed close-hauled across to make Elshoved lighthouse which we sighted about one-and-a-half miles off. It was now a dead beat on to Svendborg and with a freshening wind we reefed. It was very squally as we approached the Svendborg narrows and we envied a host of yachts sailing out with a fair wind, till, on looking back we saw one minus her mast! We turned and ran back to see if we could help, but one of her friends had also seen the dismasting so we were not needed. It was quite a struggle against the wind and tide, and as we got up to the big dry dock below the town we put on the engine and motored into the yachthaven just before the bridge, where, on the harbour-master's instructions we tied up alongside the wall with a Ø sign on it.

A wet and windy day and we wondered how the R.C.C. meet was getting on, it being the first time *Mary Helen* had missed one, since her first in 1937! Sunday was too wet and windy for us to feel like moving but on Monday we left in a moderate S.W. wind, three rolls in our mainsail and the working jib up, but we soon shook out the reefs as the wind lightened. However, beating through the Hejvestene lob the wind freshened again and we wished we were still reefed. Once through the narrow channel there was room to reef, but it was very wild and unfortunately the reefing handle went overboard, not a major disaster, but making the job more difficult. By now it was blowing hard and there was a filthy sea, so we downed the mainsail and ran back; what a waste of hard won miles to windward! Being unwilling to run right back to Svendborg we anchored under the lee of Skaro Island, hoping the wind would fall away in the evening as it usually did. The wind was now gale force with some very fierce squalls, but the anchor held and we were reasonably comfortable. It was bright and sunny with the rough water to leeward looking quite spectacular; the wave tops being blown off like horizontal rain. As the day wore on the wind increased rather than took off, so we realised we were there for the night. We kept anchor watch, this being a new experience for Francesca, and we nearly wore out the cards playing Canasta! It blew fresh all next day from the N.W., and at 0600 we felt we'd had enough so weighed anchor and ran back to Svendborg under jib and motor; there were plenty of lights so it was a good navigational exercise for James. We had an excellent meal at the restaurant overlooking the harbour, which we felt we had deserved. Later we were told that it had been a force 9 gale, and the only yachts who had ventured out had returned!

Francesca, who, with all this bad weather, had been getting a bit worried about being back for her job on Monday, left us this morning to find her way back by more reliable transport! We felt rather sad to see her standing alone, waving to us as we sailed off. She'd been an excellent crew, lively and energetic, never shirking the wettest and most arduous jobs, and it would be harder work without her. It was rather a wet sail with a moderate S.W. wind, and we were reefed most of the time, keeping the engine going periodically to help keep us to windward, and by 1520 we had tied up in Mommark, now organised for yachts as well as ferries. Several yachts who had passed us off Lyo, came in after us. James's navigation obviously better than theirs! A chap off a German boat recognised us from Svendborg and thought I was James's and Francesca's grandmother! Then, somewhat embarrassed when I put him right, he called me 'a grand old lady of the sea', which made me feel older still!

On Thursday 14 September, we slipped under sail in the rain at 0740 and then had a very hard wet sail across to Scheimunde, but as it was blowing fresh, straight out of the fjord, we decided to carry on to Laboe, our final destination. It was so wet that we even had to laugh at some of the heavier rain squalls! We had arranged for *Mary Helen* to be laid up at Laboe, as my sapper son, Edward (R.C.C.), was stationed in Germany, but I felt very sad and sentimental as we drove away leaving my beloved *Mary Helen* in a foreign land!

A final word: I do realise how incredibly lucky I am that two of my sons had suitably timed leaves which they were prepared to spend taking their elderly Mum cruising!

MARY HELEN

TABLE OF DISTANCES

Date			Distance made good	Time h. m.	Engine time h. m.
June	11	Lymington – Bembridge	21	6 30	0 10
	12	Bembridge – Brighton	39	9 24	0 30
	13	Brighton – Hastings	30	12 00	0 00
	14	Hastings – Dover	36	15 10	0 00
	15	Dover – Dunkirk	41	9 22	0 00
	16	Dunkirk – Nieuwport	15	5 20	0 20
	19	Nieuwport – Zeebrugge	25	6 20	0 18
	20	Zeebrugge – Middleberg	26	6 25	1 18
	21	Middleberg – Veere	5	1 20	1 20
	22	Veere – Kortegne (Delta Marina)	10	3 10	0 17
	23	Kortegne – Willemstadt	34	7 25	2 05
	24	Willemstadt – Dordrecht	20	3 49	0 42
	25	Dordrecht – Hollans Issel	9	1 30	1 30
	26	Hollans Issel – Alphen	20	4 43	4 43
	27	Alphen – Amsterdam Bridge	30	5 14	5 14
	28	Amsterdam ry Bridge – Sixhaven & Volendam Sixhaven	15.5	4 48	0 51
	29	Volendam – Enkhuizen	15	4 11	0 31
	30	Enkhuizen – Stavoren	14	2 55	0 00
		Stavoren – Heeg	10.5	2 38	0 05
July	1	Heeg – Leeuwarden	29	7 06	2 59
	3	Leeuwarden – Groningen	50	13 20	13 20
	4	Groningen – Delfzijl	22	4 50	4 50
	5	Delfzijl – Borkum	18	3 50	0 38
	6	Borkum – Nordeney	33	7 20	2 05
	9	Nordeney – Langerooge	19	5 10	0 25
	10	Langerooge – Wangeroog	17	4 20	1 37
	11	Wangeroog – Brunsbuttel	54	14 45	1 55
	12	Brunsbuttel – B.F.K.Y.C.	54	10 05	10 05
	13	B.F.K.Y.C. – Holtenau & Marsholm	21.5	5 40	0 50
	14	Marsholm – Sondeberg	18	6 55	0 37
	15	Sondeberg – Aarosund	18	7 00	4 00
	16	Aarosund – Middlefart	19	5 02	0 57
	28	Middlefart – Kolby Kass	35	8 25	6 36
	29	Kolby Kass – Hundsted	58	12 20	8 01
	30	Hundsted – Jyllinge	20	6 20	3 20
Aug.	20	Jyllinge – Lynaes	19	5 20	2 25
	21	Lynaes – Gilleleje	21	5 05	0 20
	22	Gilleleje – Elsinore	12	2 55	0 10
	23	Elsinore – Ven (Backviken) and Copenhagen	20	5 15	0 40
	25	Copenhagen – Dragor	9	1 40	0 20

	26	Dragor – Abbekas (Sweden)	47	9 15	0 10
	27	Abbekas – Kaseberga	16	3 30	0 05
	28	Kaseberga – Ronne (Bornholm)	27.5	5 45	0 15
	30	Ronne – Hasle	6	1 35	1 35
	31	Hasle – Skillinge (Sweden)	24	8 30	2 45
Sept.	1	Skillinge and back	12	3 10	0 10
	2	Skillinge – Kaseberga	11	4 30	0 14
	3	Kaseberga – Ystad	10	5 05	0 15
	4	Ystad – Gislov havn	15	6 15	4 30
	5	Gislov, Trelleborg, Rodvig	32	8 25	0 20
	6	Rodvig – Sandvig and Petersvoerft	23	6 30	5 03
	7	Petersvoerft – Fejo Havn	24	7 45	3 52
	8	Fejo Havn – Lohals (Langeland)	26	8 40	1 35
	9	Lohals – Svendbord	18	6 25	0 30
	11	Svendborg – Skaro Is.	5	3 55	0 30
	12	Skaro – Svendborg	5	1 35	1 35
	13	Svendborg – Mommark	22	7 18	2 58
	14	Mommark – Laboe	34	9 15	0 00
		Totals: Jyllinge to Laboe	438.5	127 38	30 17
		Lymington to Jyllinge	901.5	234 42	82 09
		Total Trip	1,340.0	362 20	112 26

WATER MUSIC III
TO THE MEDITERRANEAN

by J. C. Foot

Water Music III, a Nicholson 43, was built for us in 1970 as one of the now extinct breed of cruiser-racer; always one of the most attractive and graceful of production g.r.p. boats, she had in her early years many notable racing successes, though we have been fortunate latterly to enjoy her more in her role of a comfortable and quick cruising yacht.

After the excitements of her 1975–6 trans-Atlantic cruise, we decided to sail her back to the Mediterranean in 1978, planning our departure for the outward voyage to Corfu for 1 June, though more for sentimental than for any really practical reason. It was just our hard luck that this happened to coincide with one of the few high-pressure systems over Western Europe this year, giving us only very light airs and poor visibility, if not actual fog.

I was fortunate that Howard Gosling and Neil Wilkie, both of whom had already sailed in *Water Music* from Antigua to Warsash via Bermuda and the Azores, had volunteered to join this latest voyage. It was very comforting to have two such experienced crew, and a compliment greatly appreciated – that after one ocean voyage with me they should want to undertake another! We then added a newcomer, Peter Gavin, who proved a very happy choice – unfortunately neither Jonathan nor Stephen, both heavily committed to University exams, could join us. Above all, nor could Nick, responsible for both of them, for Lucy with 'O' Levels and for all the other members of the family. She was sorely missed, not only as my wife, but as one of the truly competent and trustworthy crew members.

There were the usual tribulations and traumas before leaving – we all know the pattern – but somehow it all comes together. Nick had worked wonders at storing and victualling so finally at noon on the 'Glorious First' of Howe's memory we were ready to depart, but of course the tide in the Solent was by then foul – it always is on occasions like this – and it made for a slow start with little or nothing in the way of wind other than light sea breezes. This meant we began with a long slow beat against the tide, not finally making our departure from the Needles until 1930, to be met there with a light north-westerly airstream and decidedly poor visibility (the log mentions 'a black thick windless night').

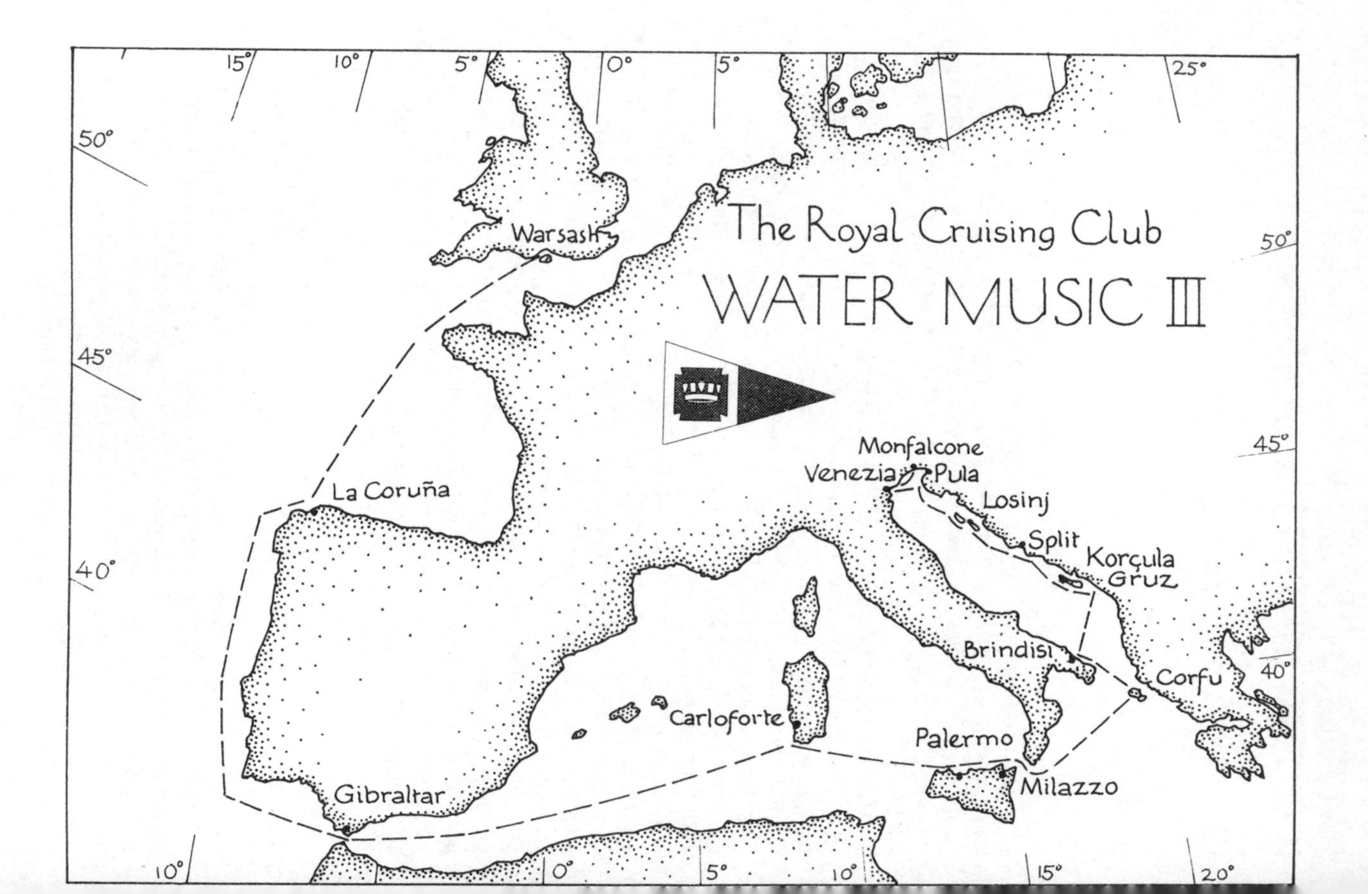
The Royal Cruising Club
WATER MUSIC III
Warsash
La Coruña
Gibraltar
Carloforte
Palermo
Milazzo
Monfalcone
Venezia
Pula
Losinj
Split
Korçula
Gruz
Brindisi
Corfu
15°
10°
5°
0°
5°
25°
50°
45°
40°
10°
0°
5°
10°
15°
20°
50°
45°
40°

And so it remained throughout Friday and indeed most of Saturday, while all at home enjoyed fine warm weather, although we never had quite the fog banks threatened by the forecast, but it was certainly cold, grey and overcast. There was some motoring, some windward work, but there was a short spinnaker run and we hoped that *Concorde*, as she banged her way over, noticed our new tri-radial. Incidentally, what an affront this aeroplane is – why must we accept these wholly unreasonable intrusions! Perhaps you need to hear her supersonic at relatively low altitudes, as over the Channel, to understand fully how obnoxious it is.

This took us to Ushant, rounding in the forenoon of Saturday 3 June, where sadly our troubles started. Earlier that morning, while carrying out a routine check, I noticed that our fan belt was wearing and this took the united efforts of Howard and myself some while to replace – as our Perkins works through a Vee drive, the engine is effectively installed back to front, so that the fan belt is as inaccessible as it could be. However, finally it was accomplished to our mutual satisfaction, Peter meantime sailing us through into the Bay with an amiable little breeze on quite the warmest day we had so far enjoyed – indeed, the only warm day.

After this was done, we checked that it was working, and felt content that a difficult job had been completed. What never even occurred to us was that shredding fan belts seldom do their work properly, particularly with an alternator to drive, and that while we were content, after the motoring we had done, that our batteries were charged, this was far from the case, as we were to find to our cost.

The sun left us – the log says 'dull and miserable', and Scotland lost in the World Cup to Peru, which upset Neil's nationalistic aspirations, but slowly we sailed our way south through a dark night with periodic thundershowers. It was not until the following morning, noticing that our Hengist, our wind-speed indicator – which works off our main batteries – was reading abnormally low, that we realised the awful truth. We were without electrics – no navigation lights, no compass light, no lights below decks and of course totally inadequate power to start the engine and recharge.

We decided, rightly or wrongly, to press on to La Coruna, rather than turn back to Brest, largely owing to the tides and press of shipping round this area, since at least we had plenty of torches and handlamps, together with dry battery-operated navigation lights; but it is best really to draw a veil over the succeeding days until we arrived at our amended destination. The nights continued dark, the weather cold, the winds light, fortunately we met little in the way of shipping and had our hearts in our mouths whenever we did. There were two watches early on Tuesday morning which produced a total between them of three quarters of a mile made good, which gives some idea of our speed – and this, at night, was still two-sweater-and-oilskin weather. (This Tuesday, incidentally, was *Water Music*'s eighth birthday – she has travelled well and far and been much loved in her young life.)

However, finally we sailed into La Coruna Harbour early on the morning of Wednesday 7 June, and here were faced with entirely fresh problems – the wind had at last decided to join in the proceedings and was blowing with some vigour from the north; and coming alongside a marina berth under sail only in such conditions is a trifle daunting. Still, it was managed quietly and successfully, thanks to good team and crew work, and while we had expected then to hire a taxi to take the batteries away for charging, we found that the Real Club Nautico could do this for us. They were on charge within ten minutes of being brought ashore, and a twenty-four hour charge meant we were able to set sail again the following morning, Thursday 8 June – one week out from Warsash – splendid help for which we were very grateful.

La Coruna is a useful port of call – all facilities are reasonably accessible, but with the constant passage of commercial traffic it is an uneasy place. We were unfortunately savaged by a Frenchman who decided to lie alongside us despite every discouragement; before he left he had pulled out one of our stern fairleads and snapped off short the new ensign staff I had fabricated with so much care during the winter. Still, it could have been worse – at least our precious and expensively painted topsides were undamaged!

Our departure on Thursday morning 8 June, with crew washed and refreshed and batteries re-charged, was a much more ordered affair, and we welcomed signs of a fair sailing breeze at last, N.N.E. apparent twenty knots, which gave us a good start on a broad reach to clear Sisargas and later Villano – a whole sail wind, running comfortably at a steady seven to eight knots, recording between fourteen and sixteen miles in a two-hour watch. But more was to come – no. 2 genoa changed to no. 4 and several rolls in the main – the log says the super day's sail now beginning to seem a trifle overdone. Still we tramped on, now on our long southerly course down the Spanish and Portuguese coasts, by evening under no. 4 headsail alone: the Irish sail, so called because it originally came from one of the boats damaged by an IRA bomb at the London Boat Show some years ago. We subsequently bought it very cheaply and it has certainly done us good service, and did this night, taking us downwind at eight to nine knots with an indicated wind speed up the tail of thirty to thirty-five knots. 'A wild roller coaster ride' says the log, and so indeed it was, everything from time-to-time disappearing in a welter of spray as we surfed along at ten knots and more (we don't know how much more, the clock stops at ten).

This was very exciting, but of course tiring. 'Percy', our Aries self-steering gear, was quite unable to cope with this excitement and though *Water Music* behaved herself impeccably, none of us truly were sorry when Friday dawned and there was an easing in the wild wastes around us – by 1000 we were able to set full sail again. Even Neil, who hankered for a gale on the way back from Bermuda, or at least said he did, seemed content when this little lot had passed through; and it all came out of a clear sky. One hundred and thirty seven miles in sixteen hours, under a small headsail for the most part, will take some beating for us, and that is without taking into account the favourable current under us.

Subsequently we proceeded at a more pedestrian pace down the length of this coast, mostly in indifferent or downright poor visibility (the sun declined to make any appearance) and it was still quite remarkably chilly.

Our tack, to close the coast, with no sight for some while past, had to be based purely on dead reckoning and intuition, and it was a very satisfying moment when Cape St. Vincent came in sight through the haze, some four cables on the port bow. Thereafter, our brave wind having left us, we had perforce some hours of motoring, since these are no waters in which to linger, particularly in conditions of poor visibility, and passing close to Pta de Sagres we wondered if the shade of Prince Henry saw and approved. Unfortunately we then had still some hours of engine work before the wind rejoined us (we were on a very tight time schedule), but happily by then it was warmer and we were able to discard at least one sweater by night.

Gibraltar finally came in sight early on the afternoon of Monday 12 June, eleven days out of Warsash as against the ten forecast, but we had had what we thought at the time was a wasted day in La Coruna. Of course, wasted it was not – the engine and electrics gave us sterling service after our battery recharge and since we came to terms with the idiosyncrasies of our new ignition switch wiring, which was just as well in the windless conditions we faced. At least, however, we had no fog, as there was some forty miles east of Gibraltar, causing a very nasty collision. Fog in the Mediterranean really is unusual.

We made fast in Gibraltar late that evening, initially in the Pens, though we were later to move to the rather more convenient waters of the Cormorant basin. Our log records that in this, our first intended port of call, all hands were in good heart – Neil cherubic and beaming, Howard rather more measured in his approach but always willing, while Peter, the new boy, was a great addition to our number. Defects were few, the minor damage caused by our Frenchman in Coruna, the disinclination of our freshwater electric pump to work, a faulty compass light connection, and 'Percy'. He had a bad voyage until then, spending most of the time sulking in his tent – we tried threats, promises, blandishments, cajolery and curses, but to little end – bar short spells he had not earned his keep in oil and rope and it was difficult to know why. He seemed unable to cope with the big seas we experienced, but it did not seem to worry him on the way out to Barbados.

Gibraltar is one of those ports at which one is pleased to arrive and pleased to leave – rather like having one's mother-in-law to stay. We found, as before, that while all there are friendly enough, there never seem to be the stocks of chandlery one would expect, and the bazaar atmosphere of Main Street gets a little wearying; indeed the whole atmosphere is raffish and it is depressing to see the number of yachts both in the pens and the marina area whose owners profess their intention, when they are finally ready, of sailing to the Antilles, to South America or South Africa, when one knows full well that it is all a pipe-dream, that they are just whistling down the wind.

But it is none the less saddening to see once high hopes and professed intentions come to naught and once fine ships decaying – we were fortunate in that through Patrick Madge we had an introduction to the Queen's Harbour Master, Keith Rogerson, and had been invited to move to the comparative cleanliness and sanity of Cormorant.

So, after re-stocking and re-storing – incidentally, with surprisingly good fresh meat considering that the border with Spain at La Linea is still closed after nine years, and spending more than I should have done (Gibraltar is no longer a wholly duty-free port), we set forth. This was at 1800 on Wednesday 14 June, a fine bright sunny evening, with a welcome westerly of apparently ten knots blowing, giving us a steady seven knots on our course of 085 °T, after we had squared-off on course at Europa Point.

We had logged in all 1,340 miles for Warsash to Gibraltar and were now at about our halfway point. If the Mediterranean were to run true to form and to our own previous experience, we were going to be faced with a lot of motoring over the next 1,200 miles (had anyone told us at this stage that while we had used twenty gallons of fuel between Warsash and Ushant, we would need only five from Gibraltar to Sicily, our answer surely would have been short and sharp.

Some while ago I was told that the weather off Gibraltar usually holds in cycles of three – if it blows from the west it blows for three days, and vice versa from the east. So, since our opening westerly had really only appeared at noon, we had high hopes, our concern being where we were subsequently to call for fuel; the itinerary included stopping-off points at Alicante and Ibiza if necessary, but at neither of these did we wish to call unless it were really unavoidable. If we had a day or so in hand we would prefer to spend it in the quieter Ionian than in the south coast of Spain and the Balearics.

And so it was, by early on Thursday 15 June, we were off the snow-capped peaks of Adra, our concern now a no. 2 genoa badly chafed at the tack on the pushpit. (Why don't we remember, on the reach, to set this on a tack strop?) And still we ran on, and by evening it was clear that Alicante and the fleshpots of Spanish paella could be dropped from our reckoning – we were now in motoring distance, even in a flat calm, of Ibiza. By the morning of Friday 16, while what the log calls 'the high hilarity of the first twenty-four hours' had dropped, we were still tramping along, recording some fourteen miles to a two-hour watch – these were peaceful, placid days, warmer and sunnier, with 'Percy' – now back from his sulking – firmly in control since we dropped Europa Point. Shipping was occasionally a problem, but more of interest than a worry – at least in these seas one can be pretty sure of reasonable visibility with few of the close encounter situations so worrying in the Channel.

By Saturday, our Meridian Passage sight gave us an O.P. of 37°58.7′N, 3°11′E (navigation throughout was by sextant, Portuguese and Spanish Radio Beacons being infrequent and unreliable), and this gave us 260 miles for the island of San Pietro off the S.W. of Sardinia, which we now decided should be our goal. The log hereabouts mentions that our breeze from the S.W. or S.S.W., was warm and dry and presumably was a sirocco – perhaps we were fortunate it did not feel like decanting any sand on us.

Neil logged this day that one of his watches, by then some seventy-eight hours and 540 miles out of Gibraltar, was the first to average less than five knots – we would have comfortably wagered odds against this sort of sailing before we left! What is more, it was now warm – both Peter and I recording 'superb, warm, moonlit watch – real champagne stuff'. Still the wind kept with us so that by Mer. Pass. we were less than 130 miles from Carloforte, and still making an average five and a half to six knots. There had earlier been a discussion on whether we should call at Carloforte or Cagliari, or indeed whether we needed a port-of-call at all before Sicily; but we decided eventually that a night's rest and opportunity to re-stock would be desirable, and, in any event, with the breezes we had enjoyed, we were well up with the clock. The remainder of the choice was simple – an island port like Carloforte was clearly preferable to the dustiness and squalor of the larger Cagliari, even if supplies might be more difficult to obtain.

And so it was, we had perforce a little motoring early on Monday 19 June, though the wind soon came back to us. Land was sighted shortly before noon, and finally we made fast in the pretty little port of Carloforte at 1600, 758 miles and rather less than five days out of Gibraltar. In terms of time and of distance run it was, in Mediterranean conditions, a supremely successful and happy leg, *Water Music* behaved as ever splendidly, even 'Percy' having apparently repented of his Portuguese Coast sins.

All had gone very smoothly, any bickering being an amiable affair confined principally to the mutual competition in biscuit consumption between Neil and Howard, and the different hours of sleep apparently needed by the four of us. Howard was occupying the port upper berth in which Will had spent so many hours on the crossing to Barbados – there must be something infectious in that particular pit!

Water Music had visited Carloforte on her way through to Malta in 1971, and it is a happy and convenient port of call: an unspoilt, simple haven with the additional advantage of leaving options open for a further passage east, either north or south of Sicily, though it must help to speak a little Italian, particularly with Customs and Immigration Officials. However, they were polite and friendly enough and all was soon satisfactorily arranged with the aid of a little mutually indifferent French. Supplies required ashore were water, fuel, fresh food and ice, but the bulk of these we decided, all banks being shut for the day, to defer till the following morning. In fact we did not succeed in changing any Travellers Cheques that evening, though we did manage, through a complicated barter system including Swiss and French francs, sterling and American dollars, to obtain for ourselves sufficient lire for an excellent meal. Being of fish and *fruits de mer*, locally caught, it was of a freshness that we had not experienced for quite a long time – Feeding ashore in Gibraltar is not exactly an exciting gastronomic experience! – but it was nonetheless surprisingly expensive, as the navigator and skipper (who had been foolish enough to win both the E.T.A. and watch run competitions and was therefore responsible for the first meal ashore) found to his cost. However, it was a very pleasant evening in a wholly unsophisticated atmosphere, though we were surprised to find how early everything, even hotels and restaurants, closed down for the night.

Peter, unfortunately, here received news of a burglary of his London flat, with the loss of a good number of his treasured personal possessions – a terrible thing to happen when so far from home and powerless to do very much about it. But he was adamant in not wishing to fly home to sort things out, and to continue with us, a much appreciated decision. To add to his troubles, he then began to suffer severe toothache from an impacted wisdom tooth, which was to last him over the next four days – whether this was pure coincidence or not we cannot say, but it certainly did not make him any happier.

The following morning, Tuesday 20 June, Peter, Neil and Howard spent re-fuelling, re-watering and re-stocking, while I had a grand cleaning session, washing all the tea-towels and pillow-cases, scrubbing the heads compartment, the cabin sole, the galley and cooking equipment, and finishing off on deck. Very satisfactory, at least to me, and nobody was allowed on board until it was all completed and dried. However, all good things come to an end, and by 1250 we were through, complete and fit for sea once more – or so we thought!

Unfortunately I did not check the engine cooling water level before starting, in accordance with normal practice, since it had only been done shortly before our arrival, and we were therefore appalled when at 1300, just as we were leaving harbour, the motor suddenly cut on us. We found it extremely hot, with a temporary seizure, and the fresh water cooling system dangerously low, which took eight pints (of warmed water, of course) to bring up to level.

Now we were in a pickle – though the engine quickly freed itself and seemed none the worse, it still needed topping up with a pint an hour when in use; curiously it lost more when not working, which explains the drastic loss in Carloforte. A moral here incidentally – always check everything before departure, even if you know it is right! The trouble was soon diagnosed as a leaking fresh water cooling pump and while for the time being we had enough wind to sail, it clearly had to be repaired or replaced sometime, somewhere. The problem was when and where?

There were clearly no suitable facilities in Carloforte; Malta was a possibility but we had already decided for other reasons – principally the cost of harbour dues for a short stay – to give Malta a miss and were reluctant to go back on this. The only remaining choice was Palermo, and while the Perkins manual mentioned no appointed agent, it seemed likely that as the capital of Sicily, and a substantial port, there ought to be facilities of some sort there.

So, Palermo it was to be. Unfortunately, during the course of all these traumas, staying at the wheel too long, hatless in hot sun, I had given myself a mild dose of sunstroke, but this soon passed. Indeed, it was surprising that despite the heat we later met, we had little trouble on this score – perhaps we had had enough time to condition ourselves, the ample use of salt tablets, or the awe-inspiring quantity of suntan lotion used. However, be that as it may, Palermo was our choice, and true to our fortune the log records in the early hours of Wednesday 21 June, the longest day, 'a pleasant sailing breeze, nice and warm' – our luck holding, it was still astern. However, by 0400 our pleasant sailing breeze had become too much for a full main and boomed-out headsail – the only occasion we took risks in being over-canvassed the whole voyage. It shows the deception easily practised by warm weather, but a gale is still a gale in warm Mediterranean winds just as much as in the colder airs of the Channel.

However, snugged down we were still making good progress and by 0840 had made good eighty-three miles in the ten hours since our departure from Cabo Spartivento – the delicate condition of our engine was not yet handicapping us. This of course was too good to continue, and while we were to make fast finally in Palermo, at 1215 on Thursday 22 June, we had in the latter stages to motor some of the way. At least the leak was not increasing and to pour in a pint an hour was no great trouble, particularly in daylight when most of our motoring took place, and there was always someone to check other than the duty watchkeeper – 'Percy' will have nothing to do with engines.

Palermo, and indeed the N.W. coast of Sicily, was one of the few ports and areas for which we had on board no large-scale chart – a cause of some concern – but it is just not possible to allow for every contingency and we had a pretty substantial folio of charts on board as it was. Fortunately, it is a simple enough entrance, at least in daylight, helped as we were by an outline sketch Howard prepared from information from the Pilot. This latter was surprisingly accurate and certainly we experienced no difficulty in finding the yacht basin, though rather more in finding a vacant berth.

An engineer was immediately contacted – we must have been very lucky – and aboard and sizing up the problem. Language again was a difficulty, other than schoolboy Latin, indifferent French and plain intuition, but we did understand him to say it was too hot and that he would be back later (though not entirely certain whether he meant the engine or the weather). However, he was comfortably built, as engineers should be (all competent engineers have large backsides), and we trusted him – after all, there wasn't much else we could do.

Palermo is a most interesting old port, redolent of history, with some most unusual Arab-Norman architecture, whose influence we had never suspected to spread so far south; even with our other problems we could not but regret that we had insufficient leisure to explore further. Street markets of every sort abound, teeming with humanity; hot and dusty by day, and by night more than a little frightening.

Unfortunately, our well-endowed engineer did not reappear until 0900 on the morning of Friday 23, by which time we were wondering whether he was as reliable as his shape suggested, and if we ought to look elsewhere. But our temporary lack of faith was confounded – he reappeared with a replacement Perkins pump, and by noon had it fitted – at no mean expense of course, but what else can one do? At least it worked and continued to work, and this is one of the problems when in the Mediterranean where a reliable engine is an essential.

It meant a trip to the bank to obtain an indecent amount of lire, and it was a nervous moment to walk back through the sleazy market districts with the amount of cash involved. This is when I had the unusual experience of causing an accident – a vast pantechnicon stopped, presumably to ask me the way (why choose me?), and when I explained politely that I had no idea what he was talking about, he laughed so much his foot slipped off the clutch and he rammed the car in front. A clear case where prudence is the better part of valour, and I disappeared quickly to pay off our excellent and competent engineer.

So now it was once more all systems go – we suspect incidentally that our original water pump may have suffered from the fan-belt incident – and so we departed at 1415, re-fuelled, re-watered and re-stocked, even personally showered, this latter always a problem in Mediterranean ports.

There followed one of the few wholly windless passages of the whole voyage, an uninteresting spell of motoring along the coast of Sicily, during which Peter had a sharp difference of opinion with an unco-operative fisherman overtaking on our starboard quarter, who seemed intent on ramming. This was very worrying, but at least with a magnificent full moon, visibility was now excellent. However, by dawn the following day, 24 June, it was clear that if this spell of calm weather were to continue, we had insufficient fuel available to reach Corfu, and we decided it would be prudent to replenish before reaching the Straits of Messina.

So we called in at the small port of Milazzo on the north east of Sicily, a deviation of scarcely a mile from our direct passage and an easy entrance, although no port in which to linger in any winds with the north in them. This was a real racing pit-stop – we made fast at the fuel berth at 0930 and were on our way again, tank and cans all filled, by 1005, now really on the last stage of our long voyage.

We then experienced one of the sudden windshifts typical of these waters – after motoring for so long in calm conditions, and on the point of turning south for the Messina Straits, we picked up a force 7, inevitably from the south, involving a dead beat to windward. This was just what we needed least, with all the shipping around, and there were scenes of frantic activity in headsail changes and reefing down before we came to the turn. At least we had timed the tide correctly, and in these Straits, especially at Springs, this is a factor very much to be borne in mind and we were swept through quickly. This is always an interesting passage, but one to be treated with some respect – in spring-tide conditions there is a difference in level between the Tyrrhenian and the Ionian seas of some twelve inches, in a distance of some three or four miles. Neither Scylla nor Charybdis are of course the menace they were to Odysseus, but even so still produce interesting whirlpools, particularly the latter; Scylla's powers were abruptly truncated after an earthquake a hundred years ago or more. So, no song of the sirens for us, and nor did I have to be tied to the mast, nor the ears of the crew stopped with wax.

But we did get very wet, with warm and very salty water – the saline content of the sea is very high in the Eastern Mediterranean – and regretted that while in Milazzo we had taken down our cockpit dodgers to get more cooling air aft, which was not very good timing!

However, all this soon passed – by early afternoon we had all reefs out, in a breeze that had dropped as quickly as it had risen, though leaving behind an uncomfortable lumpy sea, and by 2100 were past C. Spartivento at the toe of Italy and squared off on our last course for Corfu. There came then two of the most worrying moments of the whole voyage – both Peter and I when on watch in pitch darkness as the moon had not yet risen, became aware of a large unlit motor vessel steaming from dead astern at high speed, sheering off only at the last moment and shining an Aldis on us as she did so. What was it? Possibly the Italian equivalent of the Customs and Excise looking for smugglers, or more probably smugglers looking for a contact; it certainly was no fisherman, and a highly dangerous exercise. Thank heaven at least that our batteries were fully charged and our lights burning brightly.

The remainder of our voyage to Corfu was pleasant and uneventful

– the breeze came and went, so we had perforce some motoring on this 250 mile leg from Spartivento; but basically we were in the sailing business with 'Percy' behaving, and finally made fast in Kerkyra at 1605 on Monday 26 June, calling there to clear Customs and Immigration *en route* to Gouvia some three miles further north.

From Kerkyra it was but a short trip to Gouvia, where we finally made fast at 1930 local time, 1630 G.M.T., 2,798 miles and twenty-four days three hours out of Warsash, 1,458 miles and twelve days out of Gibraltar, the latter with remarkably little use of engine – a surprising statistic.

Gouvia, a protected and landlocked bay on the east coast of Corfu facing Albania, had changed considerably since we were last there in 1972. In particular, a substantial marina had been constructed at the southern end, a massive piece of reinforced concrete with solid decks some ten feet wide. Unfortunately, we found the pontoons a little high for our topsides, and it was necessary, lying alongside, to lay out a bow and stern kedge to hold us off, but once this was done we were moored as safely and conveniently as we could ever be – this we proved in strong winds a few days later. It is also dusty, but then everywhere is in Greece; its virtue is that while services, water, ice and fuel are available at a cost, mooring is free: the contractors having gone bankrupt – not surprisingly in view of the massive construction – and the Tourist Board have refused to take it over uncompleted, without electricity and piped water.

However, here we were at journey's end, after a very happy voyage, with little in the way of damage to rectify, and abiding memories of good sailing to relish. Howard, sadly, had to leave us almost immediately, but for Neil and I there were a few days of rest and recuperation, interspersed with energetic spells of cleaning and maintenance, before we also returned to the workaday world. Peter remained on board until our return – we left him in charge of *Water Music* in a very friendly and happy island, full of tourists, but surprisingly unspoilt away from the main centres, with all the gaiety and warmth typical of Greece. Gouvia is fortunately placed to be on the east coast, for it is on the west and south of the island, at Paleokastritsa and other places, that the main tourist resorts lie.

We were fortunately able to see quite a lot of Corfu with the aid of hired scooters and mopeds before the day of return finally dawned; then back to an England enjoying one of the coldest and wettest summers on record, and back to reality with a bump.

Note: All mention of time both in the foregoing and in what follows refers to the local time of the country concerned or, if on passage, the country we had left, but there is a complication. During the summer months Italy operates on B.S.T. +1, G.M.T. +2, Greece on B.S.T. +2, G.M.T. +3, while Yugoslavia is on B.S.T. In consequence, to adjust themselves to the sun they rise there early by the clock, and markets are open everywhere at 0530, the equivalent of 0730 in Greece. Perhaps they are more honest than us and do not fool themselves by messing about with the clock, but it is of course more convenient to fall in with their ways when cruising in Yugoslav waters – early to bed and early to rise. Or if you prefer to deceive yourself, and more particularly your crew, put your clocks on two hours to Greek time.

It would be pleasant, if selfish, to be able to record that England's non-summer of 1978 took a turn for the better on my return early in July, but this was not to be – the cold wet weather that had persisted throughout May and during our absence in June showed no signs of letting up. Indeed, the fine spell that heralded our departure from the U.K. had lasted only for a few days, and it seems to have been a pretty unfavourable summer throughout. When we arrived in Corfu we had reports then of yachts returning from the Aegean to avoid persistent strong winds, long before the Melteme should have started to blow.

So there was no warm welcome for us, at least not from the weather, and although there was enough to keep me occupied in my office after a month's absence, it was an uneasy interval before we returned to Corfu on 6 August.

Our intention for this second part of *Water Music*'s 1978 season was to cruise up the Adriatic as a family party, and to lay her up for the winter at Monfalcone, near Trieste, in the latter part of September. We would have preferred to sail through to the Aegean, but late summer is not the best time for those often stormy waters, and to reach the Aegean from the U.K. in one season makes for a very long cruise. Besides, we had never previously sailed in the Adriatic and while we were given mixed reports on the reception we might have, we were aware that it was a cruising ground of quite spectacular vistas, culminating with the sail into Venice; and to sail into the heart of that city, in his own boat, must surely be an ambition of any cruising yachtsman.

During this first part of the cruise we were to be seven aboard until 26 August – Nick, Stephen, Jonathan and myself, Anne and Jo Streeter, and Richard Melhuish, the latter a friend of both Jonathan and Stephen; for the remainder, when Jonathan had flown to Sardinia for the Aga Khan Cup aboard *Winsome*, and Anne, Jo and Richard returned home, we would be joined by Lucy, for once horseless, to sail as a family of four until the weekend of 16/17 September.

At last came Sunday 6 August, when Nick, Anne and I were due to fly out to Corfu, and a fitting day it was on which to leave, with a heavy downpour of rain from dawn onwards, and a greeting at Heathrow from a traffic warden of quite staggering offensiveness – as we were leaving England for a while the latter did not worry us too much, but it quite upset Caroline, who had been good enough to drive us there. Otherwise it was a comfortable enough flight, although we were disappointed on our arrival at Corfu Airport to find no Peter awaiting us, but found aboard *Water Music* a note explaining that he was away in the south of the island, doubtless not unaccompanied.

It was good to be on board again, even though it was warm and sultry, and Peter had clearly been to a lot of trouble to keep everything clean and shipshape, and it was a pity that we never saw him – even though we were in Gouvia until the following Thursday – as we would have liked to thank him for looking after *Water Music*.

Jo, Richard, Stephen and Jonathan flew to Milan by Student Chartered Flight, and then by train to Brindisi and ferry to Corfu, so we were not finally assembled as a crew until the morning of Tuesday 8 August, when all four joined us, surprisingly cheerful and relaxed after the vicissitudes of Italian railways and Greek steamers. We all decided that we must see more of Corfu, and so proceeded north up the east coast to Kassiopi on Wednesday on hired mopeds and motorcycles. There were the usual dramas – statistics prove that an average of two visitors a day are killed in road accidents through the season, a frightening but unsurprising figure. Fortunately we did not add to their number, but there were certainly thrills and spills enough, while poor Anne distinguished herself by getting shot! Presumably by a small boy with, again presumably, an air gun – no great damage was done, but it is a somewhat unconventional greeting!

This we took as a signal that we had outstayed our welcome, but one of the problems in a departure from Corfu, when northbound, is the looming menace of Albania, while the north Corfu channel is safe enough by day, it is of course only four miles wide, and for this and other reasons we decided to make a southward departure to Paxos before crossing to the Italian coast. This had the advantage of a short twenty mile settling-down passage for both boat and crew, and since *Water Music* had been immobile for some five weeks, this clearly was wise. So at 0850 on Thursday 10 August, we made our departure. Unfortunately, it was then necessary for us to sail to Kerkyra for clearance outward, as the officials concerned would not give this to us in absentia while we lay at Gouvia, which was somewhat irritating, but at length the formalities were complete and we were on our way.

Gaio, on our arrival at 1630, was its usual pleasant self, little changed since our last visit six years ago, still with its spectacular winding entrance channel, but full of boats and tourists as we had never seen it, with scarcely room to move on the attractive square for the press of bodies; finding supplies and even a meal ashore was no mean task. However, we managed well enough – Greek catering seems to have improved since 1972 as we had found in Kondakali – and had a pleasant enough dinner in company with *Lady Carola*, R.C.C.

Next morning we were away early for Andi Paxos for a swim *en route* for Otranto, our first intended port of call in Italy; this was as ever a quiet and attractive anchorage, surrounded by water of a clear Cambridge blue. It was now fine, warm and sunny, as it had been since our arrival in Corfu, with only a light north-westerly breeze and this seemed a good augury for our crossing, while to make for Brindisi, our original intention, would take us much more nearly head to wind. We made our departure finally at 1750, anticipating a passage of some nineteen hours for the ninety-five mile crossing, and by soon after midnight had covered approximately half the passage. However, a spectacular thunderstorm, which for some while had been grumbling along the Albanian coast, then decided to move out to join us and unfortunately we were just not quick enough to anticipate what was going to happen – within less than five minutes, from motoring in a flat calm, we had a sudden squall of fifty to fifty-five knots. By the time we got our mainsail down this was badly torn and the gooseneck and outhaul slider damaged, while our headsail rose up the forestay and flogged itself into a rare old mess. All this happened very quickly, and in the fashion of these electrical storms, the whole affair lasted only about an hour from beginning to end. Perhaps the only relieving feature about the whole occurrence was that the rain, when it came, was so heavy that it flattened the sea completely, despite the weight of wind.

So there we were in quite a pickle – clearly there was little we could do before daylight, and as we were very wet by the time this little performance left us we decided to motor on until dawn, by then in a calm again. Fortunately, we had aboard a spare mainsail, though this needed some small repair we could only complete in harbour, and our only alternative was our trysail, last used as a roller stopper on our 1975 Atlantic crossing. However, no further adverse incident ensued, and we finally made fast in Otranto at 1730, after an apparent run of some 130 miles. This is an easy harbour to enter provided you watch the sailing instructions, but not an easy one in which to find a berth; for lack of any alternative, and with no room to anchor, we were forced to make fast to a ferry warping buoy. This was not wholly desirable, the more so as we were warned we might have to leave at short notice, but there seemed no practicable alternative.

Ashore we found a town in *fête*, but apart from this and a cathedral with an intriguing mosaic floor, we found little to interest us; certainly the meal we had ashore was a gastronomic disaster. Our prime need was to find ourselves a sailmaker to repair our damaged no. 3 and mainsail, and so at noon on Monday, after repairing our outhaul slider (which was fractured and later had to be replaced), our gooseneck and our reserve main, we set off on our thirty-eight mile passage to Brindisi. Once more pursued by threatening black clouds and lightning flashes, we were this time a little more canny and managed to skirt around them without any difficulty; this was as well since we heard later that it produced a repetition of our troubles the previous night. However, all we had from it was a quick and enjoyable sail, making fast in Brindisi later that afternoon at 1830 – a run of fifty miles in six and a half hours – only to find another town in *fête*, with everything shut on the morrow.

Brindisi is a large port, not of the importance it enjoyed in Roman times, nor in the nineteenth century when it was a main terminal for liners bound for the Far East, but still busy enough for all that as a ferry base, and regrettably full of officials. We were berthed stern-to the quayside, opposite the Inter-Continental Hotel, and Richard's pleasure was to step ashore to take a bath in that august mausoleum, later to return in rather damp pyjamas due to some unreported carelessness.

Despite many promises, with a town in *fête* we never found our sailmaker, and in fact were not to do so throughout the Adriatic. Stephen later repaired the no. 3, a Herculean task, but unfortunately the mainsail was too badly damaged for any amateur stitching and eventually had to be brought home to the U.K. So there was clearly little purpose to be served by waiting, and it was time we were on our way.

Accordingly, re-watered and stored as best we could, we made our departure shortly after noon on Wednesday 16 August, this time bound for L. Gruz, the port for Dubrovnik (formerly Ragusa). On this occasion, for a change, we enjoyed a very peaceful passage in warm and sunny weather, mostly regrettably under engine, but with a few hours of pleasant sailing in the early hours. (In the expectation of this sort of passage, 'Percy' had been packed away – he makes it difficult to step ashore when made fast stern-to so it was perforce back-to-hand steering, but this was no hardship with seven aboard.)

By dawn, while we had seen no shore lights, the full mountain range behind Dubrovnik was in sight, and the radio beacon for that port clearly audible. Of course one of the disadvantages of closing a high mountainous coast such as this in conditions of good visibility is that the last few miles seem to take so long, and this particular entry was no exception. However, after an exemplary passage we made fast at 1000 on Thursday 17 August, immediately to be visited by the appropriate Yugoslav officials, immigration, customs and police.

This was where we had our first and most pleasant surprise – while we had been warned that we must expect to find the formalities quite severe, both on entry and on leaving, this was not to be our experience at all. Indeed, we were told by all three of our visitors that their regulations had been much relaxed, and this we found to be so – little more onerous than for a yacht cruising in French or Spanish waters.

Dubrovnik is second in its charm, its appeal, and its unique condition as a walled city, only to Venice as the queen of this Adriatic Sea. We spent several happy hours there on the evening of this day of our arrival – interspersed by an excellent meal – and indeed on the following morning. Where else can one see streets of polished marble swept and washed three times each day?

Even so, time was now running short, particularly for Jo who had to fly home on Saturday 19 August, and despite the attractions of Dubrovnik, L. Gruz is noisy and overcrowded, like any marina anywhere. So, soon after midday on Friday 18 August, we enjoyed a pleasant motor-sail to L. Janska, some fourteen miles up the coast from Gruz, the first of the many peaceful anchorages that we were to visit in Yugoslavia. There was in fact always some difference of opinion both aboard *Water Music* and with others to whom we spoke, as to whether it was preferable to spend the day at the quieter anchorages and overnight in the harbours, which were in August very crowded, or vice versa. There is of course, as ever, much to be said for both points of view.

Be that as it may, we had, early on Saturday 19 August, to return from L. Janska to L. Gruz so that Jo could catch her plane back to London, and later that afternoon motored to M. Zaton, a small creek some two miles up the coast from L. Gruz. Unfortunately we had an unhappy experience in Gruz during the nights of Thursday/Friday, 17/18 August, when although both Stephen and Richard were sleeping in the cockpit (which was a great deal cooler than below decks, particularly in our pilot berths), no fewer than four pairs of shore-going shoes were stolen from where they lay on the counter. This was surprising in an authoritarian state, though it is probable that the person responsible was no local but a member of the crew of one of the many charter boats around, but it added nothing to our enthusiasm for marina berths. Certainly we had no fear of this problem at M. Zaton, a quiet anchorage where Richard and Stephen, the fishermen of the party, tried out the net which Anne, Richard and Jo had kindly presented to *Water Music* in Gruz. Strictly speaking, to fish in Yugoslavia one ought to have a licence, but we never really felt that anyone would be very concerned at the curious varieties, and in small numbers at that, which we captured.

Then on Sunday 20 August, we were away to the islands, firstly to Mljet, spending the night at Okulje and leaving the following morning for Polace, again in Mljet. This latter was probably the most attractive anchorage we visited on the whole Adriatic coast, a well-sheltered little harbour surrounded by green hills, with only a few cottages as evidence of human habitation. Fortunately the crickets, which abound here and in so many of the islands, keep early hours and go to bed with the sun – the volume of sound they produce between them at midday is unbelievable.

Later that evening we walked south over the hill and down to lake Veliko Jezero, taking a ferry over to the old monastery, now an hotel; as it was dark when we set off back, we managed to hitch a lift in the back of an unsprung pickup truck, which was quick but not notably comfortable. We also met *Tartar*, R.Y.S., in Polace, and she was one of the only two British yachts we were to meet in all our time in the Adriatic since leaving Brindisi. We were sad to leave this happy spot, the more so as Stephen and Richard made one of their better fishing hauls – even if it did not look in the raw very appetising, the squid and cuttlefish they caught were later made by Nick into the most splendid *bouillabaisse*.

From Polace, a short run brought us to the island of Korcula, reputed to have been the birthplace of Marco Polo, which enjoys a spectacular cathedral perched on the headland above the old town. Unfortunately, this was one of the few cool and windy evenings we had at that time, after another splendidly warm day, and our appetite for sight-seeing was correspondingly reduced – indeed, throughout Yugoslavia there is almost too much to see. It could also be that we had lunched too well – and expensively – on Dalmatian ham and local wine.

U. Luka is in truth not an ideal anchorage, particularly if there are more than two or three boats there – it offers too little swinging room and is open to the north, the dreaded Bora, which is rightly treated with so much respect throughout the Adriatic. Even so, it is preferable to a berth alongside in the harbour, old or new.

Another short passage on Wednesday 23 August, brought us to L. Hvar, the chief port of O. Hvar, another historic Venetian town, but again a difficult port in which to find a berth, particularly overnight when we were surrounded by a press of dayboats and small runabouts. Conscious of the need to protect our topsides, I did not enjoy this night's stop as much as the rest of the family, but in truth, as a holiday centre, there were really too many people around for comfortable living, whatever the attractions ashore. So I for one was quite content to leave early the next morning, after considerable problems with a fouled kedge, for the quieter and more peaceful U. Lucice, on the island of O. Brac, another of the idyllic anchorages that so abound on this coast. Here we enjoyed an excellent but regrettably very expensive lobster lunch – but food is certainly not cheap anywhere on this coast. Indeed, perhaps the lesson that strikes home when cruising in the Mediterranean is just how cheap it is to live in the U.K., whatever we may think to the contrary, and it is not just a matter of rates of exchange either. We were also very interested in a discussion with our host on the political state of Yugoslavia – he confirmed what we ourselves were beginning to think, that in many respects Yugoslavia is less Communist than the U.K.!

Unfortunately, Anne had to leave for home early on the morning of Saturday 26 August, so after a quick visit to inspect Milna and a swim at U. Bobosvisce, both on O'Brac, we were on our way to Split, enjoying one of the best sailing passages we had had since arriving in Yugoslavia. This of course is a big city with all the press of people inevitable in a large port, and regrettably odoriferous; however, we were fortunate to find a berth in the Klub Labud Basin, at the entrance to the harbour, where conditions were infinitely preferable and met a very friendly welcome there, and a great deal of help and advice from Desmond and Annette Stock of *Kotare of Auckland*. He was unfortunately suffering from traumatic switches from euphoria to depression and back again as the Test Match news came in, but seemed to recover his spirits quickly enough when it was all over, even though New Zealand were soundly defeated.

Saturday 26 August, was our changeover day – sadly for us Anne left early in the morning to return home, and Lucy joined fresh from eventing triumphs at Cowdray, bringing with her not quite so triumphant 'O' Level results; while later Richard and Jonathan departed on their separate ways. This had been Richard's first experience of cruising, and while his comment in the log: 'Never had a holiday like it', may have seemed ambiguous, we think and hope we know what he meant, and all three were missed as good companions. The only consolation perhaps was the space now available – to cruise with four aboard a Nicholson 43, with seven bunks between us, is luxury indeed.

There was clearly no call to stay in Split and we wanted now to get further north and quickly left for U. Stipanska, a pleasant anchorage for a swim, and later Milna – both on O. Brac – returning to Split in the morning (Monday 28 August) to re-fuel *en route* to Trogir, with a halt on the way for lunch and a swim in the Fumija Islet passage south of O. Ciovo. It was still warm, though since our crew change day, the settled weather we had previously enjoyed seemed to have left us. Naturally, it was all blamed on Lucy, though in fairness it seems that the northern Adriatic had an unhappy summer throughout 1978, and we certainly were to meet quite a few heavy thunder showers in the weeks ahead, as we had when refuelling in Split.

Trogir we liked very much on first sight, and were delighted to meet there Harry and Sue Rogers of *Drumdoe*, R.T.Y.C., together with Sally and Caroline, with whom we enjoyed an excellent meal ashore, for once at a moderate cost. Stephen and Lucy later enjoyed the unusual experience of having four buckets of water poured over them from high level, presumably in remonstrance for an excess of noise; the prudent elders had left earlier!

But Trogir is a most interesting small mediaeval town, the cathedral alone especially being worth a visit. More particularly, despite Stephen and Lucy's curious experience, it is a clean and friendly place. Most of the mainland cities in Yugoslavia we found to be uncertain in their reception – while the islanders were normally friendly and courteous, even if on occasions a little guarded, it was always, in the larger cities, a matter of chance whether we were greeted with a welcome or plain rudeness. The explanation of this we never really deciphered; however, for whatever reason, Trogir was a pleasant port to visit and Harry was particularly helpful in his suggestions of future ports of call – it was only a pity that we missed his first recommendation, U. Sicencia, and landed up in Rogoznice instead. Never mind that this was a quiet and well-protected anchorage in rather disturbed weather, this sort of error is a black mark to any kind of conscientious navigator!

Our next port, Sibenik, though with an interesting approach through a narrow rocky channel, was to us totally without charm, and a complete antithesis to Trogir – indeed this was one of the ports which we viewed as far from friendly. Apart from fuel and water it seemed difficult to find any other sort of stores, and at the ice factory we got a flat 'no', unfortunately not for the last time, without much expression of regret. Was it really that they could not, or that they would not – it would be interesting to know. So, the log describing Sibenik as 'not a very salubrious port' we left as soon as we could after a very brief stay – it is said that the frieze of seventy-four heads carved around the impressive cathedral represents those who refused to subscribe to the building fund in 1431–1536, and perhaps it has always been a place of some independence of mind.

So we were back with some relief to the islands, this time to Prvic Luka, no more than a few miles from Sibenik, where soon after our arrival the barometer dropped alarmingly and we were penned up for some forty-eight hours in poor visibility, strong winds and surprisingly cold weather. Who among us a week previously would have thought we would be wearing sweaters and anoraks in the daytime? We could only be grateful that if we were forced to spend a day in harbour it was in such a friendly atmosphere as this island, and we only wished that one of us had the ability to sketch or draw some of the faces around us in the local taverna in the evening – they were designed for the talent of a better artist than any of us.

Fortunately, by the morning of Thursday 31 August, we found conditions once more amiable enough for us to put to sea, now bound for the outer islands of O. Kornat and Dugi, and in particular to Vrulje, though we called en route at O. Kakan and U. Lavsa. These are wild and uninhabited islands, quite devoid of any vegetation, all the trees having been cut down many years ago during the time of Venetian occupation either for building or defence purposes. The result is that they are almost frighteningly deserted, and we could not but wonder when and how the massive dividing walls had been built on each island, with no sign of past cultivation – though it must be remembered that this is one of the wine-growing areas that suffered much from the late nineteenth century phylloxera epidemic. It certainly did not help our peace of mind that we had very strong winds overnight and had to re-anchor twice after dragging: with a bottom of weed on hard sand as so often in these parts, it is not always easy to get a kedge to bite. At least that is what the Pilot says, though it felt more like rock when we touched; fortunately we found no damage from this subsequently.

However, much as we prefer the less sophisticated and crowded

Morning Sky (Oliver Roome)

Morning Sky off Hynish pier

Keeshond (Antony Linton)

icksilver locking through Sweden

Quicksilver (Arthur Beiser)

Shara of York (Kenneth Marsh)

Kio

Luxuriating in a hot spring near Estero Cahuelmo (Maldwin Drummond)

Trauco at the ice wall at Laguna san Rafael (Maldwin Drummond)

Close-hauled in the South Pacific, *Wanderer IV* sails on towards Tahiti (E. Hiscock)

The inner harbour at Hilo, Hawaii, with the coastguard cutter in the foreground (E. Hiscock)

'he crowded yacht-floats at Victoria, B.C., are overlooked by the provincial parliament buildings (E. Hiscock)

A black footed albatross feeding alongside as we lay becalmed in the North Pacific (Susan Hiscock)

Jolie Brise (Beken)

Tau, the largest twin k
yacht in the world (Rol
Riverdale)

ports, this was a little too deserted, particularly in the then unsettled weather, and we were glad to return via the Prolaz Proversa Vela, the narrow channel between O. Kornat and O. Dugi, to the relative fleshpots of L. Zapuntel on O. Molat. This was quite an exciting day in rather better weather, the Prolaz Proversa, three cables long, twenty yards wide and with a charted depth of nine feet, providing quite enough challenge to our concentration and pilotage skills, although we suspect the charted depth to be unduly pessimistic.

We were now back in greener islands, and all felt that the bare stripped rocks of Kornat and similar islands needed settled weather for a visit. We were here, after all, to enjoy ourselves, and perhaps it is preferable to cruise in company round these arid areas.

So, away early in the morning on Sunday 3 September, after an abortive fishnet experiment, for a pleasant motor-sail to the island of Losinj, calling first for lunch and a swim at the attractive little port of L. Cikat and later moving round to Mali Losinj. Here we made an error, making fast initially at the marina, newly constructed in this small land-locked harbour, but even the facility of hot showers – something we had not enjoyed since leaving Corfu – was not worth a charge in a none too comfortable berth of 230 dinars (approximately eight pounds) for one night. So early the next morning we extricated ourselves – I do not like to lie bows-on to a pontoon made fast to a steel buoy on each quarter, even were it free – and moved down to the town quay where we re-fuelled, re-watered and even re-filled two Gaz bottles; but still no ice, the machine once more announced as 'kaput'. Stephen completed the repair of our damaged no. 3, we had a good meal ashore at the Tourist Restaurant, and in general enjoyed ourselves as best we could, but stern-on to the quay of a busy harbour one is rather exposed, like a monkey in a zoo.

Only a short distance from Losinj lies the small island of Susak, described in the R.C.C. *Folio* as 'a very small . . . wine port – well worth the visit . . . wine . . . best in Dalmatia' and under 'Approach': 'This requires local knowledge and great caution'. If the first had not been sufficient incentive, the second certainly was, so we were on our way early on the morning of Tuesday 5 September, this time in heavy rain, and with the glass dropping again. We were also told of fine weather in the U.K., which is always a little disturbing in Mediterranean conditions – not, let me hasten to add, from the obvious reason of jealousy, but because it usually means that the Azores High has moved north, with the prospect of depressions slipping south under it. However, we found on arrival that the difficulties of entrance were much exaggerated (our information was admittedly years out of date), and that the wine, freely pressed on us, was nothing very special though cheap enough in all conscience. Above all we found it a very friendly island and though certainly not the cleanest we visited in Yugoslavia, it had a welcome all of its own. Geologically it is unusual in that while rock-fringed, it is otherwise all sand, which may account for the popularity of the local wine-growing activities.

With little in the way of facilities ashore, there was a noticeable friendliness among the yachts in the tiny harbour, all of many different nationalities; this was as well, since true to the portents the weather turned wet and none too warm. So we judged it prudent to spend an extra day here, leaving for Pula, on the western arm of the Istrian peninsula, early on the morning of Thursday 7 September – but Susak is an unusual island, and well worth the visit as a contrast.

Pula, our next destination, is a large town boasting a Roman amphitheatre, at one time capable of seating 30,000 people, and still the largest remaining, greater even than the Colosseum at Rome. It has again all the advantages and disadvantages of its size and we had been advised to find a berth in one of the inlets to the south, either L. Veruda or U. Konalic, and to visit Pula by bus. It was our hard luck that we initially chose the marina under construction at the former, a convenient but rather crowded place. To reach Pula was easy enough: by dinghy across the creek to the motel restaurant, with a bus trip of some fifteen minutes to the town. Once more we found there, searching for supplies, the usual problem with ice, but otherwise all the facilities one could wish for, though it seemed as a town to have a somewhat world-weary attitude as if still searching for its soul – perhaps this was not too surprising in view of its history as a cockpit of the long struggles for supremacy between Venice and Genoa, and the later complications of Occupation, in turn, by Austria and Italy.

We moved early on the afternoon of Friday 8 September to the little anchorage of U. Kanalic, another of the clean unspoilt secure harbours we grew so much to appreciate, but it must have helped that the sun was now with us again for the first time in ten days, and that the press of other yachts had now notably declined with the close of the Italian holiday months.

From here to the pleasant little port of Rovinj, where we succeeded at last in applying several much needed coats of varnish, and thence on Monday 11 September, via U. Soline, to our last Yugoslav port of call, Porec. The former, Soline, had been described to us as 'made unattractive by a slum of tents . . . the largest nudist camp in Europe'. While we felt the first comment was a little harsh, there was no question who was the more self-conscious when we were visited later in the morning by a large number of swimmers – but nonetheless, a pleasant stop for a bathe and a deck scrub!

Porec itself, although we had been told that we would prefer the southern part of the Adriatic to the northern, proved to be a charming little port with some fine Venetian buildings, well-wooded in its surroundings and with a very fine sixth century church with some remarkable mosaics. The bell tower, which we also visited by means of an unusually rickety stairway, provided a splendid view of the town and its surroundings – in all a fitting farewell to our cruise up this Yugoslavian coast.

Formalities for our departure in the morning were as simple as could be, having been much modified in recent years; so very early on the morning of Thursday 12 September, we bade our farewells to Porec, to be greeted almost immediately, as if for a final fling, by an intense but fortunately short-lived electrical storm, with the usual flat calm to fifty knot wind in five minutes characteristic. By this time, fortunately, we knew the symptoms and were well snugged down in advance – the only casualty being Lucy, horseback being no preparation for these conditions, and she poor girl was very sea sick in consequence.

However, by the time we arrived in Venice all was well, and here we were fortunate enough to find ourselves a berth in the basin at San Giorgio Maggiore, a mere biscuit toss from St. Mark's Square. It cost us about £8.00 per day, at a rate of 1,000 lire per metre overall, and was worth every single lire – to sail one's own boat into Venice right up to the Doge's Palace and almost to the mouth of the Grand Canal is one of the truly magical moments of cruising. Venice, through a curious quality of light, almost luminosity, seems to spring to the consciousness in quite a different fashion to any other port we have visited; but so much has been written of its magic that anything we could add would be quite superfluous. Suffice it only to say that the three days and nights we spent there were woefully insufficient even to begin to appreciate the treasures that were offered to us in abundance, especially in the evening when all the tourist steamers had departed; we could only be thankful once again for such marvellous opportunities and experiences. Truly we have been very fortunate.

There now remained only the domestic details – Lucy was already a week overdue to return to school, and *Water Music* herself had to be taken to Monfalcone where she was quickly and efficiently hauled out and bedded down for the winter; we can only hope that next spring we can add 'safely' as well.

So ended our 1978 season – nearly four thousand miles travelled, some top class sailing early on, with an exhilarating passage of twenty-four days from Warsash to Corfu; if latterly we had more motoring than sailing, we had these earlier halcyon days to which we could look back, and we were shown some entrancing harbours and anchorages. *Water Music* herself seemed to relish it all – she has now at one time or another worn twenty-five different foreign ensigns as courtesy flags, and it would be interesting to know what she would count as the highlight of her eight years of life, which have given us so much pleasure and enjoyment.

WATER MUSIC III

TABLE OF DISTANCES

Date		*Port of Departure/Arrival*	*Miles*	*Under Way* *days*	*h.*	*m.*	*Average Speed*	*Under Engine* *days*	*h.*	*m.*
June	1/7	Warsash – La Coruna	658	5	20	15	4.7		18	35
	8/12	La Coruna – Gibraltar	682	4	12	45	6.3		16	45
	14/19	Gibraltar – Carloforte	758	4	22	05	6.4		12	55
	20/22	Carloforte – Palermo	277	1	23	35	5.9		03	45
	23/24	Palermo – Milazzo	98		19	15	5.1		15	10
	24/26	Milazzo – Kerkyra	321	2	06	00	5.9		06	25
	26	Kerkyra – Gouvia	4			45				45
			2,798	20	08	40	5.7	3	02	20
Aug.	10	Gouvia – Kerkyra	4			45				45
	10	Kerkyra – Gaio (N. Paxos)	27		05	00			01	15
	11/12	Gaio – Otranto	131	1	03	40			12	40
	14	Otranto – Brindisi	50		07	25			01	05
	16/17	Brindisi – L. Gruz	133		21	45			05	35
	18	L. Gruz – L. Janska	14		04	30			04	30
	19	L. Janska – L. Gruz	14		04	00			01	40
	19	L. Gruz – M. Zaton	7		01	30			01	30
	20	M. Zaton – L. Okulje (O. Mljet)	20		03	10			02	15
	21	L. Okulje – L. Polace (O. Mljet)	17		03	25			01	10
	22	L. Polace – U. Luka (Korcula)	18		02	55			01	05
	23	U. Luka – L. Hvar	35		06	25			04	25
	24	L. Hvar – U. Lucice (O. Brac)	14		02	35			00	35
	25	U. Luçice – U. Bobosvisce (O. Brac)	6		01	15			00	55
	25	U. Bobosvisce – Split	9		02	00			00	15
	27	Split – U. Stipanska (O. Brac)	9		01	50			01	50
	27	U. Stipanska – Milna (O. Brac)	3		00	30			00	30
	28	Milna – Split	11		01	45			00	45
	28	Split – Fumija (O. Ciovo)	9		01	30			01	30
	28	Fumija –Trogir	4		00	45			00	45
	29	Trogir – U. Rogoznica	20		03	55			00	55
	30	U. Rogoznica – Sibenik	17		03	05			02	15
	30	Sibenik – Prvic Luka	4		00	40			00	10
	31	Prvic Luka – U. Lavsa (Kornat)	21		04	30			00	30

	31	U. Lavsa – Vrulje (Kornat)	5		00	55			00	55
Sept.	1	Vrulje – L. Zaglav (O. Dugi)	24		04	10			00	40
	2	L. Zaglav – L. Zapuntel (O. Molat)	15		02	45			02	00
	3	L. Zapuntel – L. Cikat (Losinj)	23		03	55			02	55
	3	L. Cikat – Mali Losinj	4		00	55			00	55
	5	Mali Losinj – O. Susak	7		01	00			00	10
	7	O. Susak – L. Veruda	27		05	40			01	20
	8	L. Veruda – U. Kanalic	1		00	20			00	20
	9	U. Kanalic – Rovinj	20		04	15			01	20
	11	Rovinj – U. Soline	4		02	55			00	10
	11	U. Soline – Porec	8		02	50			01	05
	12	Porec – S. Giorgio Maggiore (Venezia)	45		11	45			02	35
	16	S. Giorgio – Monfalcone	50		10	30			04	40
			830	5	20	45	5.9	2	19	55
			2,798	20	08	40	5.7	3	02	20
		Total:	3,628	26	05	25	5.8	5	22	15

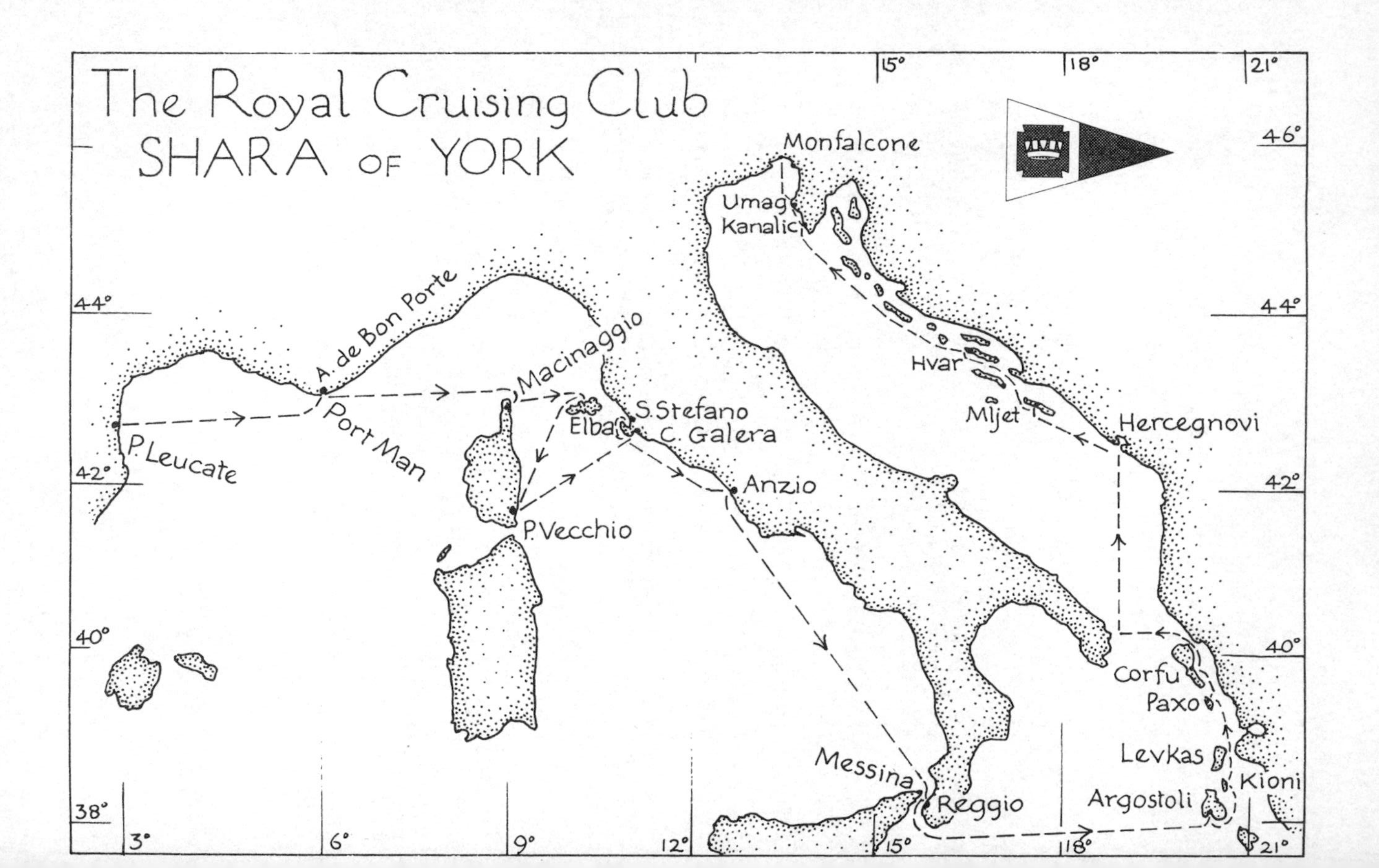
The Royal Cruising Club
SHARA OF YORK
Monfalcone
Umag
Kanalic
Hvar
Mljet
Hercegnovi
A. de Bon Porte
Macinaggio
S. Stefano
Elba
C. Galera
P. Leucate
Port Man
P. Vecchio
Anzio
Corfu
Paxo
Levkas
Kioni
Argostoli
Messina
Reggio
3°
6°
9°
12°
15°
18°
21°
38°
40°
42°
44°
46°

TO THE BALKANS

by Kenneth Marsh

Our home in Pau was too far away for weekend visits to the boat so, apart from topside repainting at Easter, she had slept undisturbed in a large shed for nine months. Two hours after our arrival at Port Barcares, she was back in the water alongside the yard quay. We had not forgotten how their small mobile crane had swayed and tottered removing the mast, so I now told the foreman we would lay it on deck. His face expressionless, he shrugged but did as I said without comment. This is one of the better aspects of life in France; because you are a foreigner and therefore of unsound mind, you will often be indulged where the French customer has to argue and explain. While Jane went ahead with the cat, I took *Shara of York* under the low road bridge and through the channel to the sea, her mast lashed between pulpit and sternguard, heading for Port Leucate and its muscular travel-lift.

During the fitting-out an awkward problem arose – we had a sick engine. Although there seemed to be more water under the valve-cover than would normally be caused by condensation, the local engineer confidently diagnosed sticking valves. This, he said was a big job and best tackled during the long, slow winter months; but if we used the engine only for entering and leaving harbour, it would probably last for our holiday. We eagerly swallowed this false hope for if the Roussillon coast had proved a good area for a winter lay-up, therein lay its only charm. And anyway, the Adriatic was our destination so the sooner we left, the better.

Next day the forecast promised north-westerly winds F.5–7, more than we wanted for a shake-down passage but last year *Shara* had amply demonstrated her ability downwind (see R.C.C. *Journal* 1977) so we decided to go.

Port Leucate – Reggio

July 5 to 7. To Anse de Bon Porte. We now feel the Golfe du Lion owes its evil reputation as much to peculiarly nasty seas as it does to the mistral. The first part of this passage was gentle. Clearing the harbour at 1100, we settled down on a course of 090° before a modest westerly, so that dusk found us sailing easily under full main and the goose-winged no. 2. As mare's tails and a mackerel sky gathered astern, we hoped for a fast run on the boat's best point of sailing.

But at 0130 a steep swell rolled up without warning from the south-west, just after the forecast north-westerly had started to blow. We were then running under only the no. 3. A little later, as the Planier light at the entrance to Marseille appeared bearing 050°, the boat felt as if she were skiing down an undulating slope thickly covered with tree-stumps. It seemed best to run off under bare pole – a mistake, as we had already learnt last year that, even in a bad sea, *Shara* is happiest when she is moving at not less than five knots before a strong following wind. Now she behaved as I should have known she would, sluggish and unresponsive to the helm, the hull offering too much resistance to wave movement. In no mood for enterprise, I carried on steering as the boat lurched and corkscrewed to leeward. It wasn't long before a breaking crest joined me in the cockpit. I pulled myself together and re-set the no. 3. With the course resumed, she at once began to swallow the miles through the rain of a dirty grey dawn. If the motion was wild, the tiller was now light and easy.

When the R.D.F. picked up Porquerolles bearing 090° the murk began to lift so that soon the dim outline of the Provencal mountains appeared on the beam. It wanted some sun to fully restore morale and this we soon had. It shone on a brilliant scene; the wind was now a boisterous friend shaping the seas into tall, regular ranks that marched up astern to lift and sweep under us with a hiss and tumble of white water; deck, mast, spars and the stalwart no. 3 glittered with moisture; here was champagne stuff of a rare vintage, made all the more heady because the wicked gulf was now behind us. C. Sicié was abaft the beam at 1115, the end of the land ahead had to be Ile de Porquerolles. In the approach to the channel between it and Grand Ribaud, the seas became steeper but a little way ahead, a graceful gaff cutter was coping manfully; under a small jib and deeply-reefed mainsail, the end of her long boom dipping close to the crests, she was a lovely sight. So we bore up and in her company shot through to the relative calm of the Rade d'Hyères.

As the islands passed we discussed what to do. To press on for Anse de Bon Porte was tempting but it was fifteen miles away, whereas close at hand lay Port Man. We were tired and remembered the tranquil calm of that lovely anchorage. The fact that it was a secure 'mistral hole' was the clincher. So *Shara* bore away towards the headland on the western side of the entrance. Rounding this, we were unprepared for what we saw. Sixty-two other yachts had decided Port Man was the place to be.

The first attempt to anchor set the pattern for the next four hours – it dragged. The problem was that, if we used the right amount of chain, we would sheer into someone else; the number of fenders on display showed this was already happening everywhere. But if we used a moderate amount, dragging was inevitable. The cause of all this lay in that widespread and insouciant Mediterranean habit of using seemingly-endless lengths of nylon warp instead of chain. Last year we snorkelled all over the inner end of the bay. While there are sandy patches here and there, the rest of the bottom consists of shallow ridges of rock thickly covered with brittle weed. The only solution (except departure) seemed to be a series of controlled drags, which meant that one of us could cat-nap while the other kept a 'drag-watch'. Some of the fleet must have thought we were mad and one crew openly laughed at us. A little later there was sour satisfaction in watching them furiously fend off an unattended yacht that repeatedly sheered into them. We draw some small comfort from the fact that, throughout that tiresome afternoon, *Shara* neither touched another yacht nor lifted any anchor but her own.

Towards evening we found a tiny slot over sand in the south-east corner and laid the anchor for the fourth and last time. Our immediate neighbours were close so we still had to keep watch, but we were able to snatch some sleep. There was much flashing of torches during the night and distant cries of '*Hola*!' and '*Oh, la vache*!' but our corner was quiet. Two hours before dawn the wind veered slightly, converting our niche into a lee shore. To leave then was more than I cared to attempt for, of all that great gathering, only seven were showing anchor lights. So we waited until, at first light, we could grope our way to the entrance. Under the no. 3 and well-reefed main *Shara* fled thankfully for C. Taillat. Passing the rugged headland, we hardened in the sheets to tack close inshore ten minutes later. At 0930 we brought up in 7 metres – sand and weed.

Here was utter bliss. The only other yacht was half a mile away beyond a small cluster of boat moorings. Gusts from the gentle hills to the north gave us an occasional sheer but the holding was fine; there was nothing to leeward but open and empty sea. Jane produced an enormous dish of scrambled eggs and *poitrine salé*, which we washed down with the good red wine of Languedoc. The sprayhood was rigged making the cockpit a perfect suntrap. I had a swim in water so cold it might have been the Channel in March, while Jane, sensible girl, immersed no more than her toes. We sunbathed, slept, ate hugely, and slept again. Between times we speculated on the fresh havoc another day of mistral was surely wreaking in Port Man. The night that followed was tranquil. We felt the Anse de Bon Port was well-named, for here were shelter and peace.

July 8 to 9. To Macinaggio. Away at 0715 we streamed the log off C. Camarat. The first main objective of the cruise was Elba so *Shara* resumed her old course of 090°. The wind, light from the north-east, held until 1215 when we were becalmed to spend the next three hours watching a procession of yachts pass under power, heading presumably for Calvi. Then catspaws from the south ushered in a fine F.4 breeze that was to last for thirteen hours. This gave splendid sailing with the boat reaching down the rhumb line and the no. 1 genoa giving of its best. At 2300 R.D.F. passed on a weak signal from Ile Giraglia dead ahead, the dawn showed the peaks of Cap Corse thrusting above the haze, log 96. Then that fine wind faded to be followed by several hours of sail-trimming and spinnaker work as we laboriously coaxed some progress from a fickle westerly. It was intensely hot. Although we were to get more used to the sun later on, at this early stage of the cruise it had a truly numbing effect on mind and body. At 1330 we were creeping past the little island of Giraglia and at 1515 we were only two miles further on, so I started the engine. Ten minutes later, as if to mock us, a strong breeze sprang up from the south-west and we were glad to berth at Macinaggio at 1545.

The landscape of Cap Corse is as handsome as the rest of the island. Green, rounded, *maquis*-covered hills rise, tier upon tier, to the jagged mountainous spine that runs south for 100 miles. But from a cruising viewpoint, it has a weakness. Nowhere at this northern end of Corsica is there a natural anchorage offering good all-round protection. The new wind was a *libeccio* which lasted for thirty-six hours, so we were content to stay in the marina. The following morning we heard that a motor-cruiser had blown ashore, a few miles north of Calvi, with a loss of two lives.

July 11 to 14. To Elba. In a brisk breeze from S.S.E. Shara close-reached in fine style for her first Italian port. Seven hours later she went too close to La Polveraia, catching a lee from that headland, but we managed to work slowly towards some white-caps and, by 1900, were beating into the great haven of Porto Ferraio. One symptom of the engine's illness was reluctance to start, so we had been encouraging it with a little ether. I must have been too liberal this time for on the second swing, the Swede coughed, the business end of the handle parted company with the flywheel and dealt me a smart crack under the chin. The cut was slight but, like all minor wounds to the head, it bled profusely so in no time, my arm as I continued to swing and the area between galley and chart-table began to look as if I had been taking a 'practical' from Lizzie Borden. Muttering about some 'B.F.' or other, Madame applied a band-aid and nobly swabbed up the mess below.

Perhaps if one has become accustomed to the Tuileries, the Villa dei Mulini would be rather a come-down. But if Buonaparte felt like that, it was his loss. None of the beautifully-proportioned rooms is too large and the view from the garden is superb. On the wall of an anteroom, we found our next anchorage; there, among a set of Weir engravings, was a charming picture of Pta delle Grotte with a frigate lying off and a boat laden with casks, pulling for the shore. *A Good Watering Place* read the inscription. We found it also good for a peaceful night, though by day there is some wash from the Piombino ferries. For the next two days there was some pleasant pottering along the island's north coast, plenty of swimming and a fine dinner at a beach cafe near Paolina Island.

July 15 to 16. To Porto Vecchio. At 1100 we were beating out of Marciana and, once clear of La Polveraia, the boat settled on a course of 215°. Although light, the wind persisted between north and west, giving us alternating periods of spinnaker and no. 1. At midnight Alistro light bore 315°, the boat was filled with the delicious, pungent scent of the *maquis* as she slowly converged with the land. The wind deserted us at breakfast, log 59, but at 0900 another appeared, this time from the south-east, so *Shara* spent the rest of the morning tacking slowly along the shore. When we opened the entrance to Pinarello Bay it looked so attractive we went in to anchor in 5 metres – sand. We would have been content to stay but at 1730 a light north-easterly produced an awkward swell, so we sailed on to Stagnolo Bay to bring up at 1945, thus ending the first engineless passage of the cruise.

July 17 to 21. After a late breakfast we drifted and sailed in a light air from the north to luff into a berth at Porto Vecchio marina at 1115.

At the beginning of May, I had ordered charts for the Ionian and the Adriatic from a well-known London agent. To our surprise, they had not reached us before we left home. A telegram and a letter asking that they be sent to Port Barcares also yielded no result, so I had asked the yard there to forward them to Bonifacio. We now went there by bus but, although we found plenty of other mail, there was, alas, no long, familiar roll marked 'Ship's stores in Transit'. Back to Porto Vecchio, where there was a quick burst of shopping before we returned aboard. The chart situation was annoying but not serious; I felt sure of finding what we needed at Messina, a large commercial port and naval base.

At 1700 we motored out of the marina. With a fresh south-westerly, *Shara* was soon back at anchor in Stagnolo Bay, but the wind rose rapidly and, with the fetch, a short sea built up. Of our four neighbours, two got their anchors and chugged off to the marina. This seemed a sensible move but we opted for Marine d'Arghi. I tried to start the engine – and failed after we had attempted every remedy we could think of. The bay is uniformly shallow so that, after I let out some more chain, there was four and a half feet under the keel. We decided against trying to sail out, since, with just the two of us on board to handle the boat and recover the anchor, we might well have needed more room to manoeuvre than we had. *Shara* pitched steeply but there was no snubbing as we had a good catenary; we were more concerned about the continual violent sheering for there was, by then, no way of laying out a second anchor to reduce it.

The night that followed was as unpleasant as any we have spent in a boat. For the first time in many years I had managed to put us in a position where we had no line of retreat, neither an engine that worked nor an escape-route to leeward. This was one of the times when you remember too late the old lessons and curse yourself futilely for not heeding them. At 0900 the gale reached its peak and held at that level except for a slight lull at noon, when I did something I had wanted to do for hours. It took time to get there even with the flippers, but what I found was heartening. The anchor was invisible; there was a scar where it had started to dig, a few feet away the chain emerged from the mud. I swam back to pass the good news to Jane, who lay down and at once fell asleep, to my relief for she was very tired by then. Throughout, she had sustained us both with good food and drink, calmly refusing to allow the weather to interrupt her normal routines. At 1830 the wind began quickly to ease so that, a quarter of an hour later, it was no more than F.3. It took some time to recover the anchor and when it came up there was a fair amount of Corsica adhering to it – dense, black, wonderful, boat-saving stuff, a quintessence of mud. With such holding there seemed no point in going far, so we brought up a quarter of a mile further into the bay where a hillside gave a slight lee. In a good bottle of wine we toasted our CQR and its staunch partner, the bottom of Stagnolo Bay. And sang the *Hippopotamus Song* until we were breathless.

The following morning, Thursday, we sailed over to Marine d'Arghi to lie close under a steep hillside, pleasantly out of the wind. Here we had leisure to plan the engine campaign. It seemed likely to involve removal of the unit and a complex repair. That had to be accepted but the success of the cruise hinged on finding competent people to do the job quickly. The service book listed only one Corsican name and he was in Ajaccio, too far in the wrong direction. The fine reputation of her mechanics made Italy the logical choice, but it was difficult to decide where to go as we had never been there, thus it seemed best to tap some local knowledge before we set out for the mainland. During the holiday season Italian yachts are as thick on Corsican waters as ducks in the Serpentine so we settled down to wait for one with, preferably, a Naples registration. We swam from a little beach and I tried for the first (and last) time to explore the *maquis*. One must be armed with a machete and clad in sheet steel; its repute as the perfect hideaway for outlaws is now clearly understood.

Good advice arrived next day on board *Swift*, a 45 ft. wedge of G.R.P., all tinted glass and high-speed diesels. No one had any English, but the owner's wife and a Brazilian friend spoke fluent French. Naples would be expensive and anyway, they said eyeing *Shara* dubiously, it was rather far to go without power. We consulted a chart and the service book. Cala Galera became the final choice and if we were unlucky there, Santo Stefano was nearby as an alternative. 'We'll see you there on Monday', they called as I rowed away. They didn't sound very confident.

July 22 to 24. To Cala Galera. A promising start with the spinnaker at 0730 soon gave way to a long period of sail-trimming in light, hesitant airs from all points of the compass. This lasted all night and Sunday morning until noon found us becalmed, the genoa on the deck and the helm lashed in a nasty swell, log 44. Montecristo is a handsome island but, by 1730, our view of it had begun to pall. Then the lightest of zephyrs appeared from the west. We set the spinnaker, holding our breath until the new breeze filled so that two hours later, when Giglio Is. showed fine on the port bow, the boat was going beautifully in F.4. A dirty sky appeared to windward but, although the breeze veered, calling for a change to the no. 1, it remained constant in strength. C. Capelrusso was abeam at 0330, two hours later we were passing the southern end of the peninsular to alter course to the north. We tacked past Ercole in calm water and Jane handed the sails off the marina entrance as *Shara* lost way to berth alongside the fuel quay. We felt she had done well in light, awkward weather to cover ninety-seven miles in forty-eight hours.

July 24 to 31. We drew a blank with the first engineer who seemed to be a collector of old iron. Walking back through the marina I ran into *Swift*'s crew, who at once went off to fetch her owner. For the next five hours that good man was on hand to interpret and advise. We can only hope that, should he one day find himself in England faced with a similar problem, he will receive as much efficient help as he so generously gave us. He telephoned Santo Stefano and soon Marcello and Adriano came aboard. They diagnosed a broken seal on the driveshaft of the water pump. The boss, Sgr. Ambrogetti, said firmly that, if seawater had lain for so long in the crankcase, there must be other damage. So I rigged a lifting tackle on the backstay and by 1400 the engine was on its way to Santo Stefano in a small van.

We followed next day with a pleasant sail round the peninsula. Berthing might have been a problem but for the friendly crew of a large ketch who welcomed us alongside. Here was a splendid surprise for she turned out to be *La Pinta*, ex-*Vanity*. That evening in her saloon, there was much reminiscing about the days when this lovely Fife 12-metre was a Solent queen, diminishing all other racing craft by her grace as much as her size. Now based on Toulon, she leads a pleasant second life cruising between the Balearics and Italy. Before they left next day, her charming owner presented us with a bottle of wine of such quality that we carefully tucked it away for the scheduled reunion with my brother in Corfu.

I haunted the workshop where Marcello worked so well that a rejuvenated Swede was back in his bed by Friday evening. However, the money for the bill had yet to arrive so we spent the weekend at Giglio Is., swimming and cleaning the topsides. Sadly, the Tyrrhenian Sea is far and away the dirtiest we have seen and must give the ecologists many a sleepless night. A Monday visit to the bank yielded nothing so we withdrew a mile to the east to a small bay, where we made a first trial of anchoring by the stern – with promising results.

Six years ago I gave Jane a small, orange sunhat. Since then it had covered many miles of cruising here and there. Faded by sun and salt, stained with *Fairlight*'s enamel and *Shara*'s anti-fouling, it had become as much a part of her as the hair it protected. Now, on this black Tuesday morning as we sailed back to Santo Stefano, an evil gust plucked it off her head and dropped it over the side. A half-hour search was fruitless. This was a poor start to the day and not one to induce the right frame of mind for dealing with bankers. However, the cash had arrived and I carried Jane off to a restaurant, where as luck would have it, we had the only mediocre meal of the cruise. Clearly it was time to go.

August 1 to 3. To Anzio. After settling with Sgr. Ambrogetti we motored clear of the harbour at 1600. There was a short swell from the south-east but enough air from the same direction for a slow beat. This lasted until we were becalmed off Civitavecchia at 0820, log 44. Mention of the hat had been carefully avoided but the shadow of its loss was still with us. Then, as we plodded under power along the filthy line which marks the effluence of the Tiber, something happened which transformed the mood on board. Jane saw a large and handsome fender that we fished out and triumphantly scrubbed clean. With morale restored, we pressed on through a hot day with light airs from the south and east and occasional help from the engine.

Approaching Anzio under power at 2300, we noticed a lot of water in the bilge. This was traced to a fast leak in the rubber water-jacket of the exhaust. It was easy enough to disconnect the water intake and use it to drain the bilge, but this meant that in time the engine would overheat since the same water would be circulating instead of being replaced by fresh. Another reason decided us to stay at sea that night. Nero has left a legacy to the unwary which is typical of the man; his old harbour works effectively obstruct the northern approach to Anzio. To circumvent these and cope with an overheating engine at the same time seemed too much. So we waited through a beautiful night in a calm sea with no moon, a sky like black velvet that not even the myriad stars could lighten. Just before dawn the fishing fleet streamed out of the harbour, giving us the line we wanted and the leisure to juggle with the water-works. Half an hour later we berthed stern-to the town quay.

Anzio made a good port of call which quickly supplied our needs. I found a new rubber tube and fitted it to the exhaust. Jane's shopping went equally well; here were fewer tourists so the Italian wine of our choice cost exactly half the Santo Stefano price.

August 4 to 7. To Reggio. Away at 1230. The light wind teased us with sail changes for four hours before settling from the south-west, F.3/4. Mt. Circeo was soon towering dramatically above the haze that hid the shore, midnight found us threading the channel between Zannone and Ventotene islands, log 53, and by dawn we were far enough offshore to have the sea to ourselves. The wind weakened but stayed in the westerly quadrant, just strong enough to keep the spinnaker quiet so that, apart from three hours of engine, our peaceful advance towards the south-east went on for thirty hours. (If it was rather too hot for comfort in the light following wind, we were now more accustomed to the sun. As it dipped towards the horizon astern, the boat slid quietly along on an even keel, leaving no mark on the smooth, blank face of the sea. Ahead the great bell of green, white and red neatly bisected by the mast, swayed delicately from side to side. Jane stood in the companionway, deftly disjointing a chicken and speculating happily about what sauce would best go with it.)

Shortly after noon next day Stromboli was abeam. We were now back in power-boat country and started the engine as the wind was becoming ever weaker and more fickle. At 1900 S.S. *Canberra* overtook us to starboard, an hour later C. Peloro light appeared ahead. Having no tidal information for the Straits of Messina, we were lucky to find the stream fair. There was heavy through traffic and many ferries, but the moment came for a nervous dash across to the mainland shore to berth at 0100. This passage gave us more motoring than any other with engine use just over a sixth of passage time.

Charts were now top priority for our last ran out a few miles south of Reggio. After breakfast I got confirmation from the customs office that Messina was the place to buy them. In the naval base, I was told, was a branch of Maridrografico, the Italian Hydrographic Office, which would sell charts to anyone, charts for the world. An officer drew me a little map of how to find it. A brisk southerly in the strait and a taxi brought us to the dockyard – where the blow fell. The duty officer said the chart office had closed for a good two months previously. He gave me the address of a bookshop, which we found was also closed for its annual holiday. The taxi-driver was eager to take me on a tour of other bookshops but the meter was now bearing a burden it seemed best to relieve, so I took to my feet. In the fourth shop was an honest man. There was not, he said flatly, and never had been a bookshop here that sold charts.

As we motor-sailed back to Reggio the swordfishing boats were seeking shelter in a rising sirocco. It seemed likely that this would soon veer to give us a wind any soldier would envy for the passage to Argostoli, a distance of 244 miles. We were ready to go in all respects – save one. If there is anything in telepathy, a London chart agent must that afternoon have been suffering.

From a nearby yacht I was able to get the course for Argostoli and make a sketch of its approaches. Into town by bus early the following morning, where Jane bought fresh food and I uselessly explored more bookshops. Then a taxi to the port office where an elderly lieutenant took me in hand. Despite my protests, he insisted on telephoning Messina. At last he put down the receiver.

'If you go to Palermo or Ancona . . .'

Outside, Jane waited patiently in a huddle of shopping bags. There remained one possibility, a last resort I was most reluctant to try, but now it seemed we had no choice for time pressed. On the southern side of the harbour was an old tanker, her sides bearing the dents and scars of a long arduous career; she flew the Italian flag. Alongside the northern quay lay a Norwegian container ship, obviously new construction, gleaming in the sunshine – intimidating. I walked south.

It must be pleasant to work on that bridge in the glow of deeply-varnished mahogany and glittering brass. One wonders if modern ships have been able to retain that atmosphere of warmth and simple elegance. The captain was a quiet, friendly man of about thirty, sensibly dressed in a pair of sandals and ancient shorts. He led the way to the chartroom, searched briefly and handed me two, for the Ionian Sea and the approaches to Corfu. Waving aside my heartfelt efforts to thank him, he asked about our cruise. When I came to Jane, he interrupted, 'Your wife sailed with you from England?' and made a gesture we shall always treasure. With his arms straight and fists clenched, he crossed the right wrist over the left.

Reggio – Corfu

August 8 to 10. To Argostoli. We lost no time getting under way and by 1100 were clear of the harbour with the log streamed. A light air from the west carried us round the ball of Italy's foot towards C. Spartivento. Here was the halfway mark. If before this, there had been some entries to make on the debit side of the ledger, the tanker captain's kindness seemed a good omen. We hoped a page was now turning which would show only profit. And so it proved.

But this was not at first apparent for, off the cape, the wind made a sudden 180° veer which threw everything aback. We managed to get the spinnaker down, luckily without damage, and soon *Shara* was close-hauled in F.5 from the north-east under a well-rolled main and no. 3. Through the night the wind slowly rose, backing as it did so to allow us to ease sheets and adopt the desired course of 085. At dawn the seas were such that the boat was becoming difficult to hold. The chart showed no irregularity on the bottom but we may then have been sailing parallel to a ridge which the soundings had missed because they were some distance apart. We changed to the rig which had proved so invaluable in similar conditions last year. With the mainsail handed, the spare genoa halyard was set up as an inner forestay secured to the large mooring cleat in the centre of the foredeck. On this was set the no. 3 sheeted to the quarter. At once the tiller became docile and *Shara* felt under control, moving easily at a little over five knots in a F.6 beam wind. An hour later the seas moderated so we were able to set the main and put the headsail back in its proper place. By 1600, with the log reading 160, the wind was north-westerly and stayed constant from this direction for the rest of the passage. Never less than F.4, rarely more than F.6, it gave us magnificent sailing, calling the changes on all the headsails except the storm jib. At 0300 a weak blink ahead signalled Cephalonia, four hours later we slipped into the lee of soft, green hills, grateful for the best passage the cruise had so far given us. Distance by log 248 miles, passage time forty-six hours.

How satisfying it is to hoist a new courtesy flag for the first time! In this case, there was almost a feeling of triumph, for to sail in Greek waters had been a dream for so long we had begun to wonder if it would ever become a reality. During the next few days we were to find all our hopes fulfilled and these Ionian islands as near perfect a cruising ground as one can find in Europe.

Argostoli makes a good port of entry. The formalities are quickly dispatched by courteous officials; a fuel bowser frequently visits the quay where water is also available from hydrants. A small chandlery has some charts in stock.

August 11 to 12. To Kioni. The same wind gave us a fast run to Kakova shoal, then a bumpy fetch northwards to Ithaca. Nearing Sarakaniko Pt. after dark, the total absence of lights ashore seemed to exclude any chance of bringing up for the night and we had just decided reluctantly to press on to Kioni when we saw some navigation lights. We followed them in cautiously to anchor in a little bay.

Early next day, an old fisherman and his wife passed in their boat to land on the rocky shore. He mounted a donkey and the three slowly climbed a zig-zag path past an olive grove to their solitary cottage, which hugged the hillside in a stand of cypress. Along a rough track below a crest, other donkeys passed, each heavy-laden and escorted by a sturdy figure armed with a stick, heading for the market in Vathi.

Our guide turned out to be an Italian yacht, *Fulvia*. In her company we had a stiff beat to Kioni, to be joined there by *Rosie Probert* who has surely strayed a long way from Duck Lane and the arms of Captain Cat! Against the wall of the quayside cafe, a pig was sizzling gently over a bed of charcoal. This powerful piece of advertising proved too much for the visitors so tables were pushed together and twelve of us sat down to a splendid party that continued long into the velvet night.

At dawn no ripple or reflection marred the sable gleam of the harbour. The small tidy houses of the village slept among the gentle hills; over all there was a silence so complete it hummed in the ears. Then, from a green shoulder to the south the hush is pierced by a hoarse inhalation, a tentative bray. 'Anybody there?' At once there is a full-throated answer from the head of the valley to the west. Somewhere a shutter bangs. So morning begins in Ithaca.

August 13 to 15. To Corfu. *Shara* wandered slowly northwards past island after lovely island: through the Meganisi and Levkas channels to spend a night at busy Port Gaio, a sort of Ionian St. Tropez and most attractive. The *Fulvia*'s came aboard for drinks and we envied them their home port of Rimini, which is so close to all this. Giulio congratulated us on our spinnaker, 'such a very **large** Italian flag!'

An early start next day for the rendezvous with my brother gave the engine an active morning in utter calm. The South Channel provided a sample of the clarity of the water in this area; weed-covered rock and even the ridges in the sand were clearly visible with the echo-sounder showing 25 metres. Passing Corfu port we found a breeze to carry us the last three miles to Gouvia Bay. There lay *Karenza*. Thanks to Ivor Holt's unremitting care she looked as if she had just emerged from the yard after a thorough re-fit instead of, as she then was nearing the end of yet another 4,000-mile cruise to Turkey and back to Antibes. We luffed alongside to a fine welcome from Norman and my nephew, Simon.

Water skiing, an exchange of family news, much valuable information for next year in the Aegean. It was hard to end what, for two reasons, has been an annual event but it seemed best to do so before hot showers night and morning and Sue Holt's wonderful cooking completely corrupted us.

Corfu – Monfalcone

August 19 to 21. To Hercegnovi. For over a week the wind had been mainly in the north-west so it seemed likely we were now faced with a passage to windward, our first in *Shara of York*. With an impressive array of Adriatic charts on loan from *Karenza*, we felt well-equipped as we got the anchor at 0840 after a peaceful night by Karagol Point. A light north-westerly made for slow progress until, twelve hours later, Fano Is. was abeam to leeward, log 39. Then, in F.5 she headed close-hauled for Italy under the no. 3 and five rolls in the main.

If one must go to windward, it is heartening to be in a boat that makes real progress in that direction. Thanks to her Half-Ton Cup ancestry, *Shara* does it well – but wetly. The boat that doesn't leak has so far eluded us but, on this sensitive subject, one can say of ours that the leaks are slight and, with one exception (the stern gland), all are on deck.

She soldiered gamely on in short seas towards C. Otranto. We tacked two miles off the light at 0415, log 77, and began the long haul to the north. During the following thirty hours, the wind oscillated between north-west and north-east varying in strength from F.2 to F.5. With some sail-changing, motor-sailing for four hours and a couple of tacks, we were able to profit from the wind-shifts to gain nothing and increase our distance from the unfriendly Albanian shore. At 1045 on August 21 *Shara* found herself in an ugly sea, caused by the coastal shelf, a residual swell from the north-west, and the slight north-going current which is normal for this eastern side of the Adriatic. The wind was then light and the engine could give us no more than two and a half knots. At 1400, wind and sea improved so we stopped the engine.

The radio beacons in this area are of that unhelpful kind which transmit only four times an hour – of no use to us as there never seems to be a timepiece on board which is entirely truthful. Thus, there is always something more useful to do than sit about, earphones to ears, waiting for a signal that never arrives. So we had taken particular care of the D.R. plot and, converging with the Montenegrin coast, were soon able to identify Mt. Lovcen. Shortly afterwards wind and sea showed signs of more discomfort to come. This sort of thing is all very well when one is driven by the competitive impulse of a race, but we were cruising and, by then, had had enough:

The bulkheads are groaning,
The young wife's a-moaning:
'My hair is a fright and I won't last the night.
This trip's been a bore, an unspeakable chore,
So get me in ***now*** *to the Gulf of Kotor!'*

So we summoned some Swedish muscle which gave us just that small edge on the wind to weather Mamula Is. and slipped gratefully into Hercegnovi. Distance made good 190 miles, by log 246, engine hours seven.

Again we were lucky in our choice of a port of entry. A lady customs officer, dressed in a pretty flowered print, came aboard with three colleagues and cleared *Shara* without delay. A visit to the Brosokomerc office at nearby Jelenika yielded no 'duty-frees' but there was a new supermarket where I was able to fill our other needs. Meanwhile, Jane had enticed a young sailor into carrying buckets of water from a tap behind a warehouse to replenish our tanks. A slow starter, he had just got to the point of asking if she was married when I returned laden with shopping. He fled back to his ship before I could thank him.

August 22 to 23. To Mljet Is. At 1130 began one of the most enjoyable passages of the cruise. After clearing Ostri Pt. with its handsome fort, we beat slowly along the rugged coast in smooth water and a light air from W.N.W. During an afternoon of bright sunshine that was just pleasantly warm, we inspected Molunat and Cavtat on the inshore tacks. At midnight we were becalmed and, with the tiller lashed, slept by turns, the boat rocking gently in rippled water. Three miles to the east Dubrovnik sparkled in counterpoint to the glittering night sky.

At 0430 a land breeze got us under way, broad-reaching to the north-west. At breakfast the spinnaker replaced the no. 1 and, through a bright morning, drew *Shara* smoothly along the shore of Mljet Island. In Gonoturska Bay a look at the mouth of the narrow channel leading into Lake Jezero revealed a popple which suggested an ebbing tide, so we anchored in an exquisite cove 300 metres to the south. While we lunched and swam, we kept an eye on a rock near the wooded shore. When this was covered, *Shara* motored round for an attempt at the entrance.

Our echo-sounder has no repeater in the cockpit so, with Jane guiding us from the pulpit, there was no way of getting a precise reading of the depth. The National Park brochure claims 2.5 metres, which is probably optimistic. However, although the boulders on the bottom seemed alarmingly close, we got through with no bumps apparently at slack H.W. as there was no stream at the very narrow inner end of the channel.

Katerina, a Yugoslav friend who lives near us, had told of pines that grew so close to the lake shore that the lower ends of the branches were submerged; on these we would find oysters growing. So no time was lost getting the boat anchored with a stern line to a tree. Alas, we found only large numbers of barnacled pine-cones and that times have changed since Katerina's childhood visits with her father. Absorbed by the hunt, we rounded a curve in the shore to come, without warning, on a cluster of nudists. Surprise was complete on both sides. They stiffened into attitudes of self-conscious and sullen defiance. We rowed quickly away. That evening we were enjoying the stillness of the lovely lake and the thickly-wooded hills when a nearby Austrian motor-cruiser shattered the peace with a selection of bumpity-bump *biergarten* waltzes better suited to Munich than Mljet. A fat man danced alone on the deck, beer bottle in hand, quivering like a jelly on a train, a living confirmation of Ian Fleming's view that only a minute proportion of the human species should be allowed to go naked.

Veliko Jezero is undeniably beautiful and well worth a visit – preferably in the off season.

August 24 to 25. To Luka Palmezana. After taking us clear of the island the light breeze died and two hours of engine brought us to Raznjic Point. By 1230 the boat was beating through the Peljesac channel, giving us a tantalising glimpse of the medieval town of Korcula, a must for next year. A long board on the port tack took *Shara* across to the Hvar Is. shore and two hours later we came to an anchor in pretty Luka Lovisce on Scedro Island.

A French couple from a nearby yacht came aboard for a gam-and-*slivovica* and shook us with their account of difficulties with the Yugoslav authorities who, for two offences had fined them a total of 3,600 dinars. As there has recently been some protest in the yachting press about similar cases, it is perhaps worth listing the common causes of trouble. These are failure to:

1. Have on board a Certificate of Registry or some other document which clearly identifies the skipper with the yacht.
2. Make a Port of Entry the first port of call.
3. Supply the police with an amended Crew List *before* a crew change takes place.
4. Keep clear of the prohibited areas listed in the Permit of Navigation which is given to each yacht on arrival.

In every case we have come across, ignorance of the regulations has been the primary cause, but it must be said that dozens of foreign yachts visit these shores year after year with no trouble at all. Because they know the rules **before** they arrive. Our own experience of the formalities has involved us in minimal effort, one hour of painless paperwork, and a routine payment of 350 dinars for the Permit of Navigation.

This seems to us, in sum, a small price to pay for the privilege of enjoying one of the finest cruising grounds in Europe. Details of the regulations and much other interesting information may be found in H. M. Denham's excellent sea-guide, *The Adriatic*.

We went on the following morning to shop in the port of Hvar and admire its dignified *piazza* and fine old Venetian buildings. Then we sailed over to Luka Palmezana for a quiet night at anchor.

August 26 to 27. To Luka Kanalic. Shortage of time now meant that *Shara* had to push on to Istria with no stops. The passage was of no particular interest though we were pleased that the land breeze and the inevitable north-westerly kept engine hours down to an acceptable fifth of passage time. On the slow beat towards Kamejak Pt. there was time for reflection on how lucky we had been on this cruise in the vital matter of wind.

For four of the six longer passages there had been mild depressions, never too close for comfort, always close enough to save us countless hours of engine. No one, we feel, can reasonably expect so much on a similar cruise in the Mediterranean in July and August. On the other passages the spinnaker had shown its worth again and again so, as never before, we have come to depend on this sail in light airs.

In the dusk and a dying breeze from the east we crept into Luka Kanalic to let go in still water surrounded by pine woods. Despite a neighbouring Finn who, for reasons unstated, objected to my use of a riding light, this last anchorage was extremely pleasant and we slept soundly.

August 28 to 29. To Monfalcone. Away early with a light north-easterly we were soon past Brioni Island. There were the gunboats in the offing so perhaps the Marshal was at home. Some engine helped us along the coast before *Shara* sailed into Umag in the late evening to take the last available berth alongside the quay.

Next morning we at last got our hands on some 'duty-free', the first of the cruise. After clearing for Italy, we slipped away under the main and no. 1. Off Far Pt., there was no wind and an uncomfortable sea, which smoothed out as we motored sadly across the Gulf of Trieste. Nearing Sdobba light it was strange to be back in discoloured shoal-water. At the last the wind, which had been such a constant friend during the cruise, returned to give us a gentle beat into Hannibal marina, *Shara*'s new winter quarters.

My brother had given us a basil plant.

Born in Rhodes, this herb steamed across the Aegean, changed horses in Corfu for a canter up the Adriatic, and then survived an arduous trek by train and car from the Dolomites to the Pyrenees.

Installed comfortably on our balcony, it celebrated journey's end a few days later. By coming into flower.

SHARA OF YORK

TABLE OF DISTANCES

Date			Miles made good	Time under way h. m.	Engine Time h. m.
July	5	Port Leucate – Port Man	149	28 20	0 30
	7	Port Man – A. de Bon Porte	14	2 30	0 10
	8	A. de Bon Porte – Macinaggio	128	34 30	0 25
	11	Macinaggio – P. Ferraio	41	9 30	0 20
	12	P. Ferraio – P. del Grotte	1.5	0 30	0 00
	13/15	North coast of Elba	18.5	12 15	0 30
	15	Marciana – Stagnolo Bay	87	39 45	0 00
	17/21	In Bay of Porto Vecchio	7	2 25	0 10
	22	M. d'Arghi – Cala Galera	97	48 15	0 00
	25	Cala Galera – S. Stefano	15	5 10	0 00
	29	S. Stefano – Cala Cannelle	11.5	3 00	0 30
	30	Cala Cannelle – P. Giglio	1	1 00	0 45
	31	P. Giglio – S. Stefano	11	2 15	0 30
			581.5	189 25	3 50
Aug.	1	S. Stefano – Anzio	56	37 30	5 40
	4	Anzio – Reggio	240	56 45	9 15
	7	Reggio – Messina	7	1 45	0 30
		Messina – Reggio	7	1 30	1 30
	8	Reggio – Argostoli	244	46 15	2 00
	11	Argostoli – Sarakaniko	45	11 15	0 30
	12	Sarakaniko – Kioni	6	2 30	0 30
	13	Kioni – Dessimo Bay	13	5 35	1 10
		Dessimo Bay – Drepano Bay	7	2 10	0 00
			625	165 15	21 5
Aug.	14	Drepano Bay – Port Gaio	37	10 25	6 00
	15	Port Gaio – Gouvia Bay	33	7 25	6 30
	18	Gouvia Bay – Bolana Bay	11	3 00	3 00
		Bolana Bay – P. Corfu	12	4 00	0 15
		P. Corfu – Karagol Pt	7	2 00	0 10
	19	Karagol Pt. – Hercegnovi	190	57 35	7 00
	22	Hercegnovi – Jelenika	2	0 30	0 30
		Jelenika – V. Jezero	63.5	26 00	0 30
	24	V. Jezero – L. Lovisce	43	12 30	2 20
	25	L. Lovisce – Hvar	13	5 45	1 45
		Hvar – L. Palmezana	2	0 30	0 00
	26	L. Palmezana – L. Kanalic	157	36 15	7 30
	28	L. Kanalic – Umag	42	12 40	1 50
	29	Umag – Monfalcone	23	10 00	2 10
		Totals	1,842	543 15	64 25

Average speed 3.4 knots.
Duration of cruise 56 days.
Engine use 11.9% of passage time. At no time was the engine used solely for battery-charging.

COMBINED OPERATIONS
Palma to Corfu on Amadea II

by C. R. Trafford

The following log of a cruise from Palma to Corfu deservedly won the Sea Laughter Trophy for Cadet Members and the account below is written by the skipper for that part of the voyage, C. R. Trafford, aged twenty-one; Dick Trafford, his father, had sailed *Amadea II* from Dartmouth and his sons took her over for the Mediterranean part of the voyage. The family then continued to cruise the Ionian islands and the Adriatic, a summer's voyage of some 4,000 miles. ED.

After leaving *Amadea* in Alicante some friends of my father spent their fortnights holiday sailing her to Palma while my mission was to deliver *Amadea* to Corfu by 24 July when the family holiday was due to begin.

This was the first time my father had entrusted his most precious possession to my care, and my first attempt as skipper. The combined ages of my crew of four was eighty! The crew comprised my younger brother James, aged nineteen (a dinghy sailor with fast tastes); his friend Mark Parry also nineteen and nicknamed 'trooper' due to his total disregard for the Queen's English; and Nick Skinnard aged twenty-one, from Oxford, fresh from the Perkins engine course. Mark had never really done a cruise before but was quick to learn, while Nick's cruising experience consisted of a single trip to the west coast of Ireland in 1976 with my father and myself on *Arabesque*. All four of us had survived several happy years together at Canford School and during the winter months had spent many hours driving from our various seats of learning to Exeter, where we all helped fit out *Amadea*.

Now at last the moment of reckoning had arrived; James and I were proud to be able to sail under the R.C.C. burgee as newly-elected cadet members. We had just twenty-one days to cover the thousand mile trip to Corfu.

We flew out to Palma on 2 July to find *Amadea* on the Marina at the excellent Club Nautico de Palma, and spent the first day recovering from examinations, storing ship, changing the engine oil etc.

On Monday 3 July at noon, we beat out of Palma into a light breeze, as yet uncertain whether to call at Cabrera for the night or to continue eastwards. As the crew quickly settled down into their watch routine, I decided that we should take advantage of the F.2–3 southerly winds and head for Sardinia. During the night we had to avoid a large fishing fleet and saw dolphins playing around us. We worked a three-hour

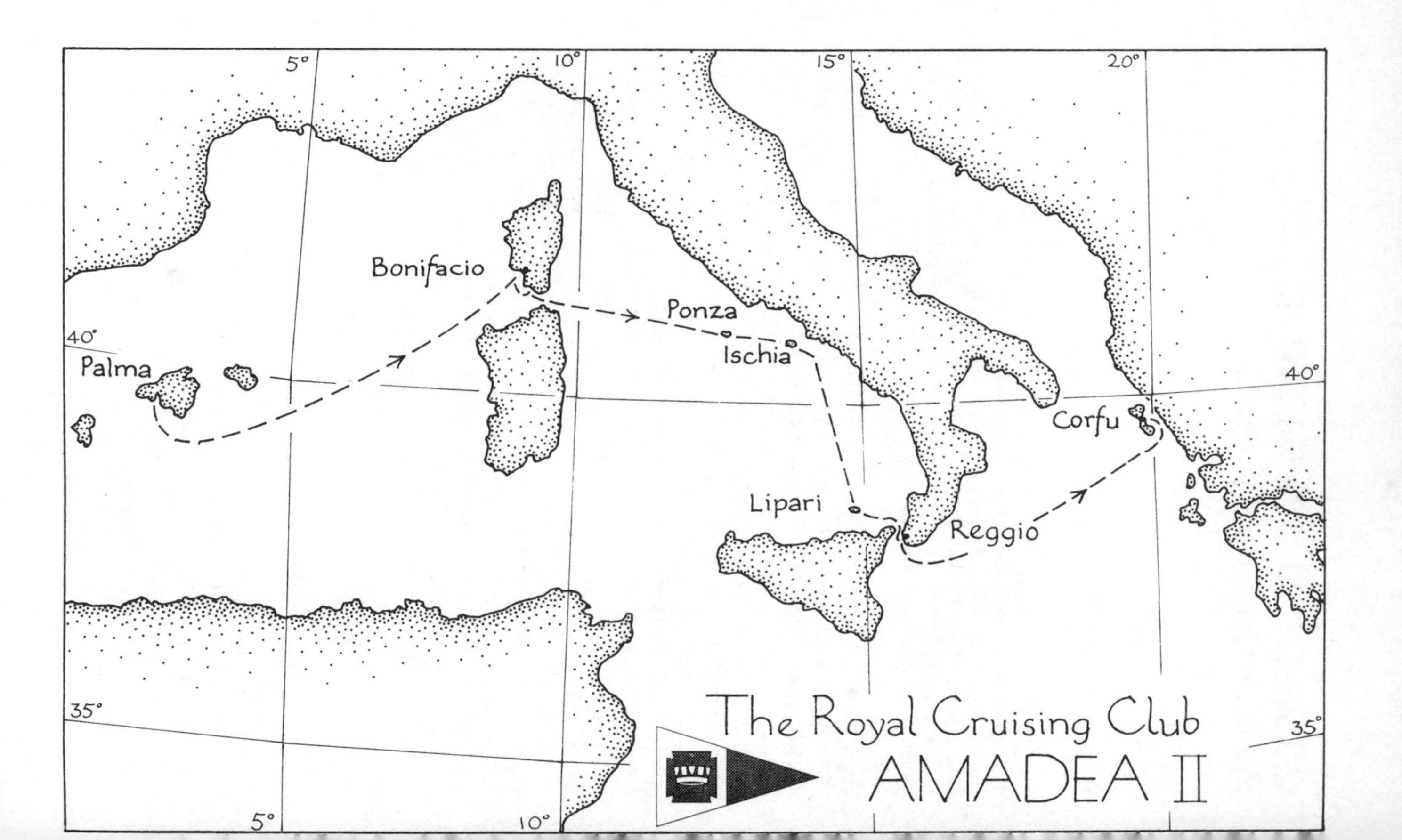
5°
10°
15°
20°
40°
Bonifacio
Ponza
Ischia
Palma
Corfu
Lipari
Reggio
35°
The Royal Cruising Club
AMADEA II

watch-keeping system in pairs which worked successfully for the whole trip, Nick and I followed by Mark and James. By 0900 on Tuesday 4 July, the wind backed slightly. In order to hold the large starcut spinnaker, which was naturally top priority, we had to alter course for Bonifaccio.

By now it was becoming apparent that Nick was the only cook amongst us, and so for reasons of self-preservation he decided to adopt this role – fortunately for the rest of us. We were, however, very willing galley slaves.

By 1800 that evening the wind had died but gave way to an impressive thunderstorm followed by a thoroughly unsettled night as the wind boxed the compass – a night of lightning, vicious squalls, heavy rain and of course bad visibility during which time we had to avoid another fishing fleet. Gradually the visibility improved on 5 July and we enjoyed a fine sail in a F.4–5 N. with reefed main and number one jib giving us at least six knots throughout the day. This was to be one of our most exciting days sailing and we were particularly delighted after hearing talk of windless hours of motoring in the Mediterranean. By midnight the wind had freshened to F.6 and we had five rolls in the main. An R.D.F. fix put us a long way north of our estimated position which was very worrying – we later found there was an error of at least five degrees which I checked by azimuth! During the winter term I attended the yachtmaster's navigation course at Gloucester which was well worthwhile and certainly helped to increase my basic knowledge.

As we were anxious not to approach an unlit shore at night, we hove to at 0300 on Thursday 6 July for a couple of hours. As dawn broke we continued eastwards in a dying wind and sighted land at 0900. We motored S.E. to reach Porto Pollo by late afternoon, 362 miles out of Palma and felt we had shortened the rather long odds on reaching Corfu!

We climbed up above the bay and confirmed the F.P.I. remark that the tombs there were not worth a visit! We looked forward to a peaceful night although we knew the holding was poor but there was no rest for the wicked, and after a calm night the wind rose rapidly and by 0500 on Friday 7 July we found ourselves in the bay, with fifteen other yachts, doing our fair share of dragging. The seemingly efficient German yacht nearby put to sea to avoid the confusion of the anchorage only to return very quickly. We listened to the French forecast which indicated the wind would remain at F.7 and not increase, so I decided that it was preferable to sail to the safety of Bonifaccio rather than remain in a potentially dangerous bay.

Sustained by a large breakfast we set out apprehensively at 1130 on 7 July, under storm jib and heavily reefed main and had the most exciting sail of the holiday surfing down the large swells. This was the biggest sea that any of the crew had ever experienced, larger than the seas off the Aran Islands which Nick and I had seen exactly three years previously. As we became more confident and the wind eased slightly, we hoisted full main and often surfed at nine knots. We soon found the magnificent entrance to Bonifaccio which we motored into at 1620 and moored next to a French charter boat. In true French style the crew were too numerous to count. We invited them aboard for drinks and had a most amusing time, after which we walked ashore to visit the Yacht Club and marina and up through the fascinating town for a meal.

On Saturday 8 July at 1500 we motored out into a F.3 W.S.W. which gradually increased to force five giving us an excellent sail to Santa Maria in the Straits of Bonifaccio. The sun was very hot but because of the wind the temperature was perfect – how marvellous it was to be sailing with this amount of wind and be wet through but still warm. At 1830 we anchored in wonderfully clear water at Santa Maria with brilliant turquoise colouring and no other boats in sight. We went in as close to the shore as possible using the lead line which we preferred to the vagaries of our echo-sounder. There followed the biggest meal of the holiday – after which we went ashore for a walk and swim in this beautiful place. After breakfast on Sunday 9 July, we decided Santa Maria was just too good to leave and so we spent the day sunbathing, snorkelling, checking the ship and generally enjoying ourselves. After a lazy day we up-anchored at 1800 and sailed east under reefed main and storm jib, wind F.6 westerly. As we sailed away from the Maddalene Straits the wind eased slightly and we hoisted twin headsails to give us a comfortable five to six knots.

At 0615 on 10 July we hoisted the main and lowered one headsail and shortly afterwards Mark and James sighted a large whale which surfaced close to the boat, stayed with us for about a quarter of an hour and then to our relief continued on its way. The wind gradually died and remained light for the rest of the day but we were determined to keep sailing. We did however drop the sails several times for a swim and Nick cooked another magnificent supper, occasionally having to feed the fish with one of his exotic sauces which were unacceptable to the palates of the simple crew! We had a night of light wind and by 1100 on Tuesday 11 July we reluctantly had to start the engine and motored into Ponza at 1600, 177 miles from Santa Maria. Ponza was really worth a visit and we enjoyed our trip ashore, made the more memorable by the excellent Italian ice creams which more than lived up to their reputation. We spent a lazy afternoon on the rocks swimming and sunbathing and ran the generator for a while because we discovered the engine was not charging the batteries.

On Wednesday 12 July at 2100 we set off for Ischia and motored right through a windless night. We felt we were ravishing the stillness of a tropical night with the throaty roar of 'Percy' the Perkins. We arrived at St. Angelo, Ischia on 13 July at 0815 and spent a pleasant day anchored off the beach swimming and spinnaker flying – our new found and very exciting sport. For those older members of the club who have not seen spinnaker flying the technique is to moor the boat by the stern, set the spinnaker and check away the halyard as far as possible while the flier hangs on a rope tied between the clews of the sail. A highly exciting and exhausting sport. After this we had a walk around the town.

At 2000 on Wednesday evening we weighed anchor bound for Lipari, sadly no wind but the lights of the Bay of Naples almost, but not quite, made up for the lack of wind. Throughout the night there was a lot of shipping and the thick fog of early morning made careful watchkeeping essential. The fog gradually cleared on Friday 14 July to leave a very light breeze, so we attempted to sail for a few hours – this was a frustrating day spent trying to sail at every opportunity but knowing we had only nine days to reach Corfu. At one stage we dived overboard for one of our numerous swims and realised we were in the midst of a sewage disposal area and we positively leaped out of the sea to the relative cleanliness of *Amadea*. The dolphins playing around did not seem to be worried – in fact they appeared to be thriving!

July 15, shortly after midnight we sighted the glow of the volcanic island of Stromboli; the log reads, 'As dawn broke abeam the spectacular sight of the Aeolian Isles was unveiled'. Stromboli itself was most impressive and also verified our position on course for Lipari. The navigation on board was a combined effort with each watch keeping a wary eye on the other! We were all eager to climb Stromboli and were disappointed not to be able to do so because fuel was short after hours of motoring and we clearly could not rely on any wind. Perversely, however, at 0905, ten miles from Lipari the wind got up and we sailed into the harbour at 1110 and anchored in nineteen fathoms, 161 miles from Ischia. After re-fuelling and taking on water, we left for Reggio on Sunday 16 July at 0815. It was very hot and the sailing conditions and visibility varied continually throughout the day. Out of the mist and well out of sight of land a 16-foot speed-boat suddenly appeared flying the French ensign: 'Ou est Stromboli?' they screamed, before ramming us amidships. Having put a dent in our topsides they did a lap of honour and roared away without so much as an apology. Unfortunately *Amadea* is pressed to manage six knots under power, let alone twenty-five, and so, frustrated, we were unable to give chase. However, later in the day an Italian yacht on the same course did give us a chase and we enjoyed an exciting race under spinnakers converging on the Messina Straits.

The entry to the Straits was one of the highlights of the trip and we sailed through sometimes reaching and sometimes running, in fluky winds. There was a great deal of shipping including the remarkable swordfish boats with their huge bowsprits often more than twice as long as the boat itself and best avoided at all times! We had read that the whirlpools were 'bad news' and so took great care to avoid these too.

We arrived in Reggio at 1930 forty-three miles from Lipari and moored stern to in the new yacht harbour with at least a dozen friendly

Italians screaming contradictory instructions, all of which we thought it wiser to ignore. We walked some distance to the town centre and in accordance with father's instructions went straight to the most expensive hotel to telephone home. After waiting two hours, we had a very good line to our relieved parents – 'Oh ye of little faith!' A good meal ashore and late back aboard after an interesting day.

Monday 17 July. I was up first for a shower on the quay but having covered myself in lather from head to toe, the water was turned off. However, the situation was saved by the kind owner of a large Panamanian power-boat who kindly invited me aboard to rinse! Later the water was turned on again and the rest of the crew were able to shower and do some washing. We also watered and re-fuelled *Amadea* and then did our shopping.

At 1530 we departed under power bound for Corfu but as we passed the breakwater we set the spinnaker and to our delight the speedo quickly showed seven knots. During a subsequent spinnaker jybe we upset a bowl of mandarin oranges and jelly all over the cockpit – a sticky mess and our last tin of mandarins; a sad loss. Quite suddenly, the wind changed from a fresh northerly to a light southerly and we beat for a couple of hours before motoring as the wind completely died away. During the night a ship trained its spotlight on us as we passed close under her stern.

Tuesday 18 July. We only had a light breeze with main and genoa and whilst running the generator to charge our batteries the fuel pipe worked loose and diesel leaked all over the locker floor; we soon repaired this and cleaned up. Apart from this it was an uneventful day at sea and at sunset we hoisted spinnaker and mizzen staysail which we held throughout the night until 1000. Wednesday 19 July was another day at sea F.2–3, and my noon sight confirmed our latitude and land was sighted at 1600. Five hours later the wind came ahead and then died so that we had to motor the rest of the way and anchored to the south west of Corfu Citadel at 0300 on Thursday 20 July, 251 miles from Reggio.

We got up late to find most shops closed for *siesta*! However, we did clear customs and obtained our transit log and then sailed up to the unfinished marina at Gouvia Bay which was full of English yachts, we moored ahead of Bill and his wife and baby in a Nicholson 38 who were very welcoming and helpful.

By now we were surprisingly three days ahead of schedule but the time was well spent having the alternator repaired; checking the gear and sails; scrubbing the topsides and generally cleaning out and preparing for the arrival of the 'Boss'. Gouvia was a most friendly place and we soon found an inexpensive and jolly *taverne* called Georges which looked after us very well.

Amadea was by now all ship-shape and tidy and on Monday 23 July we went out to the airport by bus to meet the oldies and my sister

Claire ready for our Adriatic cruise. We now said goodbye to our new found independence but hello to some good cooking!

We had had a really happy cruise during which each member of the crew more than pulled his weight and gave me his full support. There was never a murmur of discontent (except when the wind died!) and we looked forward to sailing together again in the future. We had completed our mission sailing 1,055 miles in eighteen days and delivered *Amadea* safely to the 'Boss'.

AMADEA II

TABLE OF DISTANCES

Date		*Port*	*Distance made good*	*Time h. m.*	*Engine time h. m.*
July	3	Palma	33.5	12 00	0 30
	4		118.5	24 00	4 00
	5		129.8	24 00	0 00
	6	Pollo	78.2	17 15	7 30
	7	Bonifaccio	31.4	4 45	0 15
	8	Santa Maria	17.0	3 30	0 15
	9		21.5	4 00	0 15
	10		96.6	24 00	0 00
	11	Ponza	59.4	16 00	5 00
	12		13.3	3 00	3 00
	13	*via St. Angelo*	45.1	12 15	12 15
	14		79.3	24 00	17 00
	15	Lipari	37.2	11 15	8 30
	16	Reggio	42.8	11 15	4 30
	17		31.1	8 30	4 30
	18		85.4	24 00	10 30
	19		115.9	24 00	3 00
	20	Gouvia *via Corfu Town*	19.0	5 00	3 15
			1,055.0	252 75	84 25

Average speed 4.08 knots

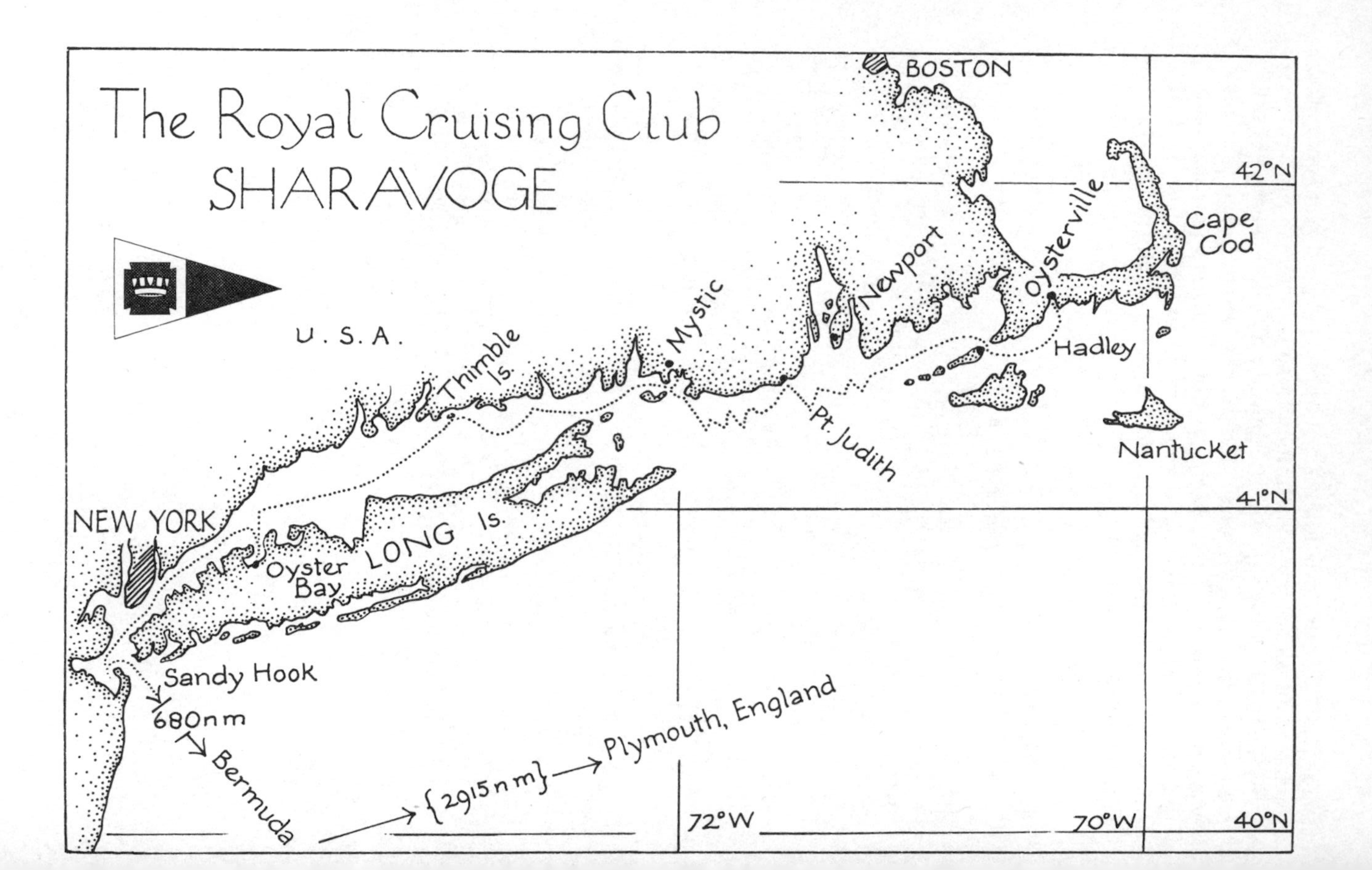
The Royal Cruising Club
SHARAVOGE
BOSTON
42°N
Cape Cod
Oysterville
Newport
Mystic
U.S.A.
Thimble Is.
Hadley
Nantucket
Pt. Judith
41°N
NEW YORK
LONG Is.
Oyster Bay
Sandy Hook
680nm
Bermuda
{2915nm}
Plymouth, England
72°W
70°W
40°N

THE RETURN OF *SHARAVOGE*
America to Britain

by Jonathan Virden

Sharavoge should be recalled, perhaps dimly, by members of the Club as a folkboat that likes adventuring in deep water. She was launched in 1963 by Cyril White at Brightlingsea, and has changed very little since launching. She has masthead rig, a Volvo Penta MD1 engine and simple self-steering. She is a model of the reasons why anyone, who knows a sea-kindly vessel, finds them and folk boats in particular quite irresistable.

In 1976 I sailed *Sharavoge* from St. Katharine's Dock in London to Plymouth, England and thence to Osterville, America via Bermuda and Newport. In Osterville all of the gear and removeable equipment, was stored in the basement of the Burnes's house. *Sharavoge*'s own resting place was in a purpose-built cradle in a shed at the yard of Chester A. Crosby & Sons Inc.: this is an old-established boat-building yard – expensive, but very efficient – to be found up the Osterville River on the north shore of Nantucket Sound.

Since leaving *Sharavoge* in her snug hide-out, Joy had become part of our menage, and we flew together to Boston on 21 April 1978. There we were met by Bunny Burnes at the beginning of a week of continuous help and kind generosity by his whole family. We stayed in a spare house and put *Sharavoge* together again. It was cold (45 °F max.) and bright for five of the seven days of refitting. The main task was simply to make everything fit together and work again, and, in addition, to fit a V.H.F. Radio Telephone which we had brought over with us. This took me some time, but with elementary knowledge of radio acquired while in the R.A.F. in 1956, I fudged the job so it worked first time. An important feature of the aerial's masthead mounting was to offset it so that a burgee would fly unobstructed. The home-made fitting is still up there, so that worked too. The burgees fly free and proud in these days of anonymity and declared devotion to the electrical gods of measurement.

Another success was that the engine started with the first swing: 'Eddie' the genius at Crosby's yard, did not believe that 'Scrap Iron' worked like that. Meanwhile, Joy was organising the commissariat and stowage, having had some practice at Plymouth in 1976.

The boundless help of the Burnes's allowed us to keep to the time-limited programme, and after exactly one week we tore ourselves away from their pier on the Seapuit River on Saturday 28 April just after lunch. We motored out of Osterville entrance in flat calm and turned west. During the afternoon a breeze arose from the west and we beat, first against the tide and then with it, to and through Wood's Hole. The tide makes 5–6 knots through this twisting channel and I was surprised to find how much of my knack of watching the true track of the boat had vanished in two years, and then how it suddenly returned. We made our way into Hadley Harbour, a deep inlet in the island opposite the town of Wood's Hole. There were only two other yachts there; in the summer there are so many it is said to be possible to walk from 'shore' to 'shore', across their decks. This is a delightful and completely safe anchorage: no facilities, as all the Elizabeth Islands are privately owned. It was quiet and I spent some time tightening the rigging in the early evening, and looked for specific leaks as *Sharavoge* was taking in more water than usual, probably only because of the long time she had spent ashore.

Bunny had given us several of his cast-off American charts: we both found the unaccustomed style of them quite easy to use; but good eyesight for detail on them is helpful. The buoy system is quite different from that in European waters, but is extremely well set out for pilotage on the part of the coast from Cape Cod through to New York.

On Sunday, we left Hadley in a calm morning and motored down the north side of the Elizabeth Islands, on the south shore of Buzzards Bay, to avoid the strong adverse tide in Vineyard Sound. The wind gradually increased all day, from W.S.W., which was exactly contrary to our intentions and was very cold at about 45°F. Passing Buzzards Tower, we spoke shortly to them, proving that the V.H.F. worked. As the wind increased so did the sea and in the afternoon I changed the genoa for a jib, getting wet in the process. We were both rather sick, this being the first time at sea for nearly two years, and the sea was unusually confused. As dark fell we came into the harbour of refuge at Point Judith. This is a large artificial harbour just south west of Point Judith at the west side of the entrance to Narragansett Bay: a most useful place for getting out of bad sea conditions. There are no facilities that we saw, though there might be some up the river at the west end of the harbour. We had motored for almost all the day, as *Sharavoge* is very slow to windward and we had limited time.

On the following day it was blowing about F.5 W.S.W. as usual, and at 39°F. Local radio stations do not give useful meteorological information, they only seem to shiver at their microphones and expect listeners to commiserate. We battened down to no. 2 jib and reefed main, and slogged along an unexciting shore to westward. It was extremely cold and ten layers of clothes were barely sufficient: we were most pleased with long Damart underwear, polar suiting, and mittens which were surprisingly good at keeping hands in working order. By hard motor-sailing all day we reached the narrow most northerly entrance to Long Island Sound at the end of the west-going tide. We then beat through Fisher's

Island Sound to the Mystic River into a low brilliant sun which made buoy-spotting hard and very tiring on eyes: two pairs were very useful. We went up the river to a marina just below the Railway Bridge where we were shown to a spare berth sheltered from the wind by a large motor-cruiser.

On 2 May, we explored Mystic town for supplies, and later took *Sharavoge* through the bridges to the Seaport Museum. No one cruising on this coast should miss this show-place, where wooden ships are preserved and lovingly rebuilt. The shore area has examples of sail lofts, mast lathes (ninety-five feet!), cooperage, pubs, rope-walks, which were all part of the maritime seaboard of the eastern U.S.A. in roughly the period 1750 to 1850. It is reported to be extremely crowded in summer, yacht berths being booked 3–6 months ahead, but we had the quays to ourselves. Six hours would be a safe minimum time to investigate all that is to be found here.

Having picked up a mooring for the night at the mouth of the river, near the deserted yacht club, we set off westward next morning at 0610. This day the tides were at awkward times and we just failed to reach the area of relatively slower currents before the adverse easterly flow started. During the morning we beat, with engine, along the middle of Long Island Sound. At 1030 we stopped the engine, and beat against a rather variable wind along the north shore to the Thimble Islands which had been recommended to us. We pass on the recommendation and magnify it as they are a charming group of little rocky islands with a few trees and a house or two on each. During the day which was rather dull and overcast, we saw an extremely sinister submarine going to sea from the Connecticut River, and various illusions; like an island which took up its anchor and went off to better fishing grounds, and a ship in the distance which eventually resolved itself into having fully grown trees and a farm house on board.

After a very peaceful night at the Thimble Islands, we sailed leisurely, off the wind for the first time, along and across Long Island Sound to the island shore. The relief from the endless motor-sailing into icy wind was great. The sun came out clearly and we even flew the cruising spinnaker for the last ten miles to Oyster Bay. Oyster Bay is a small town on an inlet of the same name. There are various yacht clubs, but, as we had an introduction, we went to Jakobsen's Boat Yard. Here they build and recondition ocean-going and big port tugs, but they also do some yacht work, beautifully, on the side. Having introduced myself to the security guard, who was a caricature of his profession suitable for any television thriller, whose boss had not told him about our arrival, and after he had checked with several supervisors we settled down in a quiet corner by a vast pontoon.

On Friday 4 May, it rained hard all day. As we were making our final preparations for the voyage to Bermuda the rain was a minor nuisance. But to compensate we met Ed and Betty Greeff, which is one of the best things that can happen to any sailor. In a few seconds it was quite conspicuous that we were kindred spirits. Ed was now retired, but organises much in the sailing world. No one could be more helpful, and under his supervision we obtained stores of all sorts in the town, and diesel fuel from the boat yard, in, for them, ridiculously small quantities. Heaven came in the form of a bath at the Greeff's home in the woods above the bay; after this Ed checked over charts and times of tides for our passage through New York. The outstanding thing about this day was the laughter, as the Greeffs enjoy linguistic entertainment just as much as we do, and have the marvellous gift of stretching any idea to a ludicrous extent just for fun. The day ended with dinner at a fine Italian restaurant, and we finally retired to *Sharavoge* thoroughly wined, dined and refreshed for the next stage of the cruise.

There was no wind next day, and it was grey with low cloud, but no rain, and very cold. We left the yard at 0730 aiming to catch the time of the top of the tide at the Throgs Neck at 1216. Having motored fairly hard into the tide down the Long Island Shore we passed under the bridge at 1215. The bridges of New York are the first spectacle one meets – they are huge. Carefully map-reading, we motored with the tide to the north end of the east river and were taken on the 4–5 knot ebb down the east side of Manhattan Island. The water was quite bouncy in places where it went over rough patches in the bottom. The cloud obscured the tallest buildings and it became colder and colder. It was quite a fascinating experience to visit New York in this way, and to pass through the city and its suburbs without touching land or being caught up in the traffic and noisy chaos of the city. Leaving Manhattan behind, approaching the Statue of Liberty we found a drift of wind from the South East. We hoisted sails and beat slowly on the last of the ebb down through the narrows under the last and greatest of all the New York bridges, the Verrzzano Bridge, which was partly hidden in the clouds. As there was next-to-no wind, we decided to anchor at Sandy Hook, N.J., for the night before setting out to Bermuda, rather than drift about the night near the entrance to the busy port and waterways. This little bay is sheltered from N. and E. and S. by the pier, but open to several miles of fetch from westerly directions. With a westerly component in the wind, it would be better to anchor close to the west shore of the Sound.

After a quiet night, without going ashore, we left Sandy Hook, N.J., at 0555 on 7 May, for the 690 mile passage to Bermuda. We were hoping that it would take about eight days, leaving us with six days to enjoy the sunshine in Bermuda before flying to England.

The passage was frustrating as the wind came from S.E., i.e. dead ahead, for a much higher proportion of the time than we expected from available information. The first day was almost calm, ending in thick wet fog, and glassy sea, such as could be seen of it. On the second day the fog cleared and with a light wind gradually increasing, we saw an oil drilling-rig guarded by a small service ship. This came to meet us in the fog, but anchored off when it saw that we were not going too close to the rig. In the evening the barometer was falling steadily and wind increasing with a wet sky, so I changed to the no. 2 jib before dark. On the third morning the wind was about F.6 from S.E. so with more reefs we had the first patch of rough weather. The wind reached F.7, perhaps, for a short period. Joy had her first experience of the noise and splash and slop of a small boat in a moderately rough sea, and found it alarming and remained cheerful nevertheless. *Sharavoge* behaved like her usual self – a perfect sea boat. But we made only slow progress against the seas. We had a quite serious leak in the forehatch sealing which allowed a regular flow of water to reach the foot of the bunks; this was extremely annoying.

When the wind dropped just after midnight on 10 May, there was a period of comparative calm followed by a light, following breeze in which we covered 100 miles under the boomed genoa. This included crossing the Gulf stream, which occurred in the middle of the night, I believe, as there was a comparatively knobbly patch of sea for two or three hours, but I did not get out of my berth. The next day, 11 May, was the only really good day on the passage: with the two boomed genoas the following wind gave us 5 knots in a diminishing swell. We spoke to a passing tanker who confirmed our position. Sadly Joy was still persistently sick, but remained cheerful when in her bunk where the discomfort was minimal.

After another short calm period the wind filled out from S.E. and remained from this direction for the whole of the remaining seven days of the voyage. There were few incidents on this stage of the voyage: the wind varied between F.2 and F.5 and occasionally F.6. For two-thirds of the time we motor-sailed, this being almost the only way to get *Sharavoge* to go to windward in moderate comfort on the open ocean against a sea. But the air and sea were warm at last. Joy suffered from incurable seasickness for all the passage: all she ate, except the juice from canned fruit, and an egg or two in the evening, was promptly returned to the sea. While in her bunk she felt quite well but activity and especially eating were not possible. In fact, we each lost a stone or more, and though uncomfortable at the time, that was good for both of us.

One happening is worth recording: in reefing the main, while motoring, the genoa was caught aback and in the confusion the port genoa sheet wrapped itself around the propellor. No damage was done as the clutch must have slipped easily, but it was a bad moment because the wind was certainly rising and there were about forty-five minutes of daylight left.

After suitable preparations I went swimming and quite easily unwrapped the sheet from the propellor. This was greatly assisted by having a face-mask, now a standard part of *Sharavoge*'s cruising equipment. The water was quite warm, and I felt very little of the wave-motion while under water. The most fascinating thing was the colour of the light underwater: a brilliant sapphire blue combined with the ultramarine of the clear summer sky in the west of Ireland. It is a curious experience to swim in more than 3,000 fathoms of water. Joy was especially glad when I climbed back onto the deck using a pre-prepared step slung on ropes.

On 15 and 16 May the wind was still consistently blowing from Bermuda and we slogged on becoming more and more frustrated because the Bermuda Harbour Radio weather forecast predicted a shift of wind to S.W. within a few hours each time we listened: but it only arrived after we had reached Bermuda. We were losing the precious days of the week we had allowed for ourselves to spend in Bermuda. On 2582 khz. the Harbour Radio gives weather and navigation information which was most useful to us because the two critical landfall buoys N. and N.E. of the reefs were not in position. Thus, we took a rather wide approach to the island. The cloudy sky made sunsights difficult, but on 17 May, we were well within RDF range of the BDA beacon. On this day each of four sunsights taken in the morning, successively confirmed our position about ten miles further north and away from Bermuda! The midday sight put us sixty miles due north of the island. The wind was becoming more southerly, naturally, still at 12–15 knots.

In the very early morning of 18 May, Joy saw the lighthouses of Bermuda. At dawn we could bear off a little and stop the engine. Bermuda looked most beautiful in that sunny morning. At 0545 we passed the St. David's Head Lighthouse and entered the channel with the wind aft of the beam for the first time for a week.

On the way round the main island to Hamilton we looked at each other to find the scruffiest scarecrows imaginable. But here was a tropical island in real full sunshine, and it was most pleasing to be there, and to see palms and casuarina and tamarisk trees and banks of hibiscus colouring the shore. The sea was quite calm and brilliant tropical blue; this was a great moment, such as always happens after a voyage.

Having sailed into Hamilton harbour we made our way to the Royal Bermuda Yacht Club. Here we were rejected by an unexpectedly unfriendly greeting and having cleared customs at an uncomfortable wall nearby, we went to the only alongside berth for yachts at the Royal Hamilton Amateur Dinghy Club. Our luck was, as usual, in good form because Richard Moss, the crew for the next stage, who was already in Bermuda to meet us, happened to be a very old friend of Martin Hutley, who was that day promoted to be in charge of all harbours, waterways, buoys and the like in Bermuda. A swift call to U.K. to calm agitated relatives and a bath put me into good order. Joy was so delighted to reach dry land that she collapsed on the pier and required reviving with brandy, followed by a bath and a round meal. The Hutleys, Martin and Tessa, gave us free-run of their home which was a real blessing.

On the evening of our arrival, 18 May, Joy collected my brother Michael from the airport and the first stage of *Sharavoge*'s voyage back home was completed with the arrival of her next skipper.

For the next two days we all worked like demons to clean and re-fit and re-victual *Sharavoge* for the voyage to England. A crate of food and other essentials was extracted from the Queen's Warehouse, with much help from the friendly customs officer. After emptying the crate it was refilled with 'excess baggage', and it was taken in charge by Commander Tim Kitson R.N. who arranged for the R.A.F. to take it to the U.K. (The subsequent adventures of the crate would make another amusing account!)

The Dingy Club is a splendid place for re-victualling, where the quay is organised by a retired schoolmaster who retails stories about almost all the inhabitants of the island while consuming endless beer. On 24 May, Joy and I left *Sharavoge* to Michael and Richard and flew home, after having a party on board, and on the quay, for everyone who had helped us so much.

Sharavoge took thirty-one-and-a-half days on the voyage from Bermuda to Plymouth. There was plenty of wind, mostly on the beam, from N., and it reached an estimated F.7 on five occasions. Michael was not well with an unidentified internal complaint for the second two weeks, but recovered. On one occasion a large wave broke on board and bent a stanchion. At home, we received three messages from *Sharavoge* kindly passed on by ships to whom they spoke on the V.H.F. which gave much reassurance to families who were not accustomed to having some members at sea for so long.

After *Sharavoge* had arrived in Plymouth, we were allowed to borrow Dick Bishop's mooring at Cargreen where the Commodore kindly looked after her, during the time we were at home. *Sharavoge* was laid up at Alec Blangdon's yard in September, and we are looking forward to next year already with a mooring arranged at Cargreen, and a cruise to Ireland all but started.

SHARAVOGE

TABLE OF DISTANCES

Date				Time			Engine time		
			Distance	*days*	*h.*	*m.*	*days*	*h.*	*m.*
April	29	Osterville – Hadley Hr.	14		5	10		5	10
	30	Hadley Hr. – Pt. Judith Hr.	39		14	35		6	20
May	1	Pt. Judith Hr. – Mystic	23		13	00		13	00
	2	Mystic – Noank	5		1	20		1	20
	3	Noank – Thimble Is.	35		13	10		4	30
	4	Thimble Is. – Oyster Bay	42		13	30		5	00
	6	Oyster Bay – Sandy Hook	45		11	00		10	00
	7	Sandy Hook –							
	18	Bermuda	665	11	9	00	4	0	00
	22	Bermuda –							
	23	Plymouth	2,928	30	23	05	1	12	00
								(approx.)	

ANTARCTIC RESEARCH IN *SOLO*

1977–8 Antarctic Research Expedition in yacht Solo. *Preliminary Report*

by David H. Lewis
President, Oceanic Research Foundation

Objectives

1. A reconnaissance to evaluate what could usefully be done by a privately financed low cost, flexibly organised expedition in a small auxiliary sailing ship.

2. Systematic measurements of sea temperature and salinity around selected icebergs, runs being made at fifteen metres and seventy-five metres depth, to help provide base lines for feasibility studies on towing icebergs to Australia (Dr. Peter Donaldson).

3. Bottom dredge sampling on Antarctic continental shelf for
(a) Ooze for foraminifera (in association with Dr. Quilty, Earth Sciences, Macquarie University).
(b) Geological specimens (Dr. Pieter Arriens)
(c) Biological specimens (Dr. Peter Donaldson)

4. Bird and whale logs (Dr. Peter Donaldson).

5. Geology, including palaeomagnetism (Dr. Pieter Arriens).

6. Weather, including ice observations. *Solo* was granted selected ship status by Meteo Melbourne, who provided instruments, six hourly observations were made meticulously in all conditions and transmitted by radio (Dr. Pieter Arriens).

7. A method of melting blocks of pack ice to produce drinking water by using the surplus warmth of the engine cooling water passed through a copper coil was to be evaluated (Pieter Arriens, Peter Donaldson).

8. An A.B.C. film unit formed part of the expedition (Ted Rayment, director-cameraman, Peter Donaldson, sound recorder).

9. A modest start was to be made in training a nucleus of Australian ice pilots, seeing that only foreign pilots have been hired ever since the time of Captain Davis.

The Ship and her Equipment

The 25-year-old three-sixteenths-of-an-inch-steel yawl *Solo*, twice a Sydney–Hobart winner, is 57 feet long, 13 feet in beam and has a draught of 8 feet. There is a 100 h.p. diesel motor and two petrol generators, autopilot, radar, echo sounder and battery charger from the free-wheeling propeller.

She was fitted for the expedition with steel deadlights over the windows, a steel companion-way door and steel stem reinforcement. An all round canvas dodger was laced round the rails. Four hundred gallons of diesel fuel were carried in the ship's own tanks. There were 320 gallons of fresh water in all, 200 in the ship's tanks and 120 more on deck in plastic cans.

A Beaufort inflatable surfboat driven by a 25 h.p. Evinrude motor was carried and used extensively, while an eight-man Beaufort emergency life raft was (fortunately) never put to use – these were provided free of charge by the makers. An Avon inflatable and experimental sledge-kyak were also carried but, in the prevailing ice conditions, were little used. Two Stingray radiotelephones were provided free of charge by the maker, Mr. Findlay and, together with a 'ham' radio, enabled communications to be maintained at all times. Electronic technician Jack Pittar kept the sets operational despite cold and damp, by installing electric light bulbs for heating. Peter Arriens was our main radio operator. Radio contact was at first through the Australian coastal stations and later, by courtesy of Senator Webster, Federal Minister for Science and the Antarctic Division, through Davis and Macquarie bases. Special mention must be made of the invaluable satellite pack ice reports from McMurdo arranged by the U.S. Navy facility at Suitland, Maryland and relayed through Davis. We are equally indebted to a number of 'ham' operators and to Campbell Island, New Zealand weather station. Walkie-talkie radios provided, also free of charge, by Dick Smith proved invaluable for ship to shore communication.

C.S.I.R.O. Cronulla provided a satellite tracking device (the 'Snow Petrel') so that our position at the time of any observation might subsequently be located. The Meteorological Office loaned a Stephenson screen, barograph, thermometers, etc. Unfortunately our own anemometer blew out shortly after the start. *Solo* carried a trace recording echo sounder which functioned throughout; the 24-mile radar froze up in the fifties and was only put right after three days' work by Jack Pittar enabling us on our return northwards to locate Macquarie Island in persistent fog.

Solo with her ship's company of eight was provisioned and carried heating fuel (kerosene) for a year. What with ski, ice axes, tents, scuba gear and general polar and foul weather clothing (much provided by Paddy Pallin Ltd.), stores, scientific and film gear, she was extremely cramped, there not being even enough bunks to go round – only six being usable at sea. It is a great tribute to the party that they did consistent work under such unfavourable conditions with remarkably good humour.

Personnel

Dr. David Lewis. Ship's master and expedition leader; ship's doctor. Experience includes research on survival physiology; leader Greenland Sea expedition 1963; single-handed voyage to West Antarctica 1972–4 in 32-foot yacht *Ice Bird*; round world and Polynesian small-boat ocean experience; studies of indigenous orientation and navigation at Australian National University, Australian Institute of Aboriginal Studies and East–West Centre, Hawaii from 1968 to 1976.

Lars Larsen. First mate and second in command of expedition. Radio operator and sledge dog expert Mawson 1976–7 year; two years North Greenland sledge dog patrol; graduate of Norwegian Army Arctic School; radio operator; diesel engineer. (Danish.)

Dr. Pieter Arriens. Geophysicist. Base leader Davis 1976–7 and extensive other A.N.A.R.E. experience; 'ham' radio operator.

Dr. Peter Donaldson. Research chemist Australian National University; amateur zoologist (birds); film sound recorder on three of Sir Edmund Hilary's expeditions.

Mrs. Dorothy Smith. All round mountaineer. (New Zealander.)

Jack Pittar. Electronics technician with National Mapping; considerable sea experience.

Ted Rayment. Film director – cameraman; a very experienced ocean yachtsman.

Fritz Schaumberg. Mountaineer; scuba diver.

General Account of the Expedition

Solo took her departure from Sydney Cove at noon on 15 December 1977 (all times Eastern Daylight time). She passed well west of Macquarie Island on her way south and it was opposite the island that she made her best noon to noon run of 185 nautical miles (under sail alone).

On 1 January 1978 between 1530 and 1830 heavy rumbling vibrations transmitted up from the seabed were experienced. The position was 61°55′S, 160°50′E. and charted depths varied from 900 fathoms over a seamount near or under our position to 1,500 fathoms to the general ocean floor.

The first bergs were encountered on 2 January in 62°48′S., and we reached the polar pack next day 3 January in 64°47′S., 160°15′E on the eighteenth day out from Sydney. Loose pack was entered under sail eighty-two miles north of the Balleny Islands at 0830 on 3rd, but by 0200 on 4th, still under sail in fog and falling snow, very heavy pack was encountered that forced us to retreat northwards in an endeavour to round a long eastward extension of the pack and approach the Ballenys from the east.

It should be pointed out that in such a low-powered and relatively unstrengthened vessel our geographical objectives were of necessity largely determined by the season's ice conditions. These had been reported to us on the eve of our departure by Dr. Bill Budd, glaciologist Melbourne University, and updated by the McMurdo satellite reports. Thus our original objective of King George V Land came to be replaced by the Ballenys and Cape Adare.

On 4 January, due to my driving the vessel too fast through loose pack, under sail, *Solo* was holed on the port side ten feet back from the stem and two feet below the waterline by impact with a floe. The hole was a bare half-inch across and was repaired with Neoprene, butyl-mastic and cement, but our ice capability was in consequence reduced. The ship was lightened by jettisoning much of the emergency kerosene.

Several frustrating days followed until we succeeded in rounding the pack's north-east extension and could shape course south-west for the Ballenys. By now the magnetic compass was virtually useless and steering was by sun compass and sun bearings by eye, coupled with alignment by the ocean swell – both ancient Polynesian methods. In the generally overcast and foggy conditions with the horizon further distorted by rough seas, sextant sun sights were difficult to obtain and often unsatisfactory. In the course of the expedition however, Lars Larsen and later Peter Donaldson were taught celestial navigation.

Young and Buckle Islands, the northernmost of the Ballenys, were sighted on 9 January. There followed gales and anxious moments in the pack and fog before a force 11 northerly storm, in which the barometer fell to 951 mb. and which lasted forty-two hours, drove the pack far southward. We followed in the wake of the pack that was being drifted south by the storm, and coasted close down the eastern side of Sturge Island, the southernmost and largest of the Ballenys, to its south-eastern extremity, Cape Smith, in the lee of which we unexpectedly found good anchorage in a partially sheltered bay, 67°35′S., 164°50′E., in 7 fathoms at 1500 on Friday 13 January. The anchorage is protected from the west and north and partly from the east; it is open to the south. It is on the south side of a half-mile long snow-covered gravel spit extending out from the main island to a 300-foot snow covered hill of volcanic rock, to seaward (eastward) of which are four stacks.

We remained at anchor for twenty hours, after which the wind turning southerly, the main polar pack began drifting north again, its outliers quickly invading the bay and we were forced to leave. During our stay two landings were made on the gravel peninsula, where the Adelie penguins and Weddel seal were filmed. A further landing was made at the foot of a rock buttress on the south-west (mainland) side of the bay. Here Dr. Arriens collected oriented rock samples. Dr. Donaldson obtained specimens of marine organisms including jellyfish from the bay. A bottom sample was dredged up.

The excellent anchorage was not marked on our charts nor mentioned in the Antarctic pilot, nor have I as yet come across records of previous landings. Further enquiries are being pursued.

After leaving the anchorage a number of bottom samples were dredged up mostly off the southern part of the east coast of Sturge Island.

On 15 January landings were effected on Sabrina Islet off which *Solo* remained hove-to in a polynia for six hours. Two landings were made on the south side of the snow covered gravel spit connecting the islet proper with the Monolith and a third on a boulder-fringed scree slope on the north side of Sabrina. Oriented geological samples were again collected by Dr. Arriens, biological specimens collected by Dr. Donaldson, penguin and seal counts made (Adelia and Weddel) and filming was done.

Heavy pack prevented any close approach to Borradaile and Young Islands so, hoping to find better conditions later, we shaped course around the eastern edge of the pack towards Cape Adare on the mainland. For the first and last time on the expedition landfall was made in good visibility, the Victoria Land mountains being sighted nearly 100 miles away. Robertson Bay was choked with ice, which was streaming anti-clockwise round the bay at about two knots and sweeping out to sea past Cape Adare. Large bergs were grounded off the cape and across the mouth of the bay.

Solo was hove-two for 5½ hours on 23 January in a rather transitory polynia off the Cave, just inside the tip of the cape, and two parties were landed in turn by the Beaufort 'rubber duck' on Ridley Beach. The historic huts were filmed and biological specimens collected. Borchgrevink's 1899 tongue and grooved hut was intact though full of snow and his store hut was also intact though roofless (as it had been in 1911). Campbell and Priestley's 1911 hut (Scott's Northern party) on the other hand, was collapsed all but one wall. An enormous ridge of pressure ice towered over the inner margin of Ridley Beach. The vast Adelie rookery exhibited the same signs of overcrowding that Priestly described.

While hove-to off Cape Adare iceblocks were collected from floes and melted by passing engine exhaust water through a copper coil (see Results).

Cape Adare – 71°18′S. – was our furthest south. We had logged 3,590 miles from Sydney, though our more meaningful noon to noon runs had totalled 3,228 miles. Less than a quarter of our diesel fuel had been used and less than half our drinking water.

On 23 January at 1130 we began heading back northward, intending to have another try at the Ballenys and to visit Macquarie Island. The first objective was frustrated by close pack encountered on 27 January when still thirty miles east of the Ballenys and we altered course for Macquarie.

An unusual observation was made on 26 January in 66°30′S., 164°35′E. of widespread patches of 'foam'. Samples were taken and the phenomenon photographed.

Three iceberg measurements were made between Cape Adare and 65°20′S., 165°45′E., where one of the last bergs was encountered, in sea temperatures varying between −3°C and +3°C. Specimens of krill and plankton were also collected.

Stormy north-west head winds hampered our approach to Macquarie Island and persistent fog, that allowed neither sun sights nor land sightings, kept us tacking on and off near the invisibile island for three days. Eventually Jack Pittar succeeded in repairing the radar, to reveal the island nine miles off. We anchored in Buckles Bay at 0400 on 11 February. We were glad of an opportunity to assist in the re-supply of huts at Ballast Bay (Sandy Bay) and Green Gully. We sailed at 0900 on the 16th.

Extremely rough weather, including a force 11 storm which constrained us to lie-to under trysail for sixty-one hours, did nothing to assist our progress northwards. Damage to sails and three stanchions was sustained. South-west of New Zealand, however, the wind freed at last to west and southwest and, in our 11th week at sea, we covered 850 nautical miles. Two days later, at 0415 on 4 March, we rounded South Head to enter Sydney Harbour.

The return passage from Cape Adare to Sydney, with the abortive approach to the Ballenys and the stop at Macquarie Island, clocked up 3,240 miles on the log, while the noon to noon runs came to 3,038 nautical miles.

Some fifty gallons of diesel fuel out of the original 400 remained. Out of the 320 gallons of fresh water taken on at Sydney, 195 were consumed, a praiseworthy 2.6 pints per person per day (all dish washing, personal and clothes washing was done in salt water – often cold.) A good deal of sea water was used in cooking.

Solo was hove-to in gales for a total of 243 hours. She was navigated in pack ice areas for a month.

The whole expedition occupied eleven weeks and two days (seventy-nine days). The grand total of noon to noon runs came to 6,266 nautical miles.

Results

(Tabulated under the same headings as 'objectives').

1. A major aim was to evaluate the efficacy of a flexible low-cost operation. It is noteworthy that the total cost of the expedition came to less than A$27,000.

2. Three icebergs were studied in sea temperatures varying between —3°C and +3°C. The latter was one of the northernmost bergs seen, being encountered in 65°20′S. Salinity and temperature runs at 15 and 75 metres depth were made from 150 metres to 30 metres off the berg. The sea temperature at the surface was +2°C and at 75 metres down +3°C. The unexpected finding was that **no** diminution of salinity could be detected on any side of this or any other berg investigated. This suggests that attrition by wave action rather than melting is the major factor in break up of icebergs south of the Antarctic convergence. These data may be of help in making calculations on the problems of iceberg towing.

3. The bottom-dredged samples mineral and biological are under examination in various centres under the auspices of Drs. Arriens,

Donaldson and Quilty, in consultation with scientists from the Antarctic Division and other institutions.
4. The bird and whale data are being written up by Dr. Donaldson.
5. The geological data are being handled by Dr. Pieter Arriens.
6. The weather observations are in the hands of the Meteorological Office, Melbourne, and Dr. Arriens.
7. The method of melting pack-ice into drinking water by waste heat from engine cooling water was most successful, the resulting fresh water being less saline than the Adelaide water supply.
8. The A.B.C. are currently editing the film and will also be publishing a book.
9. Some experience in handling a small vessel in pack-ice under sail and under power has been accumulated and will guide us in planning our larger research vessel and programming her activities.

Further Results

10. The discovery of a useful anchorage on Sturge Island may be of significance. Reports are being made to the appropriate official bodies.
11. The tectonic activity logged on 1 January in 61°55′S., is being reported.
12. Our experience in applying low-energy, low-cost technology is being evaluated. The consumption of only 350 gallons of diesel fuel in a 79-day expedition is surely significant and relevant for larger auxiliary sailing ships engaged in research in the Southern Ocean and Antarctica where enormous distances are involved, logistic problems are formidable and wind power is all too readily available. The use of modified Polynesian natural navigation techniques near the South Magnetic Pole may be useful especially in emergency situations. Similarly, locating land by observation of the behaviour of Antarctic birds and animals may turn out to be as practicable as corresponding Polynesian methods.
13. Data from the C.S.I.R.O satellite tracking 'snow petrel' is currently coming to hand.

Reporting the Results of the 1977–8 Expedition

The A.B.C. television film and book have been mentioned. The latter will contain appendices on the more scientific/technical aspects. Scientific papers are being prepared for the appropriate journals by the expedition's specialist. Popular articles are also being written. This report is being widely circulated to the various bodies and journals concerned with the Antarctic and Southern Ocean.

Solo was on show at Sydney Cove for ten days after her return and an exhibition was mounted on the quayside by courtesy of the Maritime Services Board. Another exhibition with film and slides will be held at the O.T.C. Building, Martin Place, through the kindness of

O.T.C. and at the suggestion of the Lord Mayor of Sydney (who received the expeditioners on their return).

The relatively low cost of the expedition has already been mentioned but even so it would have been impossible without vigorous fund raising activities such as the exhibitions referred to above. Further efforts are vital to pay off the mortgage on *Solo* and re-fit her for her next venture.

There is not space here to thank our many sponsors who donated money, goods or services; there would have been no expedition without them. We are glad to report that Dick Smith, a major backer, has been elected the first Fellow of the Foundation. It is most gratifying that the Commissioner of Taxation, on the recommendation of the C.S.I.R.O., has recognised the Foundation as an Approved Research Institute, whereby gifts to the Foundation for the purpose of scientific research all qualify for tax deduction.

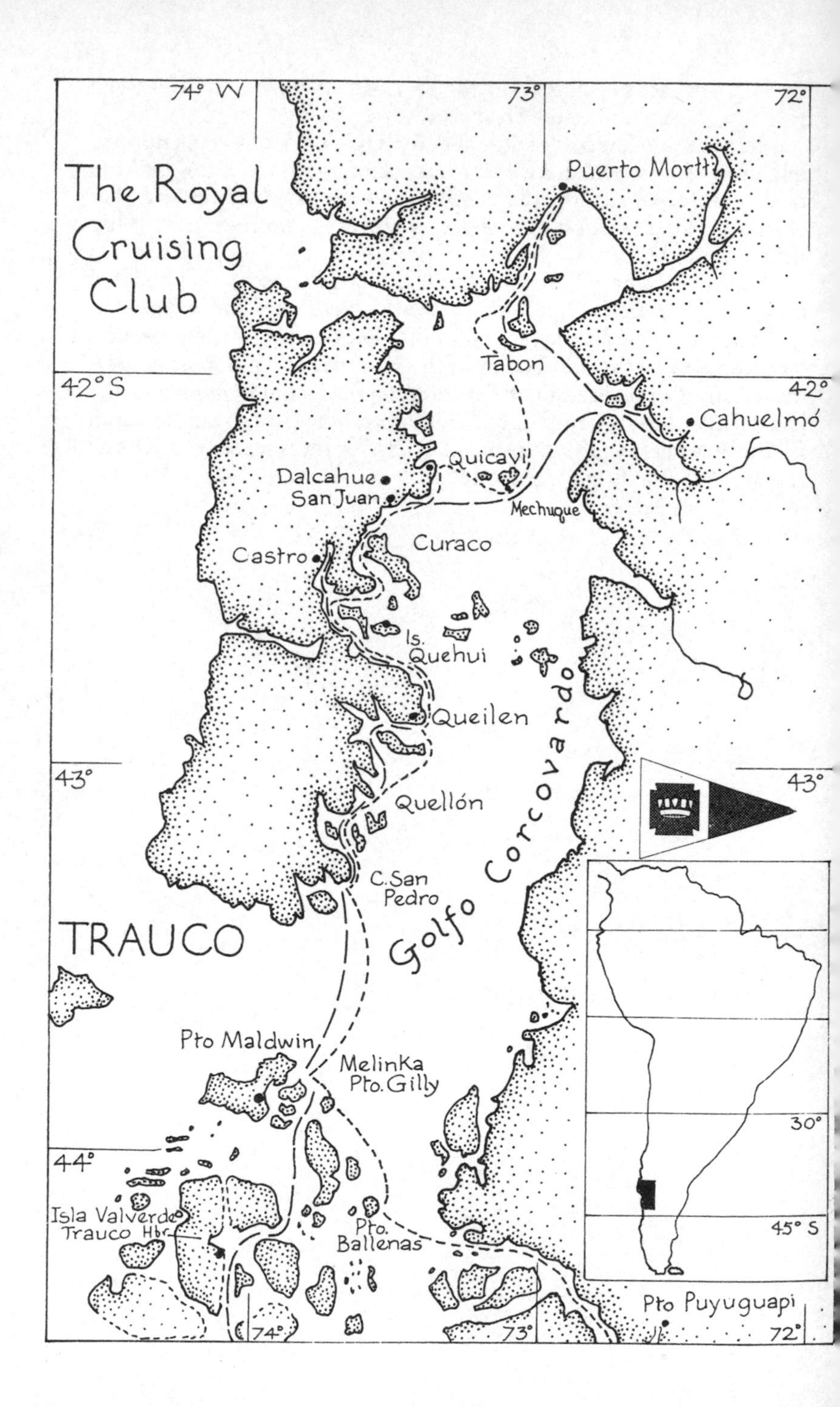
74° W
73°
72°
The Royal Cruising Club
Puerto Montt
Tabon
42° S
42°
Cahuelmó
Quicavi
Dalcahue
San Juan
Mechuque
Curaco
Castro
Is. Quehui
Queilen
Golfo Corcovado
43°
43°
Quellón
C. San Pedro
TRAUCO
Pto Maldwin
Melinka
Pto. Gilly
30°
44°
Isla Valverde
Trauco Hbr.
Pto. Ballenas
45° S
Pto Puyuguapi
74°
73°
72°

IN BYRON'S WAKE
TRAUCO *IN SOUTH-WEST CHILE*

by Maldwin Drummond

Trauco, a 50-foot cutter with squaresail, was built on a lonely beach in the north of the Chilean archipelago that stretches southwards to the Horn. My brother Bendor helped build her in 1969 and her owner, Doonie Edwards, had asked us both in that year to explore the islands that sit at the foot of the Andes, in the shelter of the large island of Chiloe (as was recorded in the 1970 *Journal* and *Roving Commissions* 11). Ten years later we were to have an extended purpose – plant hunting under sail in the Chonos archipelago, searching down as far as the Lake of San Rafael.

Puerto Montt, where we joined *Trauco*, is a busy port. It had been tidied up a good deal since Bendor and I were last there. The market that used to be submerged by the tide was now safely ashore. Little boats carried all sorts of produce to the crowded quay. There were sheep standing awkwardly on the foredecks, with vegetables and produce of the sea piled high, Samuel Plimsoll notwithstanding. Happy faces shone in the sun, enjoying the chatter.

Trauco left all this, bound for the bulk of the Andes, to the fjords that cut deep into the coastline, heading for the great cleft of Cahuelmo. We decided to break the journey by spending the night anchored under Tabon Island, a thin, sickle-like form giving shelter from southerly winds. As the light faded, a rider wandered across the beach with two children hanging onto the horse's tail. Tabon is the start of the maze of islands that serrate Chile's west coast from Puerto Montt all the way down to the Horn and are the remains of the coastal range.

There were eleven of us on board – Doonie Edwards, now a member of the R.C.C.; my brother Bendor; Colin Mudie, the naval architect; Juan Enrique Lira, a well-known photographer and world champion skeet shot; Mario, who specialised in things mechanical; Ruffino, who did the cooking; Juan, who did all the things that needed strength; and Gabriel, who seemed to be keen to do everything that no one else wanted to do; Miriam, our translator; Gilly, my wife and myself.

Before anchoring in the Estero Cahuelmo, we visited Quintupeu Inlet to the north. I remember saying that this must be one of the most fantastic anchorages I had ever been in. The white flowered *eucryphia*

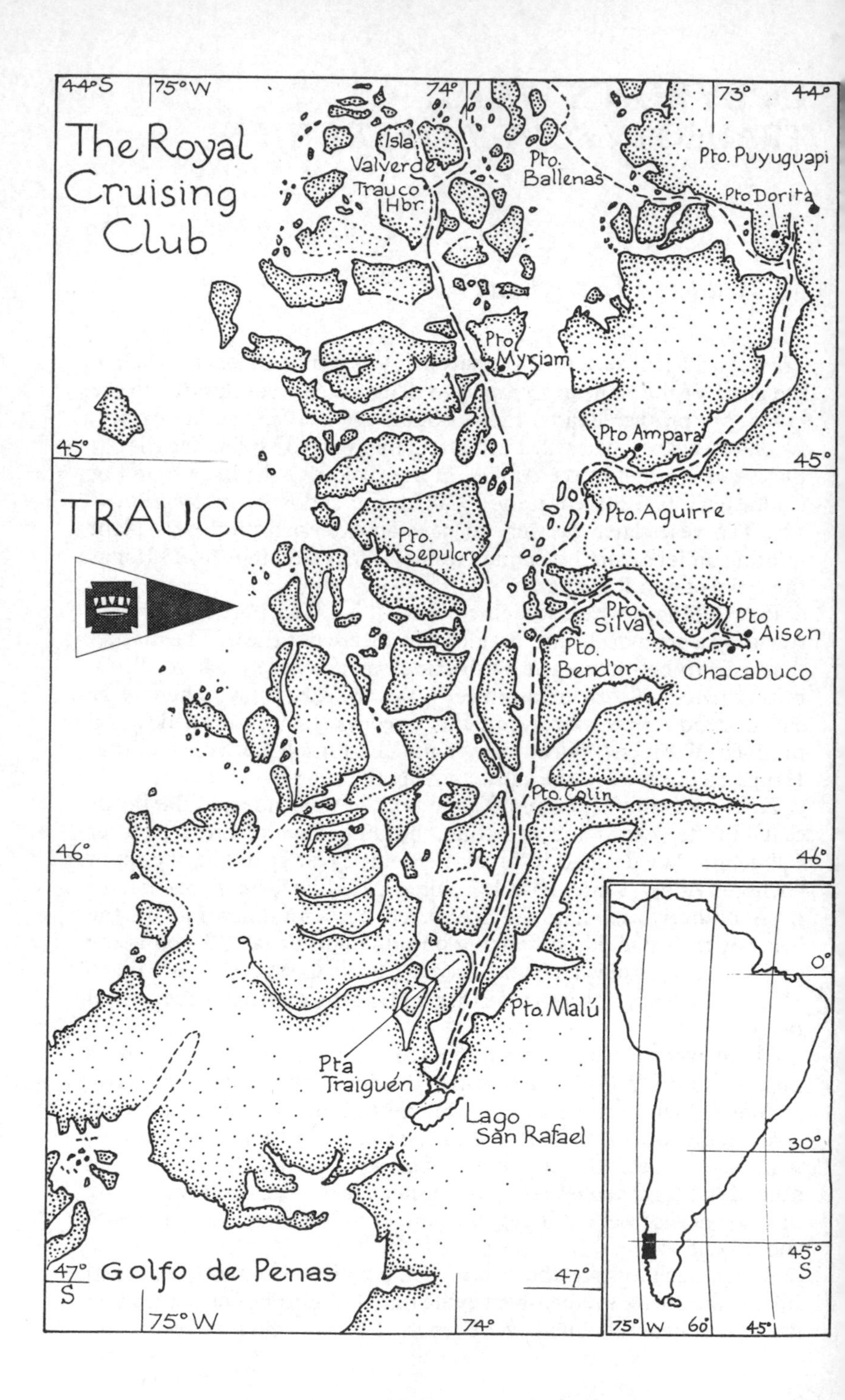

The Royal Cruising Club
TRAUCO
44°S
75°W
74°
73°
44°
Isla Valverde
Trauco Hbr.
Pto. Ballenas
Pto. Puyuguapi
Pto Dorita
Pto Myriam
Pto Ampara
45°
45°
Pto. Aguirre
Pto. Sepulcro
Pto Silva
Pto Aisen
Pto. Bend'or
Chacabuco
Pto. Colin
46°
46°
Pto. Malú
Pta Traiguén
Lago San Rafael
47°
S
Golfo de Penas
47°
75°W
74°
0°
30°
45°
S
75°
W
60°
45°

climbed the hills amongst its less decorative cousins. It was like Norway, the main difference though were the trees – their size and variety. At Cahuelmo, though, the hot springs called. There we luxuriated, controlling the water by plugging the rivulets with sods of sea grass. The water at source is 60°C. The day was Sunday 5 February and it was a good place to think of winter at home.

Day succeeded day as we worked our way down through the islands. At one stage we took in tow a small Chilote sailing boat with a man, his wife, son and a sheep aboard. This small craft was only nineteen feet long with a six foot beam and the sail was all patch. We visited the boat building centre of St. Jaun, walking by the wreck of a dugout stranded on the beach. Bahamonde's yard was as yards used to be fifty years ago – grown frames and very little machinery summed it up. Mr. Bahamonde was building a 50 foot fishing boat in the shed, employing a lofting floor for laying out his designs. He used models and half models which he proudly showed us in his house. On the walls hung graduation certificates and photographs and the bungalow was brightened by a Chilote rug in strong colours worked into a bowl of flowers. It was very clean and tidy, as though we were expected.

Trauco arrived in Castro, the capital of Chiloe, on Wednesday 8 February. Darwin had complained when he visited the place in 1834, that 'no individual possessed either a watch or a clock; an old man, who was supposed to have a good idea of the time, was employed to strike the church bell by guess'. It is quite different today – the waterfront is crowded with small sailing vessels, some with beautiful lines, some double-ended, others squat like pregnant Itchen ferries. Most of them work too hard to spare time for paint.

Bt Friday 10 February, we made the southern end of Chiloe and anchored for the night under San Pedro Island. It is a perfect place to contemplate the crossing of the Gulf of Corcovardo, which has an evil reputation, open as it is to the full force of the Pacific and troubled by strong tides and currents which further disturb the sea. I was reading about Byron's grandfather. He had been to San Pedro after being wrecked on Wager Island, a couple of hundred miles south of our destination – the Lake of San Rafael. H.M.S. *Wager* had been part of Anson's squadron in 1741 when wrecked in a gale of hurricane force on the island that later bore her name. It is a fascinating story of trials and tribulations.

Byron was with Captain Cheap and his half of the party made their way back to England by going north with the help of the Indians. The majority of the crew went south, back round the Horn in a lengthened ship's boat re-named *Swiftsure*. Few of them reached England.

But to return to recollections of the Gulf of Corcovardo; Byron records that 'it seemed to frighten our Indian guide out of his senses; and indeed there was a great reason for his apprehensions, for there ran a most dreadful hollow sea, dangerous indeed for any open boat whatever, but a thousand times more so for such a crazy vessel as we were in.'

We crossed the next morning under power. There was no wind and Byron and his friends could have achieved the voyage in a paper hat. Soon after 1500, the yacht was anchored west of the lighthouse, in the little harbour of Melinka. *Trauco* was at the northern end of the Chonos archipelago and hundreds of islands stretched to the south, some without names, though they may be five kilometres across. It is impossible to penetrate more than a few yards from the beach on any of them, as the temperate rain forest likes the place so much, that it denies any familiarity. We did not spend long in Melinka. We anchored near the head of a small *estero* on an unnamed island north of Isla Valverde. We had been at sea for just over a week. This anonymous bay was indeed a beautiful place. Great trees sprang out of the thick undergrowth and clothed the steeply rising island. I recorded that everything was so alive you could almost see the island grow. There was not a whisper, not a breath. The only sounds were made by the owners of this paradise, steamer duck, unable to fly, only to flap across the water inside a cloud of spray; the Magellanic, blue-eyed shag; black-back gulls and woodland birds. At night the sea sparkled with phosphorescence. In the early morning sun, *coicopihue* relieved the incredible green, the brilliant red flower trumpets splashing colour, as the vine climbed through the trees.

We continued our voyage southward and in the days that followed saw few people, occasionally a fisherman's summer camp with his boat drawn up on the beach, sails furled and oars stowed. The local boats are without motors and their owners dive for shellfish using ancient hard-hat gear.

We collected our water from streams, using a rubber boat. The system worked in this way. We would tow the small, open dinghy to a stream. When satisfied that we were far enough in and it was all fresh water, we would bucket it full. Sometimes a waterfall would do the work for us in seconds. The weather was unusually dry, for most years the islands are blessed with 270 inches of rain, over twice that experienced by Rhum, one of the wettest places in the British Isles. In all we had three weeks of unbroken sunshine, the rest was changeable.

On Tuesday 14 February, we passed through the Paso Tres Cruces and made east-southeast into the Elephant Channel, named after the elephant seals recorded by Fitzroy and Darwin on board H.M.S. *Beagle*. *Trauco* spent an exceptional night with scarce shelter at Puerto Traiquen, anchored close to the shore, two anchors out and a stern line to the beach. The shore party built a fire of driftwood and had a *picoroco* roast. These are huge barnacles, some were roasted, while others were boiled in an iron pot. The result resembles a 6-inch rotten and blackened molar. You can eat them with mayonnaise. The meat in the cavity has the consistency of soft roe, the top part, or muscle that works the mouth parts, tastes like the claws of a lobster. It is delicious but looks appalling.

By Wednesday 15 February we were near the river that leads up to the Lake of San Rafael and the glacier. The dinghy was employed to attack a little iceberg to replenish our ice chests and for frozen glacier water for drinks. The Rio Tempanos winds its way through to the lake. Charts are unreliable and we had to search for the channel by cruising at right angles, watching the echo sounder for signs of deeper water. The tide was rising and gradually the estuary turned into river with woods coming down to a low cliff. The Chilean beech *nothofagus dombeyii* has a Scots pine look about it, for the tree is branchless way up the trunk. Little icebergs and 'bergie' bits studded the waters of the river. Some were frosty white with highlights of azure blue. Others had a greenish tinge, some with black spots, as though they came off the top of a glacier. Occasionally, transparent blue-green ones were born under water, spawned from the bottom of an overturned berg. All around were chips, looking like ice at the end of a party. It was colder though the water was a surprising 52°F. *Trauco* entered the great lake, eight miles north to south and five miles east to west. We saw the three mile wall of ice spilling through a gap in the Cordilleras, the Ventisquero San Rafael. The lake's surface was spattered and stippled with 'ice children' and its face shone blue, green and white in the bright sun.

On one of the icebergs we saw one particularly large seal, its grey, sleek shape completely at rest as it slept. We crossed the lake, weaving through the ice flows. *Trauco* hit a small chip of ice, not more than 2 feet 6 inches square and it shook the ship, sending a tremor up the mast that alarmed Bendor and Juan Enrique who were photographing from the yard.

The magnificence of the ice wall became more and more apparent. The snow alongside the mountains, on each edge, was stained by its progress. Brown and black ice marked the movement. The wall itself was in gigantic flakes, some leaning at dangerous angles over the sea. The Admiralty Pilot warns in its peculiar way that 'the eastern shore of Lago San Rafael is encumbered by the Ventisquero San Rafael, a glacier which descends from Monte San Valentin 13,310 feet high. The icebergs which break away from the glacier are extremely dangerous to navigation, especially those that break away beneath the surface of the water and suddenly appear in the vicinity of the vessel'.

We were to see what their lordships meant the next day, when cruising some 500 yards off the ice face. A huge, white pinnacle suddenly broke the surface of the lake and soared like an ice polaris upward, well above the face, which we estimated 200 foot high, before collapsing in a boil of churning water and disintegrating ice. A new berg had been dramatically born, its sides bright blue, looking almost unnatural in its brilliance. The birth started a chain reaction. More pieces broke off the wall, their descent caused the lake itself to heave and once peaceful bergs turned over to expose their translucent blue-green bottoms. Doonie suggested a picnic on one of them but we left hurriedly when we saw that it was in danger, too, of exposing more than we wished to see. It had broken in half and the naval architect calculated its stability.

On the other side of the lake are the remains of the canal started in the 1920s that was to have been cut through the Ofqui peninsula to relieve the dangerous route around Cap Tresmontes that Byron had tried to struggle by before accepting aid from the Indians. Hebe, fuchsia and gunnera, the latter had leaves nearly 8 ft across, climb the sides of the unfinished waterway, healing the scar.

We left the lake on Friday 17 February, and made our way northward and were alongside the pier at Chacabuco in the early evening of the 19th. This was the port for Aysen, and we stored the ship by truck. Gilly and I took advantage of the situation and spent the night in an hotel on a bed with fossilised springs.

On the way north again, *Trauco* paused at Puerto Aquirre. Their local boats are still made by adze and axe. Puerto Amparo ('Protection Harbour') is a magical place on the southwestern side of the large island of Magdalena. Fishermen were working on the western side of the head of the bay as we anchored. They were studiously polite and were after the larger mussel, *cholgas*, which they harvest by grappling for it with a three-pronged, blacksmith-made, curved rake on a long pole employing a large, blunt chisel for shifting the obstinate ones. The fishermen were from Melinka and work only at low tide with their rakes. A hand air pump on one of the boats extended their range, for an experienced diver could go down ninety feet with his hard-hat. Their dog, Rondin ('Watchman') lives on a diet of shellfish. He was probably descended from the Indian dogs which were used for actually catching fish, swimming after them under water. When the crew had a sufficient pile of mussels, they took them back to the camp, cooked them, shelled them and smoked the meat. All through the islands there were large middens of shells, their history stretching back way beyond the days of Darwin and Byron.

The fishermen's whale boat was about twenty-nine feet overall and eight feet six inches in the beam. They progress from ground to ground, mostly under three oars, two oarsmen standing on one side and the other rowing, seated, on the opposite. They can travel at a remarkable rate for such heavy craft. At night the boat is beached and the sails spread tightly over the gunwhales. The sails are made of cotton, of bed sheet weight. If stretched tightly, though, they are at least waterproof.

Puerto Puyuguapi is an attractive little settlement with wooden houses built by people of German extraction. They were kindness itself and took us to see the new road they were driving through the rock and rain forest, for the town was not connected in any way with the main road system and relied on service by boat. Port Banos Termales, is a watering place, built by the legendary pilot Ernesto Hein who appears to be able to land a plane anywhere. He built this selection of little houses as a holiday resort, served by his aeroplane. The settlement is on a hot spring and we were soon testing the temperature. He encouraged us ashore by lending us one of the little A-framed houses. A huge barbecue fire was soon glowing on the beach, and Ruffino cooking lamb on a long, iron spit.

Trauco arrived back off Melinka on Sunday 26 February and the weather had broken. I remember a little notice at the police station; it read 'The Policeman is like the light, you only notice him when he is not there'. It was a good motto for that quiet little place. The wooden church dominated the road that cascaded down to the sea. *Trauco* explored the islands and leads round about and had a pretty rough couple of hours returning to Melinka, one evening, when the weather showed its true face.

The voyage back over the Gulf of Corcovardo on the night of Wednesday 1 March bore little relation to our previous experience. Poor Ruffino sat at the entrance to the charthouse feeling the motion. He looked like a seagull that had sunk for refuge into its feathers.

Trauco called at Castro again and Quicavi, a wooden village that commands a lagoon. It is said to be the home of the witches' university. The headmaster of the local school said jokingly that he was the head witch but the 'university' itself is out of the village, in the hills, according to others. Furry pigs wandered through the streets, a bullock cart helped quicken the pace of life.

On Monday 6 March we arrived at my favourite island under Chiloe – Mechuque. A narrow inlet cuts the 'capital' in two, to be joined again by an iron and wooden bridge. The western side contains the new church hall and police station. The eastern bank is clearly the original settlement. The shingle-roofed and clapboard buildings are of weathered *alerce*, Chilean cedar, and on stilts, over the water. They climb a diminutive hill, joining newer buildings, until they reach the bay on the other side, where there is a ship yard. A sixty-foot motor coaster called *Don* was under repair with adze and plane. We were followed in our exploration by Joe, a dog, belonging to an engineering student who had returned home for the holidays. Our four legged companion looked like a happy, long-legged fox. The people were sunny everywhere in these parts, smiling and unfailingly helpful, open and polite. It was a glimpse at village life in Europe, now gone, having lost, perhaps forever, that happy way. Except for the occasional motor boat and the village generator, used only for lighting, the internal combustion engine has not taken over. Perhaps there is a clue in this.

We returned to Tabon and by 1317 on Tuesday 7 March we were anchored again at Angelmo, the harbour of Puerto Montt. Before entering the narrow channel that separates the protecting island from the mainland, we had seen the volcanoes of Orsorno and Calbuco. The latter had lost a good deal of its snowcap and Doonie pointed this out as a sign of an exceptional summer. It certainly had been a memorable collection of weeks for us. Part movement under squaresail, hour upon hour spent wandering and wondering about islands and the plants on them, studying them at close quarters; surviving the shock of meeting the occasional person after days of seeing no one, the fascination of the birds, seals and shellfish. There can be few places more beautiful and few spots in the known world less explored. *Trauco*, Doonie and the weather had been good to us.

WANDERER IV FROM SOUTH TO NORTH PACIFIC

New Zealand to Vancouver

by Eric and Susan Hiscock

Our plan was to sail from New Zealand, where we had spent eighteen enjoyable months, to British Columbia, and we intended to make brief stops only in the Society Islands and Hawaii, for we did not start until early April and we wished to arrive in B.C. waters before the heavy fogs of late summer set in. The distance would be something more than 7,000 miles.

Of course one can sail direct from New Zealand to Tahiti, i.e. along the great circle track, and a few yachts of racing type have done so; but this is taking a gamble on the south-east trade wind having little or no east in it, or on its southern boundary being north of where it should be. *Ocean Passages for the World* recommends that one should go south of 40°S. to take advantage of the prevailing westerlies, and not edge away to the northward until in 155°W.; but we thought so high a latitude might be too cold and windy for us, and decided instead to steer a middle course in 30° to 35°S. (much as John Franklen-Evans (R.C.C.), did in *Kochab* in 1960), where between the trade wind and the westerlies we could expect winds from any direction, and not to head for Tahiti until we were confident of being able to fetch that island on the starboard tack. But in the event it would have made little difference which route we took, apart from differences in distance, for the autumn of 1978 was peculiar in that easterly winds prevailed over much of the South Pacific, even extending high into the forties, and as a result we were close-hauled nearly all the way and at times had to turn to windward. Often the weather was cold and damp; we had only one gale (from ahead) during which we lay hove-to, and we saw only one ship, but with the Aries vane gear doing all the steering we did not keep much of a lookout in those lonely waters. We passed south of two vigias, Haymet Rocks and Orne Bank (both have been searched for unsuccessfully) and then slanted up through the Australs, where the weather improved as we crossed the tropic.

Aware of the calms which plague the channel between Tahiti and neighbouring Moorea, we ought to have passed to windward of Tahiti to reach Papeete, which port lies on that island's northern shore; but we reckoned we could easily motor through the channel, and that we did on our twenty-seventh day at sea, first with an awkward swell on the beam, and before we had got out of that we started plunging

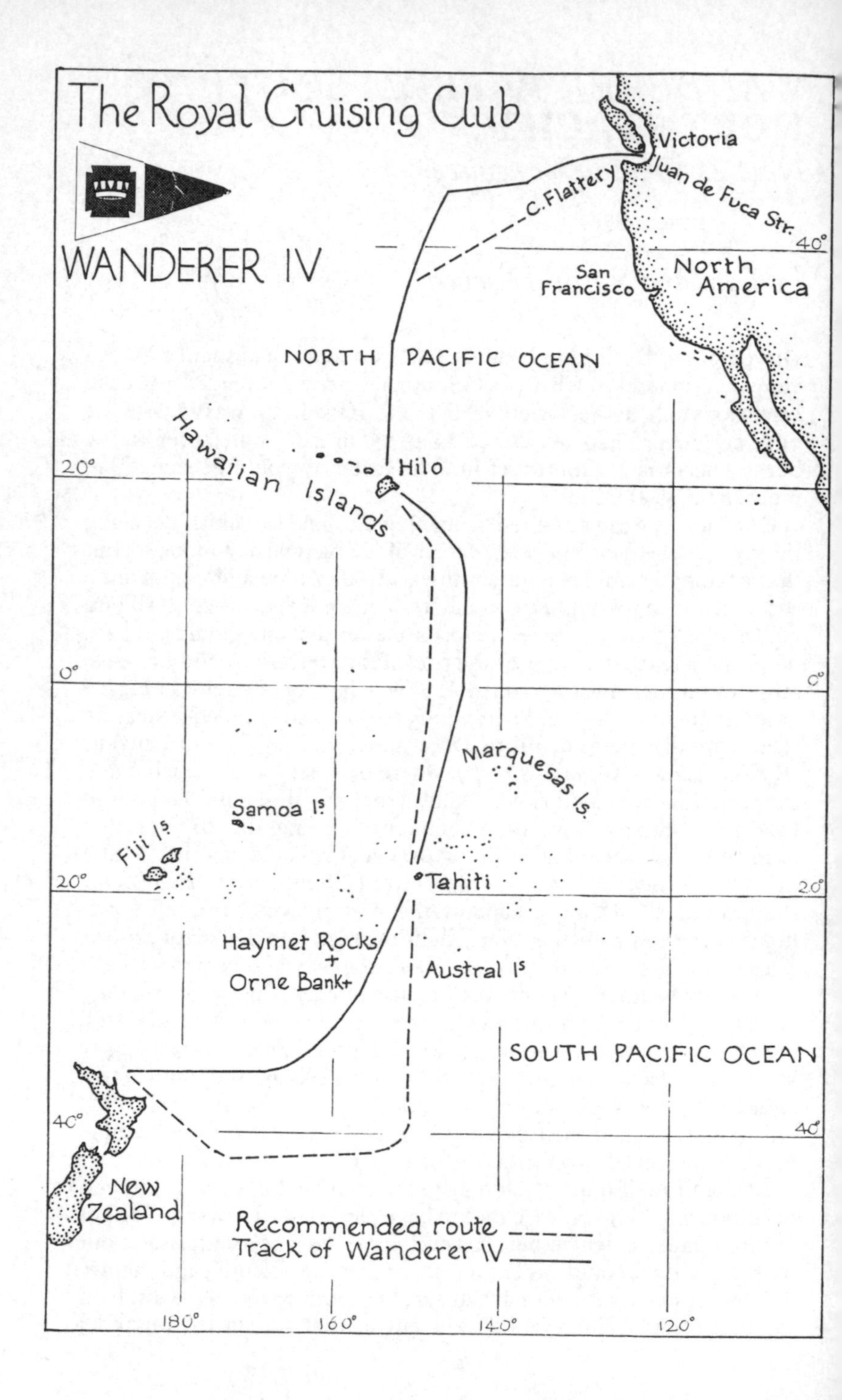

The Royal Cruising Club
WANDERER IV
Victoria
Juan de Fuca Str.
C. Flattery
40°
San Francisco
North America
NORTH PACIFIC OCEAN
Hawaiian Islands
Hilo
20°
0°
Marquesas Is.
Samoa Is
Fiji Is
Tahiti
Haymet Rocks
Orne Bank
Austral Is
SOUTH PACIFIC OCEAN
New Zealand
Recommended route
Track of Wanderer IV
180°
160°
140°
120°

heavily into a steep headsea. We plugged slowly on, and had reached a position only five miles from Papeete pass when a wind of gale force sprang at us from dead ahead; it soon became clear that we were not going to make port before nightfall, and not wishing to enter in the dark because of the likely difficulty of finding a berth, we bore away and had a fast reach to Moorea, where we found peace, comfort and a good mud bottom in glorious Cook Bay.

Moorea is not a port of entry, but the *gendarme* kindly allowed us to stay over the weekend, after which we went across to Papeete to enter. We had heard by way of the coconut radio that a bond equivalent to about £270.00 per person aboard must be posted by all yachts visiting the Society Islands, and had arranged in advance for money to cover this to await us at Papeete; but when we told the port officials that we intended to remain in the islands for only about a week they waived the bond.

Two days at the largely re-built and now almost characterless town were enough for our purpose, and when we had done our business there we returned for several days to the peace and beauty of Moorea, where we filled our tanks with excellent water and chose a berth where the shadow cast by a near-by mountain provided a long, cool evening twilight. It seemed remarkable, though a desire for shore-side electricity may have been the reason, that although Papeete's waterfront was tight-packed with yachts, mostly American, few of them appeared to spend much time at Moorea.

The success under sail of a passage between the Society Islands and Hawaii largely depends on crossing the equator far enough up-wind, i.e. to the east, so that when the north-east trade wind is met with, one's destination can be fetched, and preferably with sheets eased a little. *Ocean Passages* recommends 148°W, as a suitable longitude, but we felt that might be cutting it fine, and decided to cross in 145°W. Possibly Peter and Anne Pye in *Moonraker* had the same feeling, for although they left from Bora Bora, which is 130 miles to leeward of Moorea, they crossed the equator in 146°W.

We had expected this trade-wind passage to be enjoyable, but the first part of it was not. The day before we were due to leave Moorea an American friend took us for a drive round that attractive island, and we noticed that a heavy sea was breaking on the barrier reef all along the north and east sides. Next morning was calm and we motored out into a vile headsea, finding the wind an hour later. Unfortunately, it had no south but a lot of north in it, so again we were close-hauled just as we had been most of the way from New Zealand. It was mid-May when we set out, and the pilot chart for that month shows the wind averaging only force 3, but with us it was between force 5 and 7, and life on board was wet and uncomfortable, and it was much too hot below. The temptation to ease sheets a little was great, but we were set on crossing the line in 145°W., and to do so we even had to beat to windward for two miserable days; that is a point of sailing *Wanderer* hates almost as much as we do, and we feel it is best to regard her as a square-rigger rather than a fore-and-after, and attempt to sail no closer than 6 points off the wind except when in smooth water.

It was something of a relief to come at last into the doldrum belt, which was about 100 miles wide, and without hesitation we started up the Ford diesel and motored through in twenty hours, but in an extraordinary steep and confused sea such as may be found in the Race of Alderney. Perhaps this was caused by currents, particularly the east-running Counter Current, though we could detect no more than about half a knot. Incidentally, it is strange that *Pacific Islands Pilot* Vol. III, which covers these waters, should state that there are no doldrums, and that the one trade wind changes to the other almost imperceptibly. Thereafter we had more comfortable sailing, heading at first for a point well to windward of Hawaii to allow for the west-setting North Equatorial Current, but bore away a little when we found that the current did no more than about five miles a day. The sun shone, the sea was comparatively smooth, and we had the kind of sailing dreamers dream of but do not often get. We saw two ships on this passage, and a yacht which overtook us quickly at a time when we were repairing a broken leach-line in the staysail, and twenty days out of Moorea (2,525 miles) came to Hilo Bay on the east side of Hawaii, the big island where we passed in behind the mile-long breakwater and entered the pleasant little harbour at its inshore end. There among other voyaging yachts we anchored, took a stern-line to the wall, and were quickly entered by the most courteous and friendly customs officer we have ever had the pleasure of meeting. We remained for five days, watering, provisioning and attending to our ship's requirements, then departed on the final, and much the most interesting, leg of the voyage, heading towards Victoria, B.C.

On this passage there are two major considerations: the northern extent of the north-east trade and the position of the North Pacific high-pressure area. The trade will probably compel one to steer more or less north until it expires, and the high, if one is able to alter course towards the land and does so too soon, may keep one becalmed for many days. In June, when we were making the passage, the recommended route is to head north on the starboard tack until, in about 36°N., the westerlies are met with, then to turn and steer for the destination. Other considerations, over which one has no control, are the likelihood of encountering fog and large fleets of fishing-vessels as the land is approached, and floating or waterlogged timber which, it is said, may be met with as far as 500 miles from the shore.

We had a powerful east-nor'-east trade when we left, and sailing as usual a little free, managed to make good 966 miles in the first week. But at 36°N. there was no sign of the westerlies, the east-nor'-easter continuing unabated, and the same at 40°N. By then it was growing cold and we were glad of our diesel cabin-heater; the sky had become overcast, and so it remained for the rest of the passage; the sea, which strangely enough was rarely rough no matter how strong the wind might be, had a grey, sullen look, and often there was a chill drizzle. Not until we reached 44°N. did the wind die, and then the Leach's and fork-tailed storm-petrels and black-footed albatrosses, which had been with us ever since the weather became cooler, were able unafraid to come right alongside to accept with apparent pleasure the lumps of cooking fat and scrambled egg scraps we offered them. Meanwhile the barograph had risen to a phenomenal height, and for several days stood at 30.75 inches (1,050 mbs.), the highest it had ever been in its twenty years of seafaring. So apparently we did pass through the high, the highest point of which in June is normally only 30.20 inches, yet we had, all-told, no more than about twenty-four hours of calm.

Naturally, we expected the wind to come from the west after the calm, but it did not; although it no longer blew from east-nor'-east it was still a little east of north, so again we were almost close-hauled, but now on the port tack, and at last were able to head for Cape Flattery, the southern entrance point of the Strait of Juan de Fuca, about 1,000 miles distant.

Navigation had become something of a problem. In the final two weeks of the passage we saw stars only on one occasion when it was too rough to make use of them, and we never got so much as a glimpse of the waxing and waning moon. So we had only the sun to serve us, and because of the continuous overcast, that body was visible only faintly and momentarily on rare occasions, and sometimes one had to wait a long time on deck in oil-skins, sextant in hand, so as to miss no chance of a quick snapshot if the opportunity should offer. So faint was the sun that no index shade was needed on the sextant, and sometimes when the sun could just be seen the horizon was hidden by drizzle. The yacht with radio aids is at an advantage here, for the area is well covered by Loran, and as the coast is approached there are many radio beacons, some with a range of 100 miles, from which to obtain a fix. Apart from a receiving set, we have no radio aids, but we reasoned that as earlier navigators such as Cook, Vancouver, Smeeton and Pye had managed with Nature's gifts alone, so perhaps might we.

Two nights before we were expecting to make a landfall we were reaching at speed under very reduced sail in a force 9 blow from the north. We had shipped no heavy water so we foolishly decided to leave the companionway open to make it easier and quieter for the watch-keeper to get in and out. About midnight we did ship a heavy crest in the cockpit, and this, with considerable force, rushed down into the saloon, swamping the whole of the lee side, filling the chart space and the bookshelf above it, pouring into the chest-of-drawers where we keep papers such as passports, money and unanswered letters, burying the lee settee on which Eric was sleeping under a foot of water, and it even reached the sideboard twelve feet away where the radio-receiving set stood. We spent the rest of that night pumping out and mopping up and trying to salve the more important things, such as nautical almanac and books of tables.

The contrasts of cruising are indeed remarkable. The following night on La Pérouse Bank we lay becalmed on a smooth sea in company with a fleet of salmon-trawlers. At nightfall they all stopped fishing, switched on masthead strobe lights and, presumably, went to bed, a sensible example that we followed.

We were fortunate to have no fog in this particularly foggy area, and about noon next day made a landfall on Flattery. But instead of continuing on our way to Victoria, then sixty miles distant, we put in to Neah Bay close to Flattery on the U.S. side of the strait, and spent a fine, sunny day there drying out some of our belongings, but whether we will ever get 100 books and twice that number of charts, that were soaked with seawater, really dry, remains to be seen. The final leg, 2,571 miles, had taken us twenty-three days.

Since our arrival in Canadian waters Ronnie Scott-Moncrieff and the Swinburns (both R.C.C.), have been most kind and helpful, and we feel sure we are going to enjoy this fascinating area with its countless islands and gleaming waterways. We plan to cruise a little and winter here and perhaps start on the return voyage to the South Pacific next year.

IN SEARCH OF SEA OTTERS

by R. Scott-Moncrieff

Last year it was the arrival of Freddie's daughter which limited our cruise. This year it seemed likely to be my daughter who would do this. However after discussion and finding a report that the sea otter population in the Checkleset Bay area had shown a considerable increase in numbers, we decided to investigate. Three weeks should be long enough if all went well.

The sea otter resembles the river or common otter, but besides being larger its hind limbs have developed into flippers. It lives most of its life in the sea, chiefly in and about the extensive kelp beds found from the Aleutian Islands along the Pacific coast as far south as California. It seems to subsist almost exclusively on shell fish which it brings to the surface to eat while lying on its back. It has the most beautiful fur, and this was nearly its undoing. In a recent letter Miles Smeeton says of them: 'Sea otters look like wine bottles floating in the kelp beds – from a distance that is – and if you anchor near the kelp you can hear them munching away at shell fish.'

When Captain Cook was on this coast in 1778, he acquired in trade with the Indians a number of sea otter skins which brought unexpectedly high prices when sold in China. News of this spread, and within a few years traders of many nations appeared on the west coast of America in search of sea otter pelts. To satisfy the demand they were slaughtered in great numbers by the Indians and came very near to extinction.

Some ten years ago from a few pockets in the Aleutians sea otters were collected and small numbers of them were planted in likely places along the Alaskan and B. C. coasts, with the hope of starting up new colonies. One of these areas was Checkleset Bay, southeast of Cape Cook which lies about three quarters of the way up the west coast of Vancouver Island.

On June 20 the same two shorebirds as last year set out in search of sea otters – *Tringa*, a 33-foot C. & C. ocean racer, and *Dunlin*, my 29-foot cruising type. Again we were lent a pair of walkie-talkies, which proved to be extremely useful. *Tringa* still had her thirsty petrol engine, but this year it caused less of a problem. This may have been due in part to the new reefing jib which, being controlled with so little effort from the cockpit, kept popping up and down, and came to be known as the 'Yo-yo'.

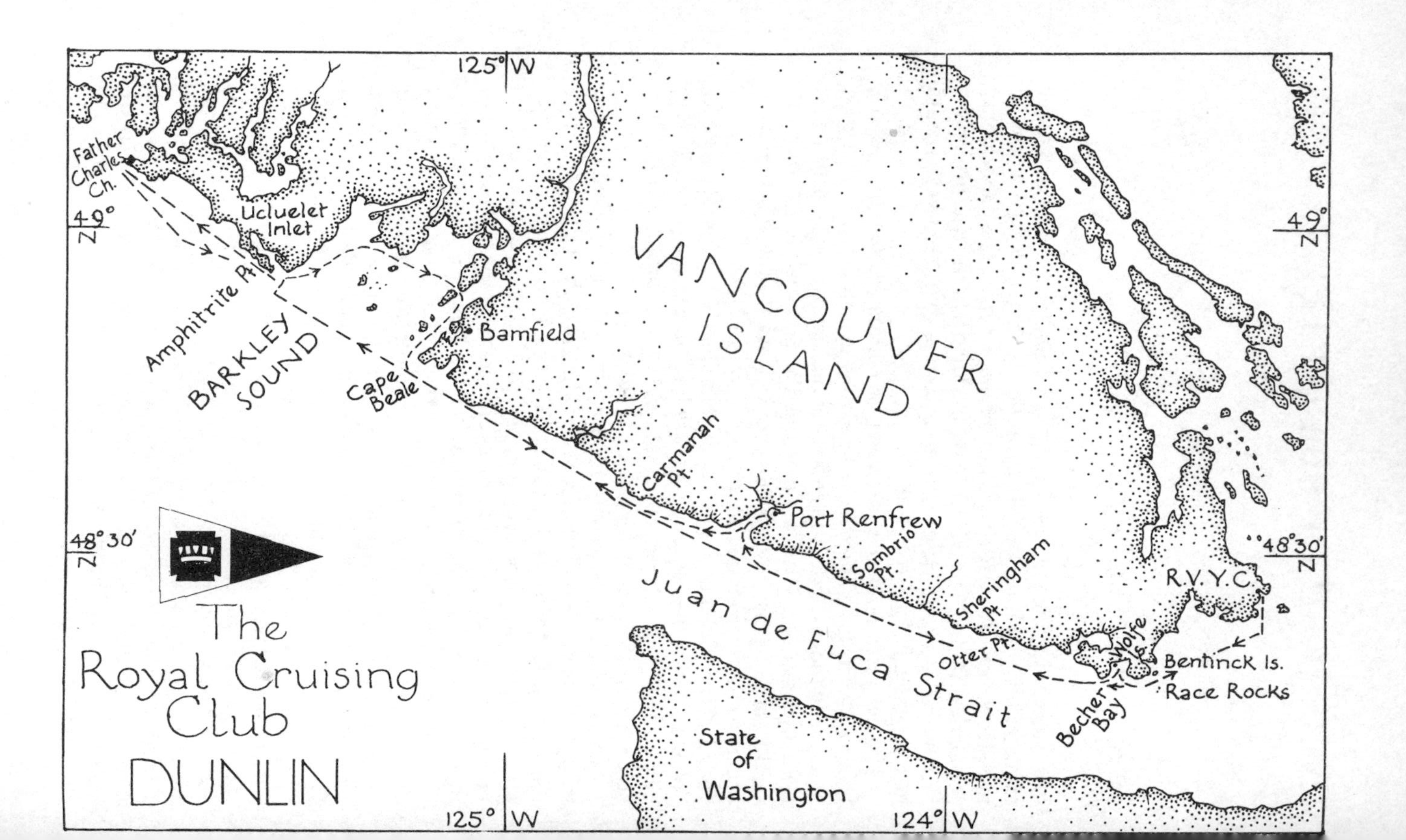
125° W
49° N
48°30' N
124° W
Father Charles Ch.
Ucluelet Inlet
Amphitrite Pt.
BARKLEY SOUND
Bamfield
Cape Beale
VANCOUVER ISLAND
Carmanah Pt.
Port Renfrew
Sombrio Pt.
Sheringham Pt.
Otter Pt.
Juan de Fuca Strait
R.V.Y.C.
Wolfe Is.
Bentinck Is.
Race Rocks
Becher Bay
State of Washington
The Royal Cruising Club
DUNLIN

The west coast of Vancouver Island, because of its high mountains and prevailing onshore winds, is given to much rain and fog. However, unlike last year, we were most fortunate in having little fog and only a day or so of drizzle. Otherwise the sun shone day after day and at times there were even complaints of the heat. This was the result of a high pressure area over the eastern Pacific. It also of course brought generally light winds or calms.

June 20. At 0601 the two boats left the Royal Victoria Yacht Club to catch the ebb. It was a calm, clear day with a few wisps of cloud over the distant mountains. 0810: We were swept by the ebb through Race Passage with its swirls and overfalls. 0830: Passing Beechey Head. This is the narrowest part of the Strait of Juan de Fuca, only about thirteen miles separating B.C. from the state of Washington. It was hereabouts that, in the early 20's during the days of prohibition in the U.S.A., a certain bootlegger is said to have begun his lucrative career by rowing by night a boat load of whisky across to the American shore. This enabled him to make his next trip with the aid of an outboard engine, and he is purported eventually to have acquired a sub-chaser in which he was able to outpace all pursuit. It was a period of violence and intrigue in which shoot-outs, sinkings and high-jackings were of common occurrence in the narrow waters separating the two countries.

At 0905 – small craft warning issued for the straits. 1140 – time for lunch after early breakfast. Consternation – no cheese on board! 1220 – small craft warning cancelled. 1425 – off Sombrio Point. The tide is slowing us considerably, and a good deal of swell is finding its way in from the western entrance.

At 1530, rounding Cerantes Rocks to enter Port Renfrew, I spotted, close alongside, a group of three Portuguese men-of-war and a little further along a pair. This was the first time I had ever encountered them in local waters. It is said to have been due to the unusually warm water along the B.C. coast this summer . . . a meander of the Japanese current perhaps. 1715 – *Dunlin* went alongside and made fast to *Tringa* who had her anchor down first.

June 21. 0105 – Wind, tide and outflow from the Gordon River were pushing us too close to a net-drying raft. Shortened scope. 0125 – wakened by a tug maneuvering a log boom near us. 0135 – log boom definitely too close for comfort. I tried to start the motor. The ignition light came on, but the solenoid would not click on, nor would the motor turn over. Shortened scope some more and began checking the electrics. Everything seemed to be in order except the starter switch.

At 0210 – wind shift and log boom moving past us. 0605 – Freddie came aboard with his professional box of tricks, but the tests were inconclusive. So I held the decompressor with a length of string (so that I could be out of the way) and Freddie swung the handle. On releasing the string, *presto*, we were in business!

Up anchor at 0625 and away along this rather dull stretch of coast

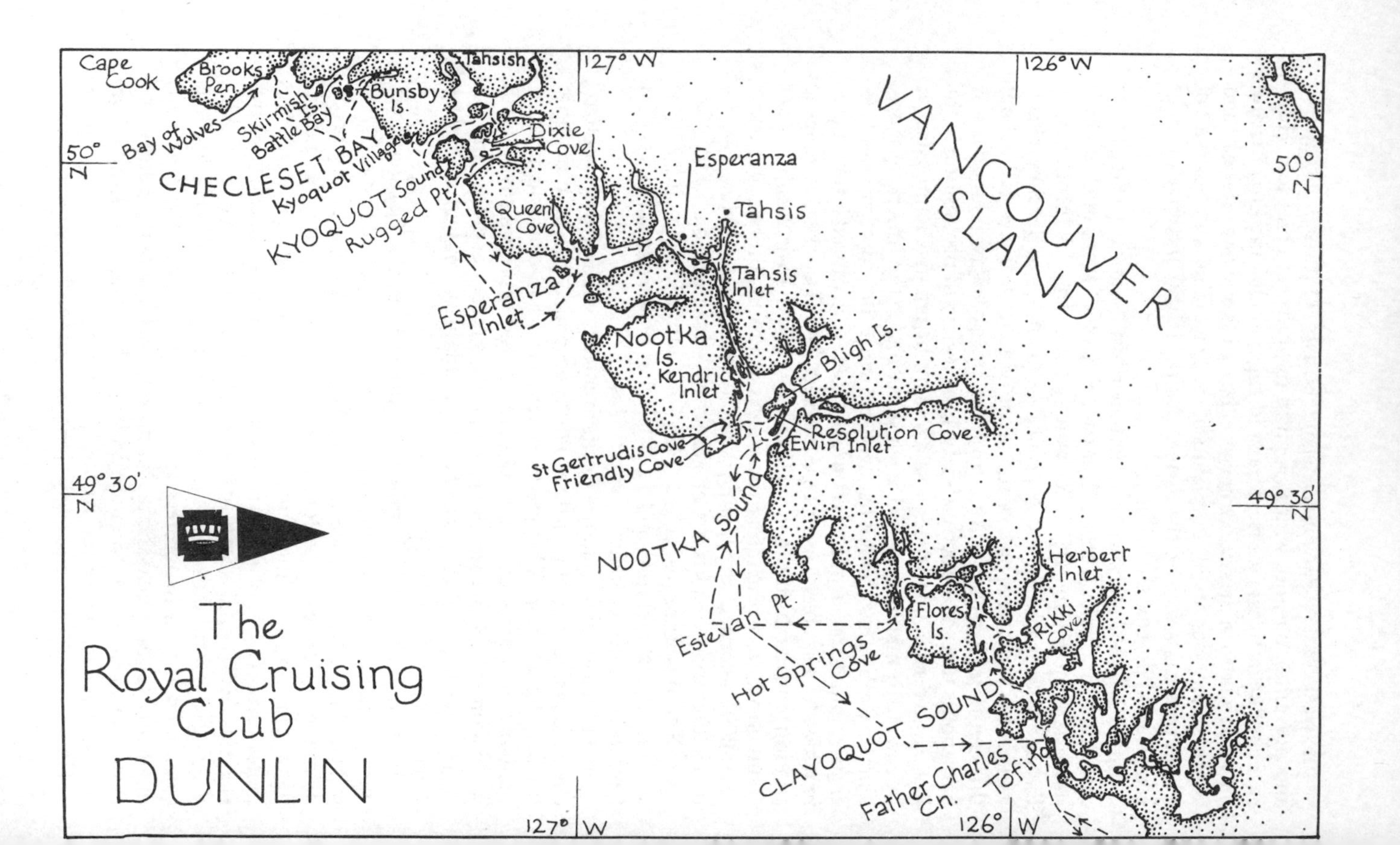

Cape Cook
Brooks Pen.
Bay of Wolves
Skirmish Is.
Battle Bay
Bunsby Is.
Tahsish
50° N
CHECLESET BAY
Kyoquot Village
Dixie Cove
KYOQUOT Sound
Rugged Pt.
Queen Cove
127° W
Esperanza
Tahsis
Esperanza Inlet
Tahsis Inlet
Nootka Is.
Kendric Inlet
Bligh Is.
Resolution Cove
Ewin Inlet
St Gertrudis Cove
Friendly Cove
126° W
VANCOUVER ISLAND
49° 30' N
NOOTKA Sound
Estevan Pt.
Hot Springs Cove
Flores Is.
Herbert Inlet
Rikki Cove
CLAYOQUOT SOUND
Father Charles Ch.
Tofino
127° W
126° W
The Royal Cruising Club
DUNLIN

towards Barkley Sound. There was a light south-westerly wind for a while, which induced Freddie to unwind the new jib and motor sail. There was a heavy overcast, at times some drizzle and a big south-westerly swell. By noon we were off Cape Beale, at the south-westerly extremity of Barkley Sound. The Sound is roughly square, about fifteen miles across in each direction and is said to contain 550 islands and islets. It is popular with family parties because of some excellent beaches, warm swimming and so many islands to explore. Over the intercom it was decided that, as we seemed to be making good time, we should push on to Ucluelet.

Alongside the government floats at Ucluelet at 1600. On trying the starter, it was found to have made a spontaneous recovery. And furthermore it behaved admirably for the rest of the cruise. The surprise of the day came as we were having a stroll through the village after supper. Familiar music attracted us to the fire hall. On looking through the half-open door we were surprised to find a lot of hot, hairy-looking people in blue jeans dancing four eightsome reels.

June 22. The day was spent in and about Ucluelet getting food, cheese for me, fuel for Freddie, making use of the laundromat and trying to find a couple of friends who lived there. It was a long hot walk to and round the old seaplane base, now a fish processing plant. Because of his time in the R.A.F. during the Second World War, this was of particular interest to Freddie and called forth many comments.

June 23. Cast off at 0610 and left in sunshine and calm. At 0845, having rounded Amphitrite Point in company with many fish boats heading for the banks, we found a complete calm with a long smooth swell. 1015 – enough breeze to warrant sailing in a gentle sort of way. 1205 – down sail and motor on before entering the narrows and its swirling tide just short of Tofino, which we visited for about an hour. It has an interesting little museum.

Time at 1345 – this was the southern part of Clayoquot Sound where there is much mud and shoal water. The channels are narrow and twisty, but well buoyed. It was the vagaries of the tide which made this area one of considerable interest from the navigational point of view.

The first of several Indian fishing villages was Opitsaht, just across the sound from Tofino. It was mentioned by many of the early traders and was involved in the massacre of a ship's company.

At 1705 – after sailing for a couple of hours we entered the narrow channel which shortly opened out into the landlocked lagoon of Rikki Cove. It was pleasantly peaceful, the only sounds being bird song, the distant rumble of logging trucks and occasional blasting for the construction of a logging road across the bare, rocky slopes of the Catface Range a mile or more across the sound.

June 24. Again it was calm and clear as we set off for Hot Springs Cove. It was another run along narrow channels, and for miles along the southwestern shore hereabouts one can see the old (I should think very old) telephone line which appears mostly to be fastened to trees. It seems to run from the village of Marktosis to Riley Cove where there is the remains of quite a large plant, possibly a cannery, with extensive concrete foundations. A U-turn round Sharp Point and there was Hot Springs Cove. We secured to the government floats and after an early lunch were soon on our way to the hot spring, which is about a mile back towards Sharp Point.

There used to be quite a large Indian village here, but it was badly swept by a tidal wave some fifteen years ago and was moved to higher ground further up the inlet. However, there is still a good trail from the site of the old village to the hot spring. Very soon after the steaming water issues from a cleft in the rock it is led into an enamel tub. Why, I cannot think. The water is far, far too hot to get into at this level. However if one descends to one of the several pools below, where the spring water mixes with the sea, a suitable temperature can be found.

Later the coast guard vessel *Racer* made fast to the outer side of our float. The unusually large crew resulted from the 'Opportunities for Youth' programme of that summer. Many of them were university students.

Sunday 25 June. There was some delay in leaving due to a nearby fish boat which spewed large greasy flakes of soot from his galley chimney over several boats, including ours. It took a lot of scrubbing to get rid of the mess.

A few miles to the west lay Estevan Point. It is one of the major promontories along the coast which deflect the northwest-flowing current sufficiently to produce a dirty sea with an opposing wind. However there was no problem on this occasion. On approaching Nootka Sound the wind gradually backed so that on entering the sound it was nearly a dead run. This is the only ship anchorage on this coast which has an entrance not encumbered with rocks and islands. Because of its distinctive, mountainous background it is easy to recognise. All the early navigators made use of it. There is an excellent sketch of this in the old admiralty charts, but unfortunately these sketches are no longer shown, which I think is a great pity.

The anchor went down in the middle of Friendly Cove for lunch and discussion. Some six or eight shacks, a church and a sort of hall were scattered about in the bushes. Most of the windows seemed to be missing. From the shack nearest the fine crescent beach the garbled sounds of taped rock music blared at us. A lighthouse stood on our left on San Rafael Island which is largely responsible for the protection found in the cove. On the two extremities of the island are commemorative plaques, one for Cook and one for Vancouver. Some three years ago I had sailed to this place to see these, but was not allowed to go ashore because I was not an Indian and the plaques were said to be on Indian land. Being alone I did not argue the point. This time the small craft float had been removed from the government wharf and there was no place to land except on obvious Indian property. The B.C. Government had asked the tribe to take part in the Cook bicentennial celebrations. After discussion they said they would have nothing to do with it.

On leaving what was thereafter known as 'Unfriendly Cove' we made for Resolution Cove where Cook's two ships, *Resolution* and *Discovery* lay for about a month for a re-fit after their passage from Hawaii. The nearly circular cove was surprisingly small, the depth seemed to be nowhere less than ten fathoms, and the bottom rocky. The shores were steep and thickly forested with the trees coming down almost to the water's edge.

It was necessary to back-track for about a mile and we then made our way up Ewin Inlet, in Bligh Island, parts of which were very narrow. However it opened out into a pool at its end, and once we had identified the several reefs shown on a not very large scale chart, it afforded us excellent anchorage.

June 26. Under way by 0810. Hereabouts there is a fine flurry of Spanish names: Pantoja I., the Saavedra Is., Boca del Inferno, a lagoon with a rocky slot of an entrance, Santa Gertrudis Cove, recently proclaimed a 'marine park', Santiago Mt. a little further along, and then the robust English name of Blow Hole Bay – and I bet it is!

The nearest fuel seemed to be at Tahsis, a logging town twenty miles up Tahsis Inlet. As we proceeded, it appeared to be buzzing with activity with planes going over every few minutes and a great many outboard boats going flat out.

In the year 1792 Vancouver and Quadra and a number of officers were rowed up this inlet all the way from Friendly Cove to be entertained by Maquinna, chief of the Nootkans, at his winter village of Tahsis. It had been previously agreed that Quadra would take the eatables and Vancouver the drinkables. They all seemed to have enjoyed themselves, including Maquinna.

The Nootkans were one of the few tribes to hunt whales with canoes. These were dugout canoes made from a single red cedar log, L.O.A. thirty-five to forty feet and beam about five feet. The eight-man crews were hand picked and had to go through a period of rigorous training, which seems to have had religious overtones. Several canoes would be in on the hunt. One of the objectives was to make a kill as near the home beach as possible so as to avoid an exhausting tow after a long hard chase. These were probably the grey whale which travelled along the coast in considerable numbers during spring and autumn.

This being a Monday no fuel was available at Tahsis. However we had better luck at Esperanza, some six miles away. There has been a mission there for many years, but now, besides the mission hall, there are only a couple of houses, several large fuel tanks and a government wharf. The incumbent at the mission was a young Englishman who apparently raced dinghies with no little success in the Solent, but how successful he had been at the mission he did not say.

Some fifteen tortuous miles further, on nearing the mouth of Esperanza Inlet to the north of Nootka Island, we turned off into Queen Cove, a snug and picturesque anchorage. About dark, three Japanese fishing boats came in. One anchored near us and with military precision the other two went alongside to port and starboard and made fast. They all fed on one boat, and it seemed as if in no time at all, one anchor light was flicked on and they had all turned in.

June 27. The Japanese boats left at crack of dawn. It was another clear, calm day with heavy dew. A few wispy clouds made 'necklaces' for the higher tops, and it was distinctly chilly in the shadow of the mountains.

Off, at 0805, under power for Middle Reef Buoy. The entrance to this inlet is about eight miles wide, but it is thickly studded with rocks and reefs, and except for fishermen there is only one safe passage and that none too wide. This day there was a very steep swell, and it was not long before there were a couple of crashes down below – particularly when the cutlery tray got loose and landed on the cabin sole. There was a general low haze, and a very large sun dog.

Rounded Kyuquot Entrance Buoy at 1155. Occasionally on top of a swell Cape Cook became visible away to the north west, at the western extremity of the Brookes Peninsula.

At 1245, the anchor went down in the little cove immediately beyond Rugged Point, where there is a fine sandy beach. The log notes: 'My last act of foolishness, after picking up the cutlery and tidying up the mess, was to upset a bowl of soup at the foot of the companion steps.'

A weather forecast came through, telling of a Pacific disturbance which would bring strong N.W. winds, with fog. There was still no wind so we motored along Nicolaye Channel towards the village of Kyuquot, the last half mile of which is really quite tricky, but fortunately well marked. The village is scattered over parts of three islands, the houses all facing a central basin. On the west side of the anchorage are a government wharf and a number of private floats. At the head of the wharf is a general store, new since my last visit. It is no longer run by Indians, and has a surprisingly good stock of necessities.

Indian boys were enjoying themselves by holding onto a large hook at the end of a hoist on the wharf and letting go when swinging out over the water. There were hoots of derision when anyone made a bad shot. It was noticeable here that all the Indians were much more friendly and forthcoming than in some other places. When we went for a walk later they each greeted us on passing. One elderly Indian was so incensed when his dog barked at us that he gave it what I thought was an unnecessarily severe beating. My feeling was that at 'Unfriendly Cove' they might well have encouraged the dog to bite.

I commented to the elderly owners on the origin of the name of their boat, *Loch Ryan*. I think it was probably pulled out of a hat, but we were later given a salmon which was much too large for two people who did not have any refrigeration. They would not think of cutting it in two.

June 28. It blew quite hard during the night. We got part of a weather forecast, which did not sound very encouraging. We therefore spent the day exploring the central part of Kyuquot Sound, radiating from which are several fjords. There was an astonishing amount of logging going on, and in three landlocked pools where we hoped to anchor, we found log booms stretching virtually from shore to shore. We eventually made our way into Dixie Cove which was surrounded by low hills and uncut trees. Although it blew fairly hard at times, the rest of the forecast did not seem to apply to us.

June 29. In a leisurely manner we worked our way back to Kyuquot village by a different route but just as full of obstructions. There was a long delay while *Tringa* lay at the fuel dock awaiting her turn and quite a queue developed. The store opened in the late afternoon, and we got there while there was still a good choice of fresh supplies.

June 30. Cast off at 0715 for the Bunsby Islands. A pleasant looking morning and a rising barometer. Having got through the islands of Kyuquot village we turned to starboard towards the north channel. Some five miles further, a black buoy to port and a red buoy one and a half miles to the north gave us a clear run through the Barrier Islands to the southeast point of the Bunsby Islands. On the chart this area looks almost impassable, but the above two buoys clarify the whole picture.

It might seem that too much of our time was spent rock and reef dodging, but in fact we felt this was necessary in that sea otters like this sort of scenery even if we prefer something different. Roughly, one can say that there are three Bunsby islands lying side by side with two channels between them which, without stretching the truth too greatly, could be called navigable. We got through both of them unscathed.

Anchored, at 0930, off a clam shell beach, which is often a sign of an Indian midden. After lunch we went ashore and found this to be the case. The twenty-foot bank above the beach was full of clam shells and occasional pieces of charcoal. The area above had been logged off some years ago and the second growth was quite young and small. It was full of flowers, including foxgloves between the huge tree trunks which had been left lying about by the loggers. Deer sign was everywhere as well as evidence of bear. There was much bird song. An eagle was whistling somewhere but we could not see it. The ridge above the beach was high enough to be a good vantage-point for looking round.

The rest of the day and part of the next morning were spent nosing about these islands. We saw a number of seals and a deer swam across between two islands just ahead of us.

There seemed to be at least two uncharted rocks, and much kelp – but still no sea otters.

July 1. About 1030, we left from north of the Bunsby Islands on a westerly course. It was interesting to speculate as to what went on amongst the Skirmish Islands and in Battle Bay. We had lunch behind an un-named island off an un-named peninsula. It would have been a pleasant anchorage, but our intended destination was a small cove under Jackobson Point on the southeast side of the rugged Brookes Peninsula. It had been recommended to me as a good anchorage, an added attraction apparently being that friends of my informant had lost their dog to wolves there. Thus, as it was not named, we spoke of it as the Bay of Wolves. Three and a half hours under power took us across the remainder of Checkleset Bay. On entering the Bay of Wolves there were three proper-looking mooring floats, with a pretty looking black cutter of about thirty-five feet made fast to one of them. The owners with their dog came back at high speed in an inflatable, at about supper time. It was so hot that for the second time Freddie spread his cockpit awning, which was affectionately known as 'Regina Africanus'.

Sunday 2 July. Before leaving at 0915 Freddie went off in his inflatable and found a very nice beach with a stream, and wished we had time to do some exploring. However, our time was getting short and we felt we should turn south.

Crossing Checkleset Bay we cut through a corner of the Barrier Islands and made for the black buoy south of the Bunsby Islands, and then followed the outward track past Kyuquot and along Nicolaye Channel. However this time instead of going outside past the south-eastern part of the Barrier Islands, we cut into the channel which lies inshore of them. This is regularly used by supply vessels and fish-packers which have to go this way in winter, since it provides something over ten miles of good protection. There was little if any wind but quite a big swell which caused much motion off the entrance to Esperanza Inlet. By 2000 we were at anchor in Queen Cove once more.

On July 3, at 0745. Up anchor and off for Nootka Sound or beyond. As I had a bit of an upset stomach, Freddie agreed to go by the smoother but somewhat longer route via Esperanza and Tahsis Inlets. Again there was almost no wind so once more we stopped at Esperanza for fuel. This time there was a second bearded young man (assistant missionary?) who worked the fuel pump. Indeed I am sure the one in charge was glad of help. There were twenty very active and noisy children there for a weekend holiday from Tahsis.

A mile or so further along I saw a bald eagle swooping down at what looked like an immature gull on the water. The third time the eagle made no mistake, and carried off his lunch to the top of his favourite tree.

As we progressed down the straight and narrow Tahsis Inlet a head wind gradually came in. As we entered the very narrow channel into Kendrick Bay, where we had considered putting in for the night, we were hit by a blast that would not have shamed Blow Hole Bay. The whole anchorage seemed to have been taken over for logging and we passed on.

Over the intercom Freddie suggested having a look at Santa Gertrudis Bay, though the coast pilot said it was 'encumbered with rocks'. In the event it was found to be full of rocks in its northern part, but seemed quite possible elsewhere. There were already three power boats there but they left a couple of hours after our arrival. A certain amount of swell was finding its way into the cove, so after supper we separated and each hung on his own anchor.

July 4, at 0655. The anchor came up with sticky mud. I went on ahead to get out into the open in time for the 0725 weather forecast . . . and drew a complete blank.

Outside Nootka Sound there was a low southwesterly swell, clouds down on the tops and a light southwesterly breeze. Two or three times *Tringa* tested the wind with the 'Yo-yo', but later gave it up. We stayed well clear of Estevan Point and its shoals. On reaching the islands west of Tofino, we cut through by Father Charles Channel and apart from the tide made an easy approach. As soon as we were tied up Freddie went off to phone home. I was duty cook and reported home later. A R.V.Y.C. boat was tied up nearby. They came and paid us a visit later on, and told us about their recent cruise to the South Pacific.

July 5. We were surprised to get an early weather forecast, and it was a good one. There followed a few chores to be done such as visits to the laundromat, the grocer and the baker, who was closed. But Freddie found a shower.

Away under power at 1140, but when we got through the narrows a breeze began to come in from the S.W. So up sail and off motor. The wind picked up a little later, and we were able to ease sheets until eventually the wind was coming over the starboard quarter. We were encouraged by meeting three U.S. boats and two Canadian sailing north and apparently trying hard each to outdo the others. We might well have continued to Bamfield, but elected to turn in round Amphitrite Point for Ucluelet before it became chock-a-block with the fishing fleet when it came in for the beginning of its four-day lay-off.

July 6. There was light fog when we woke, and weather report mentioned 'fog with zero visibility' at various places along the coast. It was decided to get out of Ucluelet Inlet and see how it looked. There was fog to seaward, but it did not look too bad to the east. So we took a swing through the inner islands where visibility was quite reasonable.

By 1630 we were alongside the government floats at Bamfield and walked along the board walk, a logical method of dealing with the excessive winter rains in those parts. We caught up with the news at Gwyer's store and used the phone to report progress and E.T.A. From a large fish boat lying close to us at the floats we acquired a fresh caught salmon – unfortunately after we had supped.

July 7. 0650 – overcast, with light variable wind and light patchy fog. 0800 – rounded Cape Beale, by which time the fog or low cloud seemed to be concentrated over the land. There was quite a heavy swell and it was interesting to pass near a troller with his stabilizers hung out, and observe how well they were working.

At 1245 we were passing Carmanah light; Freddie reported us to be well ahead of our timetable, and averaging over five and a half knots. 1320 – off Bonilla Point, where the bottom shoaled somewhat and became irregular, the swell suddenly became much steeper. Off here also there were literally hundreds of shearwaters which seemed to take off in large coveys.

1420 – approaching Port Renfrew. On our regular 'sked' we discussed the question of proceeding direct to Becher Bay, the next reasonable anchorage. The logistics officer, who was using a tiller master and, in spite of the corkscrew motion, could well spare the time for this sort of thing, reported back to say that we ought to get there before dark – so on we went. There was still little wind, but over the hills to port the leading edge of a bank of low clouds (or fog) was keeping pace with us. I thought it looked rather forbidding.

1615 – a forecast came through from Sheringham Point, a few miles ahead, to the effect that a westerly of fifteen to twenty knots should be expected soon. Although we did not hear about it till a couple of days after we got home, this was soon changed to a gale warning, which we found was no understatement.

Wind at 1820, from the west rapidly increased off Otter Point, about seven miles short of Becher Bay. *Tringa* made use of her 'Yo-yo' which with ease was progressively reduced to a very small size, but I was lazy and continued under power. As Robert Allen so aptly put it: 'It is more work without an engine single-handed I can tell you!'

2000 – rounded Beechey Head to enter Becher Bay. The wind now came off the land in furious gusts which I estimated to be fifty knots. It was confirmed by a nearby weather station. Rounding up into the wind I dropped the kedge, a twenty-five pound CQR, on reaching four and a half to five fathoms off the marina and well into the bay. *Tringa* followed suit with her thirty-five pound CQR nearby and eventually let out nearly fifty fathoms. It soon became evident that we were both sliding off down wind. Freddie spotted several deadheads to leeward, and this immediately produced a situation of some urgency. I for one rapidly found that it was quite impossible to retrieve the anchor without a long hard struggle. Over the intercom I said I was going to buoy and slip the anchor warp and try again behind Wolfe Island, about half a mile further up the bay. After a period of brisk activity, having slipped and cleared the deadheads, my thirty-five pound CQR was ready with its six fathoms of heavy chain and most of its fifty fathoms of nylon warp free to veer. The anchor dug in at once and held where the chart showed an encouraging 'M'. *Tringa* soon came alongside. Here we much appreciated a degree of protection from the wind, which did not ease until well into the small hours.

As a result of all this, *Dunlin*'s anchor can now be recovered with the use of a cockpit sheet winch, which is conveniently near both tiller and engine controls.

One of *Tringa*'s problems was that, as a result of furling her new 'Yo-yo' with such a weight of wind in it and therefore on the furling line as well, this line was all used up – i.e. there was none left on the drum – before the sail was fully furled. This also is now rectified.

July 8. Soon after dawn Freddie and I both went off in *Tringa* to recover our gear, hoping that the sports fishermen would not be attracted by our buoys (fenders) before we got to them. Our mission accomplished, we returned to a well-earned breakfast.

The remaining eighteen miles to Victoria were enlivened by having to make our way against the ebb through Race Passage. This lies between Race Rocks and Bentinck Island, the site of the old leper station. At one time a number of lepers were kept there in isolation, most of them, I believe, coming from amongst the imported Chinese labourers. Beyond that point, it was uncomplicated except for a good many stray logs, and islands of floating kelp.

At 1230 we rounded the breakwater and entered the Royal Victoria Yacht Club. We had not seen a single sea otter, but we had much enjoyed the search.

At 1300, having got straightened away I walked round to the visitors' dock and was happy to pay my respects to Eric and Susan Hiscock. They had arrived two days previously from New Zealand.

TRINGA AND *DUNLIN*

TABLE OF DISTANCES

Date			Distance made good	Time under way h. m.	Engine time h. m.
June	20	R. Vic. Y. C. – Port Renfrew	58	11 50	same
	21	To Ucluelet	56	9 45	same
	23	To Rikki Cove, Herbert Inlet	43	8 05	6 20
	24	To Hot Springs Cove	20	3 45	same
	25	To Ewin Inlet, Nootka Sound	40	10 05	5 45
	26	To Queen Cove, Esperanza Inlet	44	8 35	same
	27	To Kyuquot Village	30	5 45	same
	28	To Dixie Cove, Kyuquot Sd.	17	4 10	3 15

	29	To Kyuquot Village	15	4 10	3 00
	30	To Bunsby Is., Checkleset Bay	17	4 35	same
July	1	To Bay of Wolves, Checkleset Bay	18	5 40	4 35
	2	To Queen Cove	42	8 30	same
	3	To Santa Gertrudis Cove, Nootka Sd.	31	6 55	same
	4	To Tofino	36	11 30	same
	5	To Ucluelet	27	6 00	4 20
	6	To Bamfield	25	5 25	same
	7	To Becher Bay	79	13 35	same
	8	To R. Victoria Y. C.	18	3 30	same

THE WATERWAYS OF EUROPE
Bluebird of Thorne

by Robin Riverdale

One of *Bluebird*'s original design objectives had been the ability to traverse the inland waterways of Europe. This was about the only thing I had never done in her. Now in 1978, Howard Hilton and his brother planned a circuit of about 2,000 miles from Lymington to Le Havre, Paris, Le Marne and French canals, the Moselle, the Rhine, Holland, Belgium and back to Lymington. Would Christian and I join him for three weeks? Would we not! I have said before that Howard is a kindly and perceptive man. So in August, we stepped aboard and settled in at Kons on the River Saar.

In beautiful weather we meandered down the Moselle, a lovely river, with clean, friendly towns and villages. There were flowers everywhere, and all the famous vineyards. Yes, we **did** experiment! So to Koblenz and we turned upstream. What a change, but yes, *Bluebird* could stem the Rhine, though progress would be slow. Better, we said, to take a tow if penetrating any great distance up-stream. Down the raging Rhine, fantastic traffic, near Duisberg a huge inland port handling millions of tons, we counted over thirty large vessels under way and immediately in sight. The bridge at Nijmegan, the Dutch border, Arnhem and wartime memories, the mighty Maas, slower currents, pastoral scenes, and delta land all made from the deposits of the great rivers. Belgium, the Albert canal, the Meuse, Liege, the Sambre, Charleroi, and then the fantastic barge lift taking 1,500 ton barges in a tank for over a mile up and down 300 feet. As we descended taking photographs, I thought of the ultimate contrast. *Bluebird* with no rig, festooned with tyres, sitting in a rolling tank in Europe. Flick back a switch in the mind to the same *Bluebird* fighting for her life in force 10 in the reefs of Tuamotus in the middle of the Pacific. Could it be the same craft? Yes it could. Nothing goes amiss to her, and she did this job admirably well. The Gardner engine, now fifteen years old, never missed a beat, and as economical as ever.

So to Brussels, and when Christian and I stepped ashore on September 1, my seventy-seventh birthday, it was dull, and a cold wind from the North Sea brought vague drizzle. I felt sad. There was a fear in my mind that I might never handle her again. Howard in his turn, compelled by logic and circumstances, might sell her. Never mind. There are new challenges. With the experience gained, I came home with a design and specification for a European yacht all sharpened up in the mind.

JOLIE BRISE TO NORWAY

Racing with the Tall Ships

by Robin Bryer

My mother used to go backwards and forwards on the Gosport ferry just to see her at her mooring. I was brought up to associate her name as epitomising everything that is beautiful, fast, comfortable and seaworthy under sail. And yet I had never seen her, nor yet a photograph of her. She sailed a mythical sea, it seemed, wafted by those halcyon airs which brought her to victory in the first Fastnet race of 1924 and the Bermuda race of 1932. Her name – *Jolie Brise*.

And now I am writing this aboard that self same Le Havre pilot cutter on a brilliant October morning off the Purbeck shore. I am with the boys of my old school, Dauntsey's, and we are sailing her to her winter quarters at the Exeter Maritime Museum.

Her first active season in English waters after a Portuguese sojourn of thirty-two years has been fun, and it has been fun which I was fortunate to share.

After bottom-scrubbing hops in the Channel, *Jolie Brise* came to that miraculous marina at Brighton and there I joined her. At 0900 on August 3 we were one mile south of Roedean School and that evening lazed our way into Boulogne. *Moules marinières* the next day and by evening we were reaching down to Cap Gris Nez, a sail which seemed to justify the legend. Her long boom end skimmed the waves as she made her powerful way.

Bill Parish was the 'Daddy' of the ship and his flute-playing niece our cook. At Woolverstone on the Orwell it was her family who entertained all fifteen of us and joined us to sail coastwise to Great Yarmouth.

We were running that day, the 6 August. Lying in the bowsprit net watching her spread wings and powerful straight forefoot between my toes, I experienced another classic aspect of this great cutter.

We had torrential thunderstorms as we made Yarmouth. The pursuing brig *Marquese* appeared and re-appeared in the squalls with all the drama of a Cotman seascape.

Yarmouth was almost as full of sail training vessels as it once was with the herring fleet.

August 9 showed *JB* in one of her less admirable but understandable aspects. In 1934 she was given an engine as a twenty-first birthday present, something she has never really responded to. The 9th was the morning of the start of the S.T.A. race to Oslo and we could not leave harbour because we could not turn her under-motor, let alone make up against the flood tide. We scrubbed decks, watched others go and waited for the ebb.

Never a racing man, I found crossing the line three hours late was far pleasanter than the general fuss, jostle, bad temper and ill feeling which usually accompanies the racing scene.

At midnight we slid through some of the fleet of Smith's Knowll and sailed into a grey day of head winds and gas rigs in the ill-named Placid Field. We sailed close to one rig, happily christened *Captain Salt*, towering above us and the Dutch schooner *Sleidrecht*, one of only two other sails we saw that day.

The next day was greyer still. I had to cook my own breakfast.

But the day after was a blessed reach along the Jutland shore in pursuit of the ketch *Rona*, with Ian Procter – bully of the rugger set during my days at school – calmly sitting at his sewing machine on the foredeck mending the ravages of our two day's windward beat. Ian had viewed with equanimity 'his' Esse cooker being extinguished when we had stowed the topsail on the chimney the night before, which just goes to show that sailing makes us all more philosophical and forgiving.

The joy of *Jolie Brise* on long days at sea like these is that 117 feet of broad-capped bulwark gives everyone somewhere to sit and chat, or shelter and snooze, or they can walk round her deck, breasting the slope to her bow to run down the other side to the sweep of her counter behind.

That night we sailed anti-clockwise round the Skaggerack, with the light broad-reaching wind which the old girl really loves. This was Bill Parish's trump card. He decided on the longer route to benefit from the northward current. The direct route to Oslo fjord would risk a foul current, disastrous if the night fell calm.

And so it was that the next day, Sunday 13 August, we crossed the finishing line with the bulk of the fleet bearing down on us from the west. It was a perfect sail at sunset up the fjord.

They tell me we came second – but then that had nothing to do with us and certainly not with me. Tradition has it that *Jolie Brise* has never raced without being placed. Certainly at sixty-five it is too late to change the habit of a lifetime.

But to hell with racing. It is kindliness and looks which count, which endeared her to my mother when they were both girls – and which I think has made them both wear so well.

TAU
The Largest Twin-keel Yacht in all the World

by Robin Riverdale

This may remind you of Gracie Fields and her aspidistra, but I sing the praises of *Tau* ('My Friend' in Fijian). On a voyage in *Bluebird* in 1967, I met Colin Philp in Fiji, and for a week I worked with him on the design of a large twin-keel yacht. After much correspondence and a heroic struggle, I saw her hull complete in 1970. The outline statistics are 90 feet L.O.A., 75 feet L.W.L., beam 17 feet 6 inches., draft 7 feet, quite a light displacement, twin keels, twin rudders, Gardner 6L3B engine 150 hp., Hundested propeller, a Schooner with equal masts and a working sail area of about 2,000 sq. ft. She afterwards became a Staysail Schooner. I had originally urged Colin to make her seventy feet overall.

Now in 1978, we were sailing with him in *Tau* from Fiji. There had been two hurricanes that season. In one of them, *Tau* had dragged, wiped a tree and a rock off a cliff, and lost her backstay, but suffered no other damage. We started in bad weather. Could it develop into another hurricane? It seemed prudent to stay within the Kandavu Reef area until the danger had passed. We were not a strong team, Colin, Christian and I had 209 years between us, a splendid Fijian mate, another Fijian handyman, but not much of a seamen, and a cook, complete with Colin' son John, just nine years old. We fished, we swam, we explored the reefs, enjoyed the sun, talked and sang and played. An idyllic existence.

How did *Tau* behave? Just like a very large Bluebird. She wriggled in and out of reefs and passages and coral anchorages with incredible agility. I remembered that my nephew, John Hope, had made a passage in her under sail at fourteen knots, but to be safe in Pacific squalls, the huge sails needed manpower, so we were usually under genoa, staysail and mizzen at eight to twelve knots, and often with the incredible Gardner ticking over, slow, silent and wonderfully economical. In the huge seas and swells, she pitched and rolled more than I had expected at her size, but remained beautifully balanced, and she coped well under all conditions. A large deck shelter aft had rather spoilt her looks, but was a very practical answer when she was used with a number of charterers.

What more can I say? Would that I could own and run such a yacht in the Pacific, but for me seventy feet would be enough. Thank you, Colin. Thank you, *Tau*. Wonderful memories.

MUCKLE FLUGGA AND BACK

The Round Britain Race 1978

by Martin Read
with help from Jock Macleod, Philip Greig, John Russell, Richard Clifford, Mike Richie, Jeremy Hurlbat

Every four years, an ever-increasing number of volunteers from every walk of life and profession – boat builders, accountants, sailors, doctors, solicitors, pen-pushers various and others, all with that quiet air of determined resourcefulness – put to sea to further the development of sailing. They are dedicated and unselfish. Leaving the security of their homes they converge on Plymouth to set sail, disregarding advice and shipping forecasts, to continue pounding through headseas for remote objectives in spite of sheltered friendly harbours at hand.

However, even this rare breed are known to falter in their task. For almost all, at some remote corner of our British waters, the realisation slowly dawns that they are, in fact, foolish and misguided. This opinion normally evolves after beating to windward for an extended period in a confused sea in near-freezing conditions, soaked to the skin and having eaten nothing but 'Mars Bars' for the last forty-eight hours, with only a sodden sleeping-bag as refuge – on the rare occasions one is able to get anywhere near it.

If this didn't do the trick, Poseidon has a host of other options to play. Using a combination of calms, headwinds, rain, sleet and, of course, the unexpected cold green goffer, having just removed one's oilskins, a firm and unerring conviction slowly manifests itself that quite positively this is the last time.

Why is it then, that we are already thinking about the next Round Britain Race?

The Race this year was for all of us most frustrating. A series of calms and a succession of head winds made it much longer than normal although it did result in the fleet remaining far more compact. This year, out of seventy-four starters, the R.C.C. was represented by eight boats. Mike Richie sailing on *Gipsy Moth*, John Russell with *Haigri* and Philip Greig with *R.F.D.* were all competing for the first time, joining the growing number of two- and three-timers.

We all, of course, have our own reasons for doing the race but all agree it has its own definite character and is fun. It provides not just the excuse but a competitive challenge to sail round Great Britain, which due to the distance and conditions requires careful planning and preparation, and needs to be undertaken in a proper, seamanlike manner. Completing the course is satisfying; rounding Muckle Flugga and heading south gives one a sense of exhilaration and relief similar, I'm sure, to the way one would feel rounding the Horn – though no doubt on a much more lowly level!

We have a week prior to the start at Plymouth, when all boats are assessed, checked and cleared as being seaworthy and having all the necessary safety equipment. This week and the four other compulsory stops of forty-eight hours each produce the time and opportunity for old friends to be re-met and new friendships forged. Common experiences are shared and recounted, followed by a further leg to battle with your chosen rival and recoup for the next round of parties.

The hospitality is always generous to the extreme; each port has its own character. Jock McLeod, sailing in the Race for the second time in *Ron Glas*, has summarised the course as follows: 'The course is clockwise round the British Isles starting and finishing at Plymouth, and leaving all to starboard except Rockall and the Channel Isles. It is about 2,000 miles and is divided into five 'legs'. At the end of each leg there is a specified finishing/starting line which we time ourselves across and have to spend forty-eight hours in port. These stops are a significant factor in the enjoyment of the Race.

'The first leg, to Crosshaven, Eire, is the shortest and the fleet remains relatively bunched. This puts a considerable strain on our hosts, the Royal Cork Yacht Club, and their mooring facilities, but their new Marina allowed all but the largest boats to lie alongside, several boats deep at the peak time, and step ashore to enjoy the facilities of the Club or step across to join the many impromptu parties.

'The second leg, to Castlebay, Barra, spreads out the fleet and the density of yachts at each port gets less and less while the period of activity for our hosts get longer and longer.

'Castlebay is the only typical "cruising" anchorage on the Race where we all have to lie to our own anchor. It is a magnificent scenic anchorage in fine weather but is exposed to the wind and can mean dragging anchors and other anxieties when bad. The focal point is the small Castlebay Hotel (with a large bar!) and the technical facilities are provided by Mr. McNeil, the lifeboat mechanic, who operates a ferry service for competitors unwilling to use their dinghies, and undertakes many other tasks as well.

'The third stop, Lerwick, is just over half-way round the course and is remarkable for the exceptional hospitality extended to the competitors. The small but very hospitable Lerwick Boating Club makes us very welcome and each boat is adopted by a member's family who provide baths, undertake laundry work and cope with lists of requirements. The harbour has been extended and reorganised as a result of the oil activities and we were all able to lie alongside in sheltered basins clear of the wash from shipping.

'The fourth leg is the only leg where the rhumb-line course is a straight line to the next stop, at Lowestoft, where the Royal Norfolk and Suffolk Yacht Club have the daunting task of providing a welcoming service for almost a fortnight to greet the extended fleet. The final approach close to the coast allows the Coastguards to spot most yachts and alert the Club, who provide two launch crews on 24-hour watch to offer a tow for those who require it and a pilot vessel to guide us in. The strong tides and heavy overfalls that sometimes exist can make the entrance tricky and this service is a great help.

'Most yachts were able to lie alongside in the yacht basin directly in front of the Club house with its excellent catering facilities and willingness to remain open to greet finishers at all hours. Unfortunately the oil spill from a tanker wreck had polluted the basin and in spite of valiant efforts by the Club to provide cleaning teams and detergent, many boats had to leave with oily topsides to be cleaned at Plymouth.

'The final leg down channel returned us to the finishing line off the Royal Western Yacht Club of England, our organisers and hosts before the start and when we finished.'

'Competitive events provide the main impetus for refinements in design and techniques irrespective of the sport or requirement. The Round Britain Race has as one of its main objectives 'to encourage the development of suitable boats, gear, supplies and techniques for efficient short-handed cruising'. It is therefore entirely relevant to cruising, providing the test bed for new ideas and systems.

All of us got round in one piece, though style varied substantially. Robin Knox-Johnson, driving *Great Britain II* designed for a racing crew of 18, down to a minimum comfort capsule such as *R.F.D.*, a thirty-foot trimaran with myself and Philip Greig, both to be seen off Dungeness for several hours locked together during one of the many calms. After all, it would have been most uncivil not to accept invitation to dinner. Jock McLeod in *Ron Glas*, I understand, did have to put on his oilskins and remove his bedroom slippers on one occasion and I learn that John Russell in *Haigri* is running a close second in the comfort ratings, maintaining his eight hour's sleep per day without trouble. Jeremy Hurlbat, sailing a new thirty-two foot racing machine was reduced to wearing oilskins inside as well as on deck. I hear that the most efficient piece of go-fast equipment was a bottle of scotch and measure permanently secured to the chart table bulkhead. Proves he must be a cruising man at heart.

Michael Pipe, sailing for the third time in *Slithy Tove*, but without the Pipe special twenty-two foot spinnaker pole, Richard Clifford with *Robertsons Golly* and Michael Richie in *Gypsy Moth IV* completed the R.C.C. Fleet.

The sailing highlights are as varied as the sea and coastline that exist around the British Isles. The comic antics of the greedy puffin to the graceful precision of the gannet; the looming mystique of St. Kilda and the bare coast of East Anglia; blistering calms, thunder squalls and the surge of tide rips round Muckle Flugga. This year, the unexpected bonus was the dolphin. Several large schools were sighted; ten stayed with us for half an hour as we had a northerly force 6 on the nose. There were, however, no illusions of being a long way further south!

We felt that rather than have a succession of logs covering the Race from each member's boat, which, though no doubt in their own right witty, edifying, and awe-inspiring, may be regarded as being repetitive. We have therefore tried to highlight only those aspects of the Race which were felt to be relevant either to our own enjoyment or worthy of note as a 'lesson learnt'. Attached to this article are two annexes covering safety and navigation. John Russell has recorded some valuable notes on safety relevant to their race and Mike Richie has commented on various aspects of navigation, which indicate some of the hazards but also point out several failings of our coastal system.

Victualling for the race is very similar to normal coastal cruising, where one expects passages in the region of five days. Emergency stores should, of course, always be carried in the event of a misfortune. For those weight watchers, without multiple burners, grills and ovens, unless one is content on a diet of 'Marmite' and 'Mars Bars' the problem becomes slightly more taxing. Necessity being the mother of invention, various solutions emerged. Philip decided on black pudding, hot, cold or taken with strawberry jam. Robin relied on a staple diet of Welsh rarebit (the grill was the only thing that worked) and I grew partial to the combination sandwich of Marmite, cheese and strawberry jam – three courses in one without any washing up! Apart from that, our most successful culinary creation was a porridge, chicken soup and tuna fish mix which we strongly recommend in times of great need. Fortunately, we were never down wind of Jeremy, who maintained his diet of roast beef and Yorkshire pudding throughout the race.

One of the great assets of the Round Britain Race, and of credit to the organisers, the Royal Western Yacht Club, is that it is alive. It promotes questions and confronts convention. Sponsorship for instance. It is here to stay, and indeed should be welcomed, providing further facilities and resources. But how can it be integrated into sailing events without damaging or jeopardising the traditional sporting attitude which we all value so much?

Is there a handicap system that could accommodate yachts of such varied design and concept to race against each other, or is one necessary? Are the personal incentives enough; the challenge of the elements, navigation and mutual wagers? How should the formal prize facilities be dispersed?

To what degree should one permit electronic aids for navigation, weather forecasting and handling? Drake never had them, but then he didn't have some of the problems we now have, or is it loading the odds up against the non-sponsored entrant?

The Round Britain Race has faced the challenge of change over the last twelve years, and has evolved into a classic. We have no doubt that with the continued guidance and proper direction of the Royal Western Yacht Club, with we hope a little help from ourselves, it will continue to 'encourage the development of suitable boats, gear, supplies and techniques for efficient short-handed cruising' for many years to come.

* * * *

Annex I – Safety. John Russell – *Haigri*

All but a minute proportion of accidents happen because someone made a mistake, failed to foresee a possibility, to take precautions, to study and rehearse, to judge correctly and act effectively. The risks of short-handed racing are much the same as those that have to be thought about when cruising, but the extra pressure of racing requires a corresponding increase in attention to the health and well-being of the crew.

Living and working conditions were, as might be expected, most favourable in the modern pure cruising boats like *Haigri*, whose crew report that the only strain they experienced was caused by the frustration of prolonged calms and light variables, and most punishing in the more extreme racing craft and some of the multi-hulls whose crews were subjected to acute discomfort. There is scope for much improvement in cockpit design with more attention to ergonomics and less lofty disregard of the fact that for most of the time the thing is leaping up and down at an angle of twenty-five degrees. The demands of a good dockpit are contradictory; it must give a good all-round view, yet it must shelter the crew; it must enable people both to work and rest without having to adopt strained postures (inferring that alternative postures must be possible since any posture becomes strained if maintained for long); winches for short-handed sailing need placing where the operator can see the results of his efforts; and communication between cockpit and cabin should always be possible.

A vital factor in preserving crew efficiency is having a good watch-keeping system and sticking to it. A good system is one that serves the crew; if the crew have to serve the system then it is not good. When short-handed there is a justifiable tendency for the system to get bent from time-to-time, so it must be flexible. This flexibility is a feature of the system used aboard *Binkie* in the 1970 race and described by Mike McMullen in that year's *Journal*, and which we decided to try out on the first leg. The essentials of this system are the division of the greater part of the day into two long watches which allow the opportunity of the best part of five hour's kip, and the inclusion of overlap periods of from one to three hours' duration when both are on watch; night watches are sensibly limited to three hours. We made two changes to suit our own inclinations for the subsequent legs: (1.) we shortened the evening overlap from three to two hours and introduced a one-hour overlap into the middle-of-the-night watches where a snack and chat is useful; (2.) we reversed the cooking duties so that these were done by the person next to be relieved as he was hungrier, colder and less in need of fresh air than his mate who had just turned out of his bunk.

Thanks to an effective watch-keeping system and *Haigri*'s extreme ease of handling, we did not suffer undue tiredness, though there is no denying that we were both less alert towards the end of a watch. We slept well in canvas root-berths which we found better than the foam-cushioned bunks. Bunks allow the motion of the boat to roll one around so that one is always braced to some extent, but a well-designed root-berth makes it possible to relax completely. Cooking was for us and no doubt for many others the most wearisome task, though my wife Joanna eased the load tremendously by her thoughtful victualling, accurate and comprehensive stowage plan, and book of recipes arranged according to the sea state. We have a sort of safety belt to stop the operator flying about, but in rough going the only answer is a seat capable of holding him securely while leaving both hands free. Besides reducing the extent to which he becomes tired and infuriated, having the use of both hands for the job reduces the risk of injury. We followed our usual precaution of wearing oilskins and deck-boots while cooking.

Having only one man on deck calls for additional precautions against two common hazards – falling overboard, and colliding. We wore harnesses all the time we were on deck for the obvious reason and also for the peace of mind of the man below. Lookout is difficult for a lone watch-keeper with many calls on his attention, but it is still top priority. I nearly hit an enormous ship which had appeared to be crossing at right-angles about a mile ahead so that I judged it safe to go below to rouse Dan and put on a kettle. It wasn't, because she stopped and was right athwart our bows when I came on deck again.

We once had to start the engine while lying becalmed in hazy weather off the Fastnet with a ship approaching head-on, but she turned aside at the precise moment that I decided it was now up to us and reached for the gear lever. Becalmed again eighty miles N.W. of Eagle Island, by night this time, a small ship showing both sidelights and a single, steaming light came straight towards us from the east; I made 'D's by lamp until she showed a single sidelight; she closed to 100 yards, circled, and made off to the south, which suggests that she had been aware of our presence before I had seen her. Dan reported several incidents involving fishermen whose movements are always difficult to predict until you are close enough to see what they are doing; a few of them altered course to produce a collision hazard at close quarters out of an apparently safe situation, and we learnt to be wary when making sail changes if they were about.

Whilst we unquestionably learnt a great deal about sailing the boat, and enjoyed the race enormously, it was uneventful and produced no new insights into the subject of safety. We endorse every one of Mike McMullen's 'Lessons' in his excellent account of the 1970 race, adding only that as it now seems suicidal for a yacht to expect a larger vessel to honour her obligations under the International Regulations for the Prevention of Collision at Sea, she should assume that she has not been seen until the other vessel makes it clear by her actions that she has done so; much more use could be made of Rule 34(d) if there were the means of making sufficiently powerful signals.

* * * *

Annex II – Navigation. Mike Richie

The course demands a substantial wardrobe of charts even though only a proportion of them is likely to be used. To some extent this is due to the Hydrographer's inflexible policy of leaving detail – of lights, soundings, etc., off small-scale charts. The days of hydrographic affluence are no doubt over and the cloth must now be cut according to the measure, but the modern, say, 1:750,000 series does seem extraordinarily uninformative.

The best planning chart is the small-scale of the British Isles on which the various legs can be laid off; it can then serve as a track chart if that should be thought useful. The charts of the west coasts only go out to about 11–12°W. and it is not difficult to run off them by taking a long board to the Westward. It scarcely seems necessary to carry a chart of the North Atlantic against this eventuality and one simple solution is to use Mercator's sailing using a pocket calculator; there are, of course, others.

Navigationally the course is fascinating because it demands the whole range of navigational skills – deep-sea, coastal and pilotage; it also involves navigating in three very different types of sea, the Channel, the Atlantic and the North Sea. The coasts round Britain are well-lit and the d.f. coverage good. Some boats never achieve a satisfactory d.f. calibration curve and then it is a question of assessing the reliability of the bearings on each occasion, which is not to say that the aid serves no purpose. Rounding unlit islands such as Flannan and Sula Sgeir by night can be demanding but the hours of darkness are few in those latitudes and one's reckoning would have to be fairly coarse to miss seeing them. Fog would be another matter. For most people no doubt, astro proved the principal aid – certainly on the long leg down from Shetland to Lowestoft.

For some, at least, Lowestoft proved the most difficult landfall with thick fog, little wind and strong tides. The shifting sand in the approaches, too, this year precluded an approach from the eastward. Barra had been more hospitable although at least one yacht had been so deceived by the scale of the islands as to navigate seven miles further out than he need have done. Approaching Lerwick from the North has its difficulties. 'It is imprudent', says the Pilot, 'to navigate among our skerries by night or in poor visibility', as one can well believe, but there is little alternative making for Noss Island from the northward and those happen to be the conditions. The prudent mariner would no doubt give the island a decent berth and wait until he had picked up Kirkabister Ness light before turning north-west up the sound to Lerwick. However, the coast is steep-to and the less cautious will surely have relied on sighting the Head before the crunch: some, indeed, sighted it on both sides! It seems strange that the limited arc of visibility of Kirkabister light should nowhere be referred to on the chart or in the Pilot.

Shipping becomes the major preoccupation from Lowestoft across the Thames Estuary and down Channel, and how best to negotiate the Dover Strait traffic separation scheme in the light of the ambiguous and ill-thought out Rule 10 of the Collision Regulations. Most who were on the wind will no doubt have sought merely not to enter the opposing stream of traffic.

* * * *

Annex III – R.C.C. Entries. 1978 Round Britain Race

R.F.D – Martin Read, Philip Greig
Slithy Tove – Michael Pipe
Great Britain II – Robin Knox-Johnston
Attila – Jeremy Hurlbat
Robertsons Golly – Richard Clifford
Gipsy Moth IV – Mike Richie
Haigri – John Russell
Ron Glas – Jock McLeod

GIVE A DOG A BAD NAME
The Falkland Islands

by Ewen Southby-Tailyour

The only chart to cover the area discussed is 1354A. The Admiralty Pilot for South America (Part II) should always be consulted. The Argentinian Chart is H-410 and if this is the only one to hand I have included (on their first mention) the Spanish names where these appear on this chart.

Three hundred and fifty miles east-north-east of Cape Horn, in one of the windiest corners of the world, lies the archipelago of the Falkland Islands. It stretches for nearly 150 miles west to east and eighty miles north to south. The group is made up of two main islands surrounded by well over 200 smaller islands most of which are uninhabited. This gives a total coastline of about 10–15,000 miles of sandy beaches, towering cliffs, fjords, narrow passages, sheltered harbours and 'bolt-holes'.

There are no yachtsman's facilities; the weather and tides are dramatic and largely unpredictable; there are no navigational aids except the lighthouse at the entrance to Stanley Harbour on the east coast; the waters are poorly charted and in places totally unsurveyed (although there is a hydrographic programme under way) and the charts show the last resting places of many fine ships not all of whom were sailing vessels with primitive instruments and equipment. In short, the islands have a bad reputation among seamen which I humbly believe they do not deserve. Yachtsmen regard the islands as a convenient place to lick their wounds as expeditiously as possible before hurrying north for the more enjoyable climate of the lower latitudes.

I certainly would not encourage anyone to sail the 7,000 miles from England just to visit the Falklands, but I would seriously advise anyone with the adventurous spirit (in all true cruising men it must be present in those who have sailed this far) to take a more thorough look at the beauty, solitude and challenge that lies beyond the Stanley waterfront.

Westerly winds dominate the weather as the depressions track through the Drake Passage. The average yearly windspeed is about sixteen knots (Plymouth is four!) and the temperature about 43°F. There are a surprising number of calm periods, often in the early morning and, contrary to popular belief some of the worst gales are in the southern summer. It usually snows at some time in every month of the year.

How I came to be in a position to spend a good part of my one year's tour, commanding the small Royal Marines garrison, actually at sea compiling a 'Yachtsman's Guide' to the islands had best be left untold for the moment. Having been prevented by a shortage of time and money from shipping out my 24-foot sloop *Black Velvet* I was determined to recoup my loss in some nautical manner. Under command I am fortunate to have an 140-ton motor vessel skippered and crewed by local men with great experience of the waters. I realised early on that to cover all the 'bolt-holes', anchorages and passages in a year I would have to steam – literally – and so the MV *Forrest* is proving to be the ideal vessel. Sad though it is to admit it, she gives me a greater chance of achieving my aim than would have been possible using *Black Velvet*.

Yachtsmen have probably been reluctant to sail these waters without local knowledge, for the unpredictability of the weather means that a yacht would have to nip from one safe anchorage to another, and to plan for this, these 'bolt-holes' would need to be known in advance. Currently this information is not to hand. The compiling of this knowledge is my ambition for the year. Of course, sailing instructions alone will not entice a yachtsman unless coupled with some extra 'carrot' such as those ingredients which, to my mind, make up the ideal cruising ground – isolation, a navigational challenge, wildlife, self-sufficiency from the sea and beaches and dramatic scenery. In other words, everything that is available in the Falklands.

Let me show you what I mean by giving a very brief outline of one October day in which we covered only ninety miles but which contained all I personally seek when cruising. (Albeit under power – but at least flying the R.C.C. burgee).

We had made Port Pattisson, the settlement harbour of Carcass Island (I. del Rosario), the night before and repaired ashore for dinner with the only family on the 4,500-acre island. The visitors' book in the house bears testament to the increasing importance of this wildlife sanctuary. It contains entries by such eminent people as Prince Bernhard of the Netherlands and Sir Peter Scott. Sir Peter Scott had followed his signature with a lovely sketch of a male protected kelp goose saying to his mate as a rare Antarctic cruise ship steams into the settlement harbour: 'Isn't it amazing how they find their way back to the same place year after year!'

On the morning in question, before dawn, I took the rubber boat away to seek out an alternative anchorage at the eastern end of the harbour for southerly and easterly blows. I was well rewarded after an hour of soundings and bearings with an excellent position two cables off the southern end of the east beach, in two fathoms of water over a clear sandy bottom. I also discovered that the water to the north and east of Beechams Island was clear despite kelp patches.

The golden rule with kelp is to avoid it at all times. It is probably the single most important factor in safe navigation amongst the islands for it grows along the edges of almost all the passages and over almost all rocks. It is better than any buoy system once the basic rules are understood. It can also act as an efficient breakwater for there are many beaches and coves which are guarded by kelp across their entrances through which it is possible to sail in search of a peaceful anchorage. However, it 'runs under' in strong tides and thus its 'absence' can not always be taken as a guarantee of safety. A little practice is all that is needed to understand how to use kelp to one's advantage.

We sailed shortly after dawn into a fresh north-westerly breeze (warmer than usual) out of a clear ice-blue sky. The barometer was high and steady (and the Magellanic oyster-catchers had not been calling – thus no rain!). Our first destination of the day was the inner Jasons (South, I. Pan de Azúcar and Elephant) which are part of a chain of islands stretching for forty miles out into the South Atlantic from the north-west corner of the Falkland group. They are uninhabited and guarded by some of the fiercest tides in the region. The Admiralty Pilot warns the casual visitor off the islands for very good reasons. In 1969 the last visit to check on the fur seal population was made. The Falkland Island Government (and I) was now anxious to see if the mass exodus reported earlier this year was true. We were hoping to see upwards of 14,000 and if not, our suspicions of unlawful sealing would rise. We saw only twelve, and although this is worrying there could be a natural reason for their absence. If they are not back by the time of my next visit in the new year our worries could, sadly, be well founded.

The passage west along the northern edge of the Gibraltar Reef (which should be made with the last half of the ebb) is straightforward providing a careful check on one's position is kept, for the tides run directly across the reef at up to ten knots. This part of the Falklands is renowned for its landmarks which are all dramatic in their individual ways (unlike the east coast which is low and largely featureless) and which makes fixing reasonably easy. I spent some time taking horizontal angles with the sextant in preparation for a more comprehensive study in the new year and came to the conclusion that the Gibraltar Reef extends a good two miles further than charted. Later on, off the north-east coast of Elephant Jason, further observations were to reveal more examples of the chart being at variance with nature.

The Jasons are the graveyard of many ships but, in common with most of the islands, they do offer a wide range of survival 'aids' as compensation. The tussock grass covering most of the smaller islands is a spiney-leaved plant which grows in great profusion to a height of some eight feet, providing excellent cover from the wind. Its roots, when skinned and boiled taste like horse chestnuts.

The stories of shipwreck and survival on the Jasons are still told with much gusto around the peat fires of the western settlements, and the one that interests me most, and which is absolutely true, concerns the 1,200-ton Belgian barque the *Leopard*, with a crew of twenty under Captain Couzeman. At 0500 on the 12 April 1858 she went ashore on the north coast of Grand Jason (I. Los Salvajes) in thick weather. The story has it that one crew member was perched on the very outer end of the jib-boom when she ran up the steeply shelving beach. The crewman was flung rather unceremonially into the tussock. He stood up just in time to see his ship slide back into the murk to sink instantly with all remaining hands. He lived for eighteen months before being discovered in a rather deranged state.

To survive should not be too difficult – indeed a great supplement to sound yachts' rations can be found around the shores. There are mussels and clams everywhere at all seasons. In the summer months the rivers are teeming with mullet, trout and smelt. There are plenty of crabs and krill. Squid can be caught occasionally in rock pools near the beaches. Those hills which are not tussock-covered support what is almost the national plant of the islands – diddle-dee. This is a heather-like plant with bright red berries that can be fermented into a delicious wine, turned into jam or eaten raw if necessary. The diddle-dee branches are always dry enough to burn for signalling or heat. Before the present island-wide radio network, which is used as a telephone system for medical problems or hot gossip, diddle-dee fires arranged in certain ways spelt different messages to watchers on neighbouring islands.

A sweeter berry than the diddle-dee is the tea berry which grows close to the ground amongst the diddle-dee. It is a pink and white berry, larger than the diddle-dee and very good to eat. Where the geese feed on the beaches is the most likely place to find the 'sea lettuce', a light-coloured seaweed which when boiled is, I am assured, delicious. Survival purposes only as far as I am concerned.

Penguin, goose, shag and albatross eggs are found from September to December along many of the cliffs and beaches; these breeding grounds are a sure sign of fresh water. There are no dangerous animals, reptiles or insects although the seals should be treated with caution in the breeding season. It is safest to approach the elephant and leopard seal from the front (despite their teeth) as they have the remarkable ability for such large animals more at home under water, to flip over backwards onto an unwary animal or human who would naturally consider an approach at the 'stern' to be wisest. Be warned, for they often lie in wait in the tussock.

The smaller tussock islands are the cause of an illusion common to visitors for, from a distance, they resemble the palm-covered islands of the Caribbean in 'texture' and colour. But, unlike the palm, the tussock grows to only eight or so feet thus giving the island an appearance of being further away than it really is. After 6,000 miles' sailing around the islands I am still being caught out by this potentially dangerous problem.

The bolas is a hunting device still used in the settlements for catching the edible upland goose and is the easiest weapon a ship-wreck survivor can make. In addition, there are many rabbits and hares to supplement the diet. Wild celery, rhubarb and mushrooms grow in abundance, particularly on the sites of deserted settlements.

There is no watch kept on Channel 16 or 2182 (except on the mainland of South America). A yacht would be advised to use 4.5 Mhz in emergencies for every settlement has its set permanently switched on to this frequency. Each settlement has a government-controlled medical box; the doctors in Stanley conduct a 'surgery' over the air every day at 1000 for an hour and the Beaver float planes based in Stanley will fly back emergency cases at any time except at night.

Steaming between South and Elephant Jason was a wonderful sensation for the sea in the channel was absolutely flat and a deep, deep blue, broken only by the odd patch of kelp reaching up from nearly twenty fathoms. The passage edges are steep-to and so we took the opportunity of keeping within fifty feet of the south shore of Elephant Jason to look for the fur seal.

A fascinating sight was the way the bull elephant seal, each with his harem of eight or so wives, lies nestling in great hollows made by wriggling down into the sand or shingle. When settled they look for all the world like dismasted hulks of old wooden yachts lying in a mud berth up an East Anglian creek.

As always, the birds provide the greatest fascination and command the largest part of one's attention. Here is a potted list of the birds seen in this short voyage of ninety miles:

One wandering albatross. The largest and most graceful of the species. His thousands of friends had already departed for the breeding grounds in the Antarctic.

Dozens of black-browed albatross. Feeding in the most repulsive manner on huge jellyfish caught in the tide eddies; often eating so much that they were incapable of flight without regurgitation. Breeds on these western islands.

Thousands of great petrels, known to the islanders as the 'stinker' and, after the gulls, the most common of Falkland Island sea-birds.

Kelp gulls. The most common gull not unlike the herring gull in behaviour. One of its habits is to drop mussels and clams repeatedly from twenty or thirty feet until the poor bi-valve gives in and is eaten.

Dolphin gulls. An attractive grey-headed bird with bright red beak and legs.

The first of the great skuas back for the breeding season and ready to live off penguin eggs, in addition to young lambs.

Snowy sheathbills. The only sea-birds in the Antarctic without webbed feet. Known as the kelp pigeon.

Pink-breasted gulls. Correctly called the brown-hooded gull. The smallest and least common gull in the Falklands.

Diving petrels. Apparently often confused with the slender-billed prion which I have yet to see. (Or have I?)

The Falkland Islands flightless steamer ducks whose wings are too small for flight forcing them to progress across the water at great speed and with much spray in a rather idiotic fashion. I feel very sorry for them.

The beautiful silver-grey fulmars.

The cape petrel (my favourite bird to watch) known as the whale bird or cape pigeon. I find its black and white colouring most distinctive and attractive.

We returned to Westpoint Island (I. Remolinas), once known as Albatross Island, having given Flat Jason, North Fur Island and the Seal Rocks (Is. Los Llaves) a cursory inspection with the compass and sextant in preparation for the more thorough visit planned for January. Shortly before lunch we anchored in the settlement harbour having skirted the Cat Reef to the west of the entrance which is not as straightforward as the chart might suggest. The harbour itself is an excellent example of how kelp can be used as an aid to navigation, for the edges of the entrance are well marked at all stages of the tide. At night this is one of the few harbours that can be entered with safety for the kelp shows well with a good moon, and at dawn and dusk. In the half-light it shines with an unmistakable sheen.

Lunch was ashore with one of the two families looking after the 2,500 acres and as is usual for an island which is almost completely self-sufficient in the basics, the hospitality was much more overwhelming than that found in the settlements closer to civilisation. We left with a number of freshly-killed veal and mutton carcasses to see us through the remainder of our circumnavigation of the Falklands and to distribute amongst friends in Stanley. A month later and we would also be laden with gentoo penguin eggs – delicious but too fishy for my liking in any quantity – after a night ashore.

As Westpoint Harbour is notorious for its 'woolies' (known in the rest of the world as 'williwaws') I was anxious to seek out an alternative anchorage nearby in which to shelter from the westerly gales which produce these unpleasant local winds. The best place appeared from the chart to be somewhere in Hope Harbour to the east. At the head of this harbour is Death Cove into which flows one of the better mullet rivers. It is a shallow shelving beach very sheltered from the east and could be an alternative even in a westerly blow for although the wind would run straight in, it would at least be constant. However the best place of all is in Grave Cove beneath a gentoo colony in two fathoms over sand and mud. It is a very pleasant little 'bolt-hole' worthy of closer attention in the new year.

Wooley Gut passage took us south with the flood tide towards our final destination for the day – the rather grandly named Bense Harbour. I had heard that many years ago local sailing craft collecting the wool clip would use it for shelter from all quarters. The chart gives Wooley Gut a benign appearance but it is well named for although steep-to and, navigationally, an easy passage it should never be attempted in strong westerly winds by a sailing vessel.

As is often the case in these narrow passages (although by no means unusual in open water) we were joined by the most attractive and amusing animal I have come across in these waters – the puffing pig. His real name is *Cephalorhynchus commersonalii* (or Commerson's dolphin) and is found solely in the Falklands and the Straits of Magellan. I have been able to find only one very bad sketch of him and his friend the Peal's dolphin (*Legenorphynchus australis*) in an Argentinian tourist guide to Terra del Fuego so I have studied these mammals at some length and finally painted their picture which I hope is an accurate representation. Commerson's is about four foot in length with a rather more rounded dorsal fin whereas the Peal's is six foot and its fin is more scimitar-shaped. The Peal's dolphin is more graceful and sedate in its movements than the puffing pig and consequently much less fun to watch.

I was keen to visit Stevelly Bay in Port North (Puerto Norte) for I had heard that it is a natural depository for all manner of South Atlantic flotsam, making it a beachcomber's paradise. Some quirk of nature washes up masses of nautical rubbish; in the last year a frogman's flipper (the cause of a dramatic rumour in the Stanley pubs); an unnamed ship's lifeboat; a submarine's smoke float (more rumours) and two years ago the bodies of seven sperm whales (their bones still remain). The beach is also littered with the only tree trunks in the Islands; they drifted ashore from the South American mainland. Undoubtably this is a very pleasant anchorage but only in easterly or northerly winds. Incidentally, everywhere else in Port North is too deep making it advisable not to become embayed by a strong westerly.

Shortly before sunset we slipped around the eastern end of Little Bense, skirting the kelp and keeping the northern edge of Bense Island in line with the northern edge of Cliff Island. We anchored in three fathoms between the kelp patches about half a cable from the nearest point of Bense Island. As we poured the first of a number of glasses of Chilean whisky the puffing pigs continued to dive under the keel and around the cable, their white flanks touched with pink from one of the most colourful and peaceful sunsets I have seen.

Anywhere with names such as Cape Terrible (Pta. de los Desvelos), Deaths Head and Grave Cove and where so many of the isolated rocks are named after the ships they have claimed; where the weather is never really bad for long; where the likelihood of ever seeing another yacht is minimal; and where there are so many unvisited places to explore and so much wildlife to see and study, must be unique. Such a collection of islands with names straight from *Treasure Island* such as Wineglass Hill, Driftwood Passage, Stick-in-the-Mud Pass and Crouching Lion Rocks must be worth visiting for there is a story behind every one.

The weather is never bad – nor good – for long; the next day it blew a 60-knot blizzard from the south-west but by then we were tucked-up in New Island Harbour thirty miles away eating fillet steak followed by rhubarb crumble with fresh cream scooped out of a full three-gallon washing-up bowl followed by bottles of homemade black-currant rum – but that really is another side of Falkland Island life. I shall be sad to leave but will do so with the consolation of knowing that I will return under sail to finish my survey in the proper manner.

AN AVIATOR IN SQUARE RIG

by Lieutenant Frank Scott, Royal Navy: Cadet Member

The Prelude. In August this year I was lucky enough to skipper the 3-masted barque *Marques* in the Yarmouth-to-Oslo leg of the 1978 'Tall Ships Race'. The trip was not without its problems and surprises, as I should have expected, for my own involvement was pure chance.

Normally, I lead a very comfortable life as an Observer in the Fleet Air Arm and am currently serving in 826 Naval Air Squadron. It is a very pleasant, sheltered and professional way of life; one telephone call was to change all that. In late July, I was at home on weekend leave when my father received a telephone call from a chap called Erik Abranson, who runs an organisation called 'Mariners International'. It transpired that despite being let down by two charters they had managed, at short notice, to charter *Marques*. Their problem was that this charter did not include a skipper and they wanted my father or someone recommended by him. Unfortunately, nobody else with square rig command experience was available and my father had business commitments. Thus it was that I, with extensive square rig experience, and R.N. tickets finally passed the 'catch twenty-two' barrier and got a chance to command. In fact the deal was fairly complicated, because even with maximum time off from the Navy I could only join on 7 August, and the Race started on 9 August, so we arranged for Colin Faulkner (ex-Sailing Master of *Royalist*) to deliver the vessel to Great Yarmouth.

I knew nothing of the vessel, except that since she had just been out to South America and back, filming for the B.B.C., she was basically seaworthy. Furthermore, I knew nothing of the crew and my naval duties precluded me taking time off to sort out either problem. In fact the schedule was so tight that I was still flying on Sunday, with the race starting on the Wednesday.

The situation was obviously far from ideal. On the other hand I needed the experience of commanding such a vessel and the chance was too good to miss. I was cheered up by the attitude of my squadron mates who were totally unsurprised by the whole affair, they just thought I was mad. My arrival on board in Great Yarmouth however caused even me to have my doubts because I had a little surprise in store for me.

Great Yarmouth. August 7 to 9. I knew that the crew was to some extent 'mixed' but no one had warned me that that meant mixed nationality as well. Consequently, the tirade of French that greeted my arrival late Monday night was quite a shock to the system. Fortunately Colin Faulkner, who is an old friend, had some encouraging words to say at our brief handover, otherwise I doubt that I would have lasted the night!

The crew were really my biggest worry initially because no matter how well founded your ship, if your crew is rotten you have problems. Furthermore, as a Training Ship we were odd, because the crew were amateur, mixed and generally in their twenties, which is older than normal, all of which meant a different brand of leadership to the standard Sail Training Association Sea Cadet Corps style. This concerned me because all my Training Ship experience had been in professional Training Ships (all male) and even my recreational sailing, cruising/racing had been semi-professional, with all male crews.

Marques had a complement of twenty-three: 'mix one' was fourteen men to nine women; 'mix two' was twelve British, ten French and one German. Obvious problem areas were language and afterguard. The language problem was in fact the easiest to solve. Erik, who was mate, is bilingual and this combined with goodwill and my pigeon French usually won the day. In fact some of the French proved very good seamen, particularly two of the Bretons, Loic and Daniel who were by trade respectively, a physical training instructor, and a Parisian taxi-driver!

For the afterguard I had Erik Abranson as mate, and two of the permanent crew, Geoff Redpath and Dave Martin as engineer and bosun. Geoff and Dave were great characters and excellent practical seamen, although neither would have fitted the pukka R.N./Yotti mould. I was fortunate in having a small nucleus of three experienced square rig hands, all of whom had sailed together in *Phoenix* in the 1976 Trans-Atlantic races. These three were Brian Rice (a young ex-Army officer now trainee Naval architect), Doug Phelps (retired power station engineer) and Jenni Atkinson (PRO for British Airport Authority). Their overall experience varied, Brian had the most experience in sail – yacht-master's ticket, STA Schooners, *Captain Scott* – and I later appointed him mate, while Doug – the old man of the sea – had started as a stoker in corvettes during the war. The rest of the crew were unknown and unqualified so I had also to act as navigator and, to a large extent, mate.

Marques herself was a rugged old ship built in Spain sixty-six years ago as a trading schooner and recently converted to three-masted barque rig, and otherwise altered, to act as a replica of H.M.S. *Beagle* for the B.B.C.'s 'Darwin' documentary. She was neither fast nor showy, but she was proven. She was also 'twin screw' which was good news because square riggers are notoriously difficult to maneuvre under power owing to the windage of their large top hamper. The bad news was that the starboard propeller was missing. We attempted to rectify this using a diver but ran into problems and were unable to finish before the deadline for leaving for the start came up.

The Race Start. Wednesday 9 August. We still had one good engine and so rather than delay indefinitely, which would have been a bad blow to morale, I decided to press on. Great Yarmouth is semi-artificial and the tidal stream is notoriously strong. *Marques* was bows north, the exit was south and the stream was in full flood at departure time. 'Twin screw', I would have departed early at slack water; 'Single screw', I took a tug and went out stern first. This may not have been daring or glamorous, but as one other vessel found out, it was safer than trying to turn with inadequate power and maneuvrability.

When we slipped the tug outside the harbour I did at least feel that we had left some of our problems behind. In fact, as we motor-sailed out towards the cross-sands buoy I thought to myself that things could be worse. Too true, for just then Geoff came up on deck and asked me to shut down the port engine because the shaft was overheating.

The problem was that the stern gland had been spiral packed and the force of being pulled-out stern-first against a five-knot current had shifted the shaft back and jammed the packing solid. This left us with no engines, unable in the light airs to go either forward or back. 'Problem one' was solved by getting one of the spectator boats to tow us to the start line. 'Problem two' was less easy, and we arranged to *rendezvous* with the diver next day if we could not fix our problem and he would carry on re-fitting the port engine.

We dropped the tow a mile from the start, so that we could drift and disconnect the shaft without inconveniencing the other participants. We then set all plain sail, but with the absence of wind it was for show only. The much delayed start eventually occurred at 1500 and the committee boat left us to make our own start, and at 1629 we finally crept across the line.

Geoff and Dave were meanwhile toiling down below re-aligning the engine and re-packing the stern gland. Morale was obviously low so I ordered up a large bottle of whisky, tossed the cork over the side, and spliced the mainbrace. I don't know what it did for anyone else but it made me feel a lot better. In fact, as I recall I regaled the crew with ribald comments about the Crab (R.A.F.) Buccaneer that was performing some very tame low-flying round the fleet. The wind meanwhile continued to pick up until we were doing a steady three knots close-hauled to the port track. This created too much drag on the propeller for Geoff to be able to reconnect the shaft, so I backed the foremast and hove-to while he completed the task. At this stage (2000) *Jolie Brise* passed us, obviously totally bemused by our strange race tactics!

Conditions in the engine-room were far from ideal, but Geoff and Dave were not burdened by engineering degrees and used their farm management/chartered accountancy training to advantage. Geoff was, in fact, the ideal engineer for instead of making false promises he just gave the facts and said that he would give it a try. Fortunately his best was enough and after a struggle the port engine was once more operational.

This allowed us to square away and sail on, but towards nightfall the wind fell away again and we were forced to kedge. These light conditions persisted until about midnight when the wind came up sufficiently for us to sail out the anchor and round Smiths Knoll Light Vessel. This operation showed me how much we would all have benefitted from a pre-race work-up. Standards obviously improved during the voyage but the schedule was not flexible enough for me to work the crew – or myself – up to the standard that I would have liked.

The race itself was a pure speed-time-distance problem. If the wind was strong from the south-west, our incredibly low time correction factor would have guaranteed victory, provided we finished. If on the other hand we experienced northerlies, we would make little ground and there came a time when we would have to retire and motor in order to make the 'Parade of Sail'. Sponsorship required us to make this event and I calculated that five knots was a fair average under power and the deadline was when we could just make it at that speed. This was a depressing fact of life, but I had to bear it in mind from the start, since 'Mariners International' could not afford to let down their sponsors. I had arranged an up-to-date forecast from R.N.A.S. *Culdrose* on the morning of the start and their forecast of persistent light northerlies was to prove far more accurate than the shipping forecast.

Thursday 10 August. Thursday was the critical day and throughout I hoped against hope that something would come up. Effectively we were getting nowhere – and slowly too. For those of you who have never attempted to beat to windward in light airs in a square rigger, I should say that we made good about 090° on the port tack and when we wore ship that night we were then heading 275°! The only bright spots of the day for me were a very low pass by a Dutch *Atlantique* at midday and at nightfall exchanging passing honours with H.Neth.M.S. *De Ruyter* and *Friesland* who diverted to have a closer look at us.

Retirement. Friday 11 August to Saturday 12 August. I have never retired from a race before but it was obviously pointless to continue sailing up and down the same 'hole'. Consequently at 0120 on the Friday I reluctantly gave the order to start the engine and furl the square sails. The sea was still too heavy for the wind and under port engine and staysails we were pointing 025° and making good four to four-and-a-half knots. Even in these light airs the ship would not go dead to windward under power and we had to put in a short tack towards evening to get back on our rhumb line. Generally, in fact both the Friday and Saturday were very dull with the wind never above force 2 and the sea gradually dropping away. We did however take the opportunity of tidying up below and carrying out painting and general maintenance on deck.

The Calm before the Storm. Sunday 13 August. Sunday started a beautiful day, sunny and the wind backed sufficiently to set the squaresails. We scrubbed out down below and then at midday Erik conducted a bilingual church service. By this stage all hands had gained their sea legs and food consumption reached its peak. I should perhaps stress one advantage of having a partially French crew, namely, the high standard of food. Usually on such trips my stomach is assaulted by an uninterrupted diet of baked beans, corned beef and poor quality stew. On this trip, however, *la cuisine française* took over and with much the same basic ingredients they achieved minor miracles. We also, as a matter of course, had wine with every meal – I always knew that there was something in the *entente cordiale* business.

Meanwhile the mundane ship routine continued and about 1400 we sighted the west coast of Denmark. When we were about six miles off, I altered to parallel track until I obtained a good fix. The coastline is a bit featureless round there and after a couple of days of DR I needed an update. It is fortunate that as a professional navigator I live by DR because had I been one of those electronic amateurs, problems would have arisen. *Marques* navaids consisted of a Walker log, echo sounder (both very useful) plus radar and DF. It was these last two that could have created problems. The DF never provided better than class 'C' bearings – which are worse than useless – and the radar had such a poor signal to noise ratio that I could see land with the naked eye well before it painted on the tube. Such aids are very handy when they are operating correctly. I sometimes wonder, however, how many people use them without the knowledge or training necessary to operate them correctly or how to assess their efficiency.

Sunday evening started off very pleasantly with the wind freshening to force 4 and *Marques* doing a comfortable six knots. Since we were no longer racing I reduced to easy sail at nightfall and ran on under spanker, main topsail, main staysail, fore topgallant and topsail and forecourse and inner staysail. This was a fortunate decision because about 2100 it suddenly came on to blow. Geoff had the watch on deck and immediately clewed up the fore course and topgallant and shook me.

By the time I got on deck it was blowing a good 7–8 and the vessel was careering along at seven-and-a-half to eight knots. Stowing the fore topgallant was no problem, but the course required more people and I didn't want inexperienced people aloft in such conditions. I, therefore, shook the watch below and sent the more experienced among them – like Jenni Atkinson and Dave – up to help Geoff and Brian. The remainder I used to furl the spanker and inner jib and set the storm jib. Wind and sea continued to increase in very gusty conditions until I estimated the wind at force 9 and sea state 5–6. All in all I quite enjoyed it because *Marques* was ploughing along beautifully and in the right direction. It's only a pity that we didn't have that wind the whole way.

Marques rode the storm well, but she is an old wooden ship so we did have to rig the pumps to keep the water level down. Conditions down below were none too pleasant but Sally Clarke, a rather petite 'nice' young English girl surprised everyone by taking very firm charge down there. The only thing that worried me in fact was a Danish naval vessel that maintained steady course and eventually passed ahead at about a cable, which I considered rather too close in those conditions. All good things come to an end, however, and, as the sky lightened, the wind and sea went down gradually. By breakfast time the wind was down to force 3 and we needed the engines again to keep us up to schedule. It was really quite amazing how quickly weather can come and go in that area, at 0400 it was still force 7–8, by 1000 it was virtually flat calm.

Horten Anchorage. Monday 14 August. All Monday we motor-sailed along the south coast of Norway eventually entering Oslo fjord at 1830. We had no allocated berth in Horten and rather than try for a temporary berth alongside, I elected to anchor off among the other class 'A' ships. At 2215 we sighted *Gorch Fock* in the anchorage and for practice I carried out a proper blind pilotage anchorage using radar and echo sounder, eventually coming-to with port anchor in fifteen fathoms.

Parade of Sail. Tuesday 15 August. The main part of the voyage was now over but we still had the parade of sail to come. This event seems to have become part of the 'Tall Ships Scene', though this was my first personal experience. In good weather it would have been quite pleasant, but Tuesday 15 August saw the weather change for the worse with wind southerly force 4, rain showers and poor visibility. We maneuvred out of the anchorage by bracing the bare spars of the foremast to run around to port, and proceeded in line astern.

Oslo. Tuesday 15 August to Monday 21 August. The parade ended as we passed the Royal Yacht *Norge* and gave three cheers for King Olaf. Our problems did not end however, for we found ourselves a pariah again as we had no assigned berth in Oslo. Fortunately the Harbour Master was very helpful and found a berth which we took even though it was well away from the main body. The approach was downwind port-side-to, and worrying about damaging the bowsprit I went astern too early and the ship sheared to port as the wind caught the stern. We did not damage the *Marques* at all but I was glad to be out of the way of critical eyes as a tug helped us back alongside. As a first alongside it was not terribly auspicious, but at least, we had arrived and I could get some sleep!

Our berth really was out in the 'bundu', but fortunately we had a powerful ally in Mariners International's contacts with British Airways. They had planned a public relations party on board for the Thursday and so wanted a prime berth for the publicity. As expected they fixed a berth very quickly, but because of the poor weather we were unable to take it until Thursday. Our new berth was on the main quay inboard of the brigantine *Phoenix* (driven by my old friend Mike Wheeler) and I had my second attempt at putting *Marques* alongside. This was much more successful than before and *Phoenix* and ourselves were soon moored up together. Both vessels were traditional working craft and berthed alongside each other they made a nostalgic sight.

In the last few days before I left we shifted berth quite a lot, first going over to the marina near the *Framhaus* where the diver had clear water to operate. We shifted berth twice there, eventually ending up stern-to, having laboriously warped ourselves in. By this time I really was getting the knack of handling an underpowered square rigger with an offset propeller and on the final shift back to the main town executed a perfect alongside in *Gorch Fock*'s old berth.

In a way this summed up the trip, our time was almost up but only now had I and the crew gained the confidence and experience necessary to handle the ship correctly. The initial 'Tower of Babel' confusion was replaced by lots of *d'accord* and *entendu* and we were really working together as a crew.

Reflections and Conclusions. As a voyage our trip from Yarmouth to Oslo was nothing remarkable and yet it was surprisingly worthwhile. In some way we had failed, being forced to retire and use the engine to keep up to schedule, but we had also overcome more than our share of trials and tribulations *en route*. There was a whole crowd of 'young' people of all ages – our oldest was in his fifties – without the formal bonds of uniform and the Naval Discipline Act who had eventually become a proper ship's company. Some people are only too willing to adversely compare such outfits with the immaculate turn out of the professional Naval Sail Training Ships. If you read Jenni Atkinson's *A Girl in Square Rig*, however, you will realise that in many ways the true spirit of the races lies with organisations such as Mariners International, amateur, slightly untidy, and disorganised though they may be. I've been involved in both sides and can appreciate that although each has its merits, each has its shortcomings and they are really aiming in the same direction. Professionally the amateurs are far more demanding – and rewarding – and I really quite enjoyed my conversion to mixed sailing. They proved beyond all reasonable doubt that given the chance women are just as good – if not better – than any man. Few of the professional Sail Training people seem to agree, they tend to have a rather patronising attitude, but they will come round in time. Nelson may spin in his grave, but it will not be too long before we see a female square rigger captain!

I would like to end by thanking some of the many people who gave us assistance when we needed it. In Yarmouth, Captain Taylor, the Harbour Master, was wonderful, as was the diver and the tug skipper. While in Oslo, British Airways, the harbour authorities and the skippers of *Zenobbe Gramme* and *Phoenix* were unfailingly helpful.

The next race is to Leningrad (St. Petersburg) in 1980 which may create problems for professional servicemen, such as myself, still I hope to be there and to see my old friends, make some new ones and hopefully see another participant flying the Club burgee.

Regretfully the U.S.S.R. authorities have found it impossible to invite the International Sail Training fleet to Leningrad with the Olympic Regatta [Ed.].

CRUISE WITH A DIFFERENCE

by Basil Watson

When my wife Heather suggested that I should write an article about my 1978 cruise in *Hermione*, I was hesitant. *Hermione* has no sails, no amateurs in her crew. She carries many more offensive weapons than the average yacht. She is, of course, one of Her Majesty's Ships of the Leander class of frigate, and it is only because of the firm bond that exists between the R.N. and the R.C.C. – many of us belong or have belonged to both clubs – that I have dared to attempt to put pen to paper.

Since the withdrawal of a permanent Fleet from Far East waters in 1971 the concept of group-operating has evolved. By this process the R.N. is able to continue to show the flag far outside the N.A.T.O. area and self-supporting groups of ships deploy each year for six to eight months. Every opportunity is taken to exercise with other Navies and to visit Commonwealth countries and our remaining dependencies overseas. There is a benefit for recruiting too, because men join the Navy to see the sea, to visit those magic far away places and to return home with a box full of 'rabbits' and their 'knees brown for leave'.

Deployment Group 7 sailed from home ports in May. At the rendezvous south of Portland Bill we peered anxiously around, sizing each other up, counting heads. There was the helicopter cruiser-flagship *Blake*, frigates *Hermione*, *Leander*, *Juno* and *Ambuscade*, stores ship *Stromness* and fleet tanker *Tidespring*. Ahead somewhere, unseen, lurked the nuclear attack submarine *Conqueror*. The guided-missile destroyer *Birmingham* and tanker *Green Rover* were to join later. These were to be our companions for the seven-month voyage; a living, moving, working team of 2,500 men, made up of all sorts of surprising people including seven Chinese laundries, five doctors, three chaplains and a dentist.

A day later we arrived in Brest to prepare for joint exercises in the Bay of Biscay. Command of the French language varied from excellent towards the end of the evening receptions, to less than satisfactory at the formal briefings held at a more temperate hour. However, all went well and the group proceeded on a fair weather trans-Atlantic passage by way of the Azores.

In Bermuda *Hermione* lay in charming St. Georges, regularly visited by yachtsmen. Heather joined by air to take up the offer of a berth in the stores ship *Stromness*, and we attended a reception at the yacht club in Hamilton to mark the end of the Bermuda Race. We chatted to the Commodore and other officials of the Cruising Yacht Club of America who administer this 'deepwater classic'. *Hermione* then departed for Santo Domingo in the Dominican Republic, *Stromness* to Cartagena in Columbia, with both ships arriving at Colon on the same day for our first Panama Canal transit, an unforgettable experience. One marvels at the enormity of this engineering achievement which enabled man to divide continents and link oceans so many years ago.

We edged under the Bridge of the Americas and out into a calm and sparkling Pacific Ocean, alive with marine life, gorgeous sunsets and glittering nights. At latitude 25°N, as we entered the cold Californian current, the sea temperature dropped 10° overnight. We had left the Tropics. Soon the seal-adorned fairway buoy at San Diego was abeam and we were steaming into this vast U.S. Navy port for our assisted-maintenance period and shore training for exercises that lay ahead.

For Heather and I this was a period of relaxation: the unique magic of Disneyland, visits to Los Angeles, San Francisco and Mexico, Californian 'Hot Tubs' under the starlight sky. The time passed all too quickly and on 17 August *Hermione* slid to sea and Heather flew home. At the end of the month the ship was back in Long Beach, the port of Los Angeles. Hermione Baddeley was received on board and I caught a glimpse of the Marina del Rey with its capacity for 98,000 boats. Everything is 'King Size' in California, which, if independent, would be among the top ten richest nations of the world.

We headed north to British Columbia with its stunning scenery and snow-capped peaks. For those who do not know this incomparable cruising ground its one drawback is the four letter word – 'logs'. The foreshore and beaches are piled high with the 'beasts' and for every one safely ashore there is another bobbing about at sea. This is a real hazard to yachts of all sizes and night passages inshore should always be avoided. My Canadian friends tell me that the new method of transporting lumber in barges rather than by a chained tow will result in far fewer logs breaking adrift – good news indeed. A highlight in Canada was the fleet of R.N.S.A. yachts that met us on our entry into Vancouver, some of them 'cheering ship' as we passed. And so we reached our furthest point and turned for home by way of San Francisco and Acapulco. The one elegant, cosmopolitan, striking, go-getting America; the other charming, casual, unpredictable, enigmatic Mexico. Both magic names from schoolboy atlases, influenced but not yet entirely spoilt by the traumas of the modern world.

I write now from happy Barbados, where Heather has joined me again for a further glimpse of the sun. Ahead lie the final stages of the deployment, a major exercise in the Gulf of Mexico and home by way of the Bahamas. What shall I remember most from this memorable year?

Perhaps I should top my list with the enormous number of people I met everywhere who spoke with genuine affection for our country. Their generosity and warm-heartedness made our own offers of friendliness and hospitality seem inadequate and small. Other incidents spring to mind: beating around the bushes for my golf ball in Santo Domingo, helped by my caddy, numerous small boys and two armed bodyguards who were there to preserve my life (it seemed far more likely they'd end it at any moment); Heather and I clinging to a steeply descending cable car in San Francisco when the driver was wrestling with the controls, saying: 'This one ought to be in the god-damn museum – the brakes don't work!'; my lunch with the Mayor of Acapulco at the famous Las Brisas Hotel with two hours of back-slapping conversation and neither understanding a word the other said.

Yet despite the adventure, the climate and the fun, seven months is a long time away from home. *Hermione* spent the evening before arrival at Barbados in the lee of the island of St. Vincent enjoying a good old-fashioned ship's company sing-song on deck. Coming through loud and clear were those nostalgic songs which remind us of and beckon us home. The best place of all will be Guzz on 12 December and we won't mind at all if it rains!

NEAR-MISS

by Robert Franks

Anyone who does much voyaging in a small boat needs a fairy godmother. Some of these ladies have to work harder than others and of course sometimes one is 'absent from place of duty' and there is a crunch. For the last sixteen years, over about 28,000 miles of cruising, the lady looking after us in *Matawa* had a splendid record of devotion to duty. This year we had a situation in Bantry Bay which set me thinking of other situations in years gone by, and this article recalls some of these, tries to draw a lesson here and there for interest to others, and acknowledges the luck we've had.

Basil Payne and I bought *Matawa* in July 1962 and after a refit in the yard of her designer, F. Morgan Giles, and the Dartmouth regatta, the Franks family set out on its first cruise. We crossed the Channel successfully, navigated round the Minquiers and approached St. Malo with a rising wind from astern. Son Harry was at the tiller as we tore past the Jardin lighthouse with the lights just coming on – we were all keen to get in to shelter. As we approached the locks I started the engine in neutral.

'Right, Harry, I'll take her now. Stand by to get the sails down.'

I tried to put the tiller over to come into wind but something prevented me. I tried to put the engine astern – no effect. Nor ahead either. *Panique!*

'*A bas les voiles* and stand by the anchor.'

The jib came down but the mainsail stuck half-way with the halyard winch fouled up. But the boat slowly came to the wind and we let the anchor go, veered all the cable and it held. The halyard was then dealt with, the mainsail stowed, and I went over the side and discovered that the propeller shaft had detached from the engine coupling, come aft and jammed against the rudder. Luckily the rudder did jam, otherwise I suppose propeller and shaft might have come out altogether and water come in through the hole. We spent a disturbed night at anchor and in the morning towed into harbour where repairs were made. But I might mention that shaft trouble has dogged us for some years.

Fire Our fairy godmother's French duties were not done, for we had the beginnings of a fire two days later. Our galley stove was a two-burner primus with a pressure cylinder at the back. Supper was cooking with everything very hot when the washer round a burner disintegrated and paraffin squirted out and caught fire. We could not release the pressure through the flames and there was quite a flare-up. A blanket proved very effective in putting it out, but not before the French fire engine was on the way. After this we changed to a Calor gas cooker! I think it was the next year at Falmouth that we were close to a motor-yacht which had a petrol fire and burnt out very quickly. This was a very sobering experience indeed and I think everyone should see one of these to encourage them to take adequate fire precautions.

Navigation in Fog The next time I recall the fairy godmother being on serious duty it was a navigational matter and a near-miss indeed. We were going to Guernsey and decided to try Vale, the quarry harbour then recently opened. The approach from the north was therefore to the east coast of Guernsey. The weather turned thick but we got very good reception of Casquets and Roches Douvres on the Radio Direction Finder and, full of confidence, we stood on. I got an apparently good series of fixes and had son Tom to check me independently.

'No danger.' I told our somewhat uneasy crew.

'Isn't that land ahead?' was the next call.

'Can't be,' I replied. 'We should hear or see Platte Fougere on the starboard bow later.' But, by Jove, it was land, and about half a mile away with rocks everywhere. We stopped in our tracks and eventually discovered we were just east of Cobo Bay in the centre of the north coast of Guernsey. We had come between Les Grunes de L'ouest and Grand Saut Roche – one of the few clear passages into this coast with rocks generally extending some miles off the north coast. I forgot whether we were using the echo-sounder – I hope so – but I doubt if this should have warned us in this case. I still don't know what was wrong with the D. F. bearings but it shows that the third bearing is essential if fixes are to be relied on. I learnt this first at Dartmouth forty years before!

A Leak The next incident to be related was a crisis suffered by partner's son, Antony Payne, skippering a crew in a cross-channel voyage.

Matawa had recently had cockpit drains fitted and they consisted of flexible hoses from either side of the cockpit to a seacock down next to the engine.

Antony was having quite a rough passage back to Falmouth and it was discovered that there was a lot of water in the boat. The bilge pump was started but the level didn't reduce. Buckets were then resorted to, and to save carrying them up on deck, the water was thrown into the cockpit. Still the level rose and the leak could not be found. It was not until the fairy godmother suggested Antony should look under the cockpit floorboard that he discovered one of the cockpit drain hoses had been carried away by the spare Calor cylinder which we used to keep there; water was entering freely from the seacock and furthermore water pulled out by bucket and thrown in the cockpit was coming straight back. We found another stowage for the Calor!

Anchor Drag Like most voyagers we have dragged our trusty C.Q.R. on occasion. I remember once in very light weather in Alderney we were ashore and kind friends in a neighbouring yacht assisted our fairy godmother. Kelp was the reason I think, as it usually is. But the drag I remember best was at Omonville. The place was very crowded as usual and as the weather was set fair westerly, I chose an anchor berth rather close in under the breakwater to be clear of the other yachts. We had our supper on board and just as we finished there was a clap of thunder, buckets of rain and then – horrors – a sharp squall from the south. As I struggled on deck and my eyes became accustomed to the darkness I suddenly saw that our stern was only a few feet from the breakwater. Our engine has not always been noted for quick starting but on this occasion I pressed the starter, went into gear and clawed off with very little to spare. I thought our fairy godmother deserved an engineering degree. Relying on 'set fair' conditions is not an action to be recommended.

Forestay Failure This occasion was on the way to Madeira in 1973, on a rather grim evening of rising wind. We had fully reefed the main and set no. 2 jib and Bill Hasker, our Australian doctor, was on watch. I heard the cry 'Forestay's parted', followed by 'Fore halliard's parted'. A very bad moment! A bottle screw had failed due to metal fatigue and the halyard had pulled the welded fitting off the mast. Thankfully we had a second forestay but I have often wondered whether it came close to parting when the sudden strain came on it. Of the two forestays, the one with the sail on it of course takes all the weight. No doubt our fairy godmother was also on watch at this time. But I do think it is nice to have two forestays.

Overhead Wires Cruising inshore in Norway in 1976 we motored up a lovely wooded fjord, Strandfjorden, with friend Michael Douglas at the tiller while I 'navigated'. Suddenly Mike shouted 'Wires overhead' and put the engine full astern. We lost way with our metal mast just resting against the first of three wires. We supposed that with a bit more way and hitting two wires, there would have been big trouble. I have since read of someone being killed this way. The Norwegian chart which I was using did not mark these power cables as they had recently been erected, nor did we notice the rather inconspicuous warning signs. The banks of the fjord were heavily wooded and the wires difficult to see. Luckily our fairy godmother induced Mike to look up in the nick of time. A good look-out is about the most important 'gadget' in a boat.

Underwater Obstruction From overhead snags to underwater snags! In 1977 we approached Vannes in Brittany one evening. We had heard there was a new marina with a lock or barrage but no details were in our books nor did we find anyone at Conleau (in the approach) to tell us the hours of opening. High water was at 2030 and we arrived just after 2100 so we thought our way would be clear. However there was a red traffic light so we stopped. We waited and nothing happened so we landed one of the crew who went ahead and found the control box empty and locked but the lock apparently open. After waiting another quarter of an hour for the *éclusier* to return from his supper we (or perhaps I should say 'I') decided to go ahead. All appeared clear but as we approached the *écluse* I slowed right down. Lucky I did because we hit the top of the gate which was about three feet below the surface. The damage to our bottom was slight but thank goodness the fairy godmother had urged me to slow down. We discovered later that there is a gate which is lowered two hours either side of high water, but the gate-keeper goes off duty from 2100 until 0700 when he raises the gate to keep the water in during the night. The moral, I suppose, is not to disobey traffic lights!

Crisis in Bantry Bay And so we come to 1978 and our fairy godmother's Irish spell of duty. We sailed to Ireland in late June in fresh north-westerly weather which continued as we made our way west. Consequently we used very little engine and the lights a lot, and when we came to leave Crookhaven it was not altogether surprising that the battery was flat and the engine 'no-start'. However there was plenty of wind and we proceeded on our way and beat round Mizzen Head. The wind then fell very light although the sea remained rough. With full sail we nursed *Matawa* round Sheep Head and into Bantry Bay. I felt a bit uneasy with the light wind, no engine and the rough sea. However, lunch was just on when 'whoosh' the wind hit us without warning, perhaps thirty knots (no anemometer). We were laid flat with our full sail and I went forward and released the main halyard winch band brake. The sail tumbled down half way and then stuck. The winch guard had worked a bit loose and the wire halyard had jumped between the winch and the guard and completely fouled up. With the ship still over at thirty degrees and continual spray drenching us and half the mainsail flogging, Bill Haynes and I attempted to unravel. The lee shore didn't look far off at all and John Pringle tried to keep us sailing with the jib and half the main. Eventually, Bill and I managed to unscrew the winch from the mast in these draughty conditions, untangled the mess, got the mainsail down and the trysail up. We do in fact keep a good pair of wire cutters on board but I'm glad we didn't have to use them, as it would not have been easy to reeve a new halyard. The moral here is to realise that the main halyard winch is one of the very important bits of gear which needs careful maintenance. More important still, as I said at the beginning, and repeat now, is to have a really good fairy godmother.